HEIST AND HIGH

Anthony Curcio and Dane Batty

Portland, Oregon

Heist and High
Nish Publishing
PO Box 91630
Portland, OR 97291

Chapter Four contains a quote from *The New York Times* article "When a Drug Addict Isn't Ready to Accept Help" by Paul Christopher, M.D., published on October 1, 2012; reprinted with the permission of Dr. Christopher.

Pictures taken by the Monroe Police Department used by permission of Detective Timothy Buzzell.

United States Attorney statement is from the website [http://www.justice.gov/usao/waw/press/2009/jul/curcio.html]

Cover by Kit Foster, www.kitfosterdesign.com
Interior design by Robin Simonds, Beagle Bay, Inc.

Trade Paperback ISBN: 978-09857945-0-7
eBook ISBN: 978-0-9857945-1-4
LCCN: 2012953647

First Edition
Printed in the USA

18 17 16 15 14 13 1 2 3 4 5 6 7 8 9 10

Dedication

This book is dedicated to young people who are faced with an enemy that they do not even know exists. I hope that this book can help. Also to those who have already met this enemy, who are just like me, trapped by their insecurities and addictions. I pray you find your way out, because there is a very special purpose waiting for us.

Acknowledgements

I'd like to acknowledge the following people who helped throughout this journey of creating the book you are about to read.

To my wife, Emily: Her loyalty and patience has been unmatched throughout the process of this book. She's stood by my side and fought in the trenches when I couldn't fight myself. She is my best friend and I love her and our little girls more than anything in this world. The three of you are my motivation.

To my grandparents Poppa and Grammy, my Aunt Cheryl, Aunt Mary and Uncle Mario: You never quit writing to me. Your consistent love and support during my toughest times will never be forgotten.

To Dick and Kathy for watching over my family like angels: You deserved retirement but instead were helping raise my children and being there for Emily. And took care of that damn cat who scratched up everything in the house. A million thank yous would never be enough for all you have done.

To my parents, who traveled to the end of the world and back to see their baby boy that they never stopped loving: You've taught me everything I needed to know . . . . I just wish I had listened earlier. I love you both with all my heart.

Contents

Foreword

The best books teach us something new about something we thought we knew, and do it in a way that captivates us so thoroughly we don't even realize we're learning something. These books change our worldview, usually in subtle ways, short-circuiting our preconceptions and forcing us to think rather than simply react.

So it is with the book you're about to read. The next time you're tempted to write off a criminal as just another low-life junkie chasing his next fix, you're going to stop and think, if only for a minute. It's going to occur to you that maybe this perp wasn't born evil, that at one point he was just another loving son in a loving family, that he hadn't intended to become an addict and that maybe something happened that overwhelmed him and derailed his ambitions.

Anthony Curcio was just such a kid: charming, athletic, full of ambition and blessed with possibilities. As of this writing, he's in prison. His was one of those stories in the local paper that barely merits a shake of the head before you turn to the sports page. But it's a story worth paying attention to, except that you're not going to get it from the beat reporter who took down the bare facts, crafted it into the standard set of sentences, turned it in and then forgot about it. You're not going to learn anything useful from that story and there's a lot to learn.

It takes a special hand to convey chaos and direction at the same time, so that when a turning point is finally reached, it can be seen as a natural progression of the turbulence that preceded it rather than just another in a long series of random inflection points. This narrative clearly details Anthony's harrowing story.

There is a temptation for a biographer, eager to spare us tedium, to forego critical detail and blithely hack out entire weeks or months until the life in question appears to be a series of tightly connected, well-planned and precisely executed episodes. But no life is ever like that, and this is especially true of Anthony Curcio's. *Heist and High* makes order out of a disordered life without contorting it into an invented structure, yet while still providing a meaningful arc where only discord was present, discovering underlying themes when only chaos reigned on the surface.

To read *Heist and High* is to watch a train go over a cliff, but also to see just how it got there. Like watching a disaster film for a second time, you find yourself hoping that things will turn out better, knowing all the while that they won't. Every time Curcio swears that he's clean and will never again backslide, we believe that he believes it, and we hope it's true, even though we know it isn't. The book puts us deep inside the tormented man's mind and has us rooting for him, and rooting for his wife and his mother and for his life to turn out okay.

Whether it will or not is still an open question. But I'm rooting for him, and that's because *Heist and High* has shown me a human beneath the sound bite.

Lee Gruenfeld
Palm Springs, California
Co-Author of *Confessions of a Master Jewel Thief*

Heist and High

One

Monroe, Washington, September 30th, 2008

Anthony pulled the trigger on the can of bear mace, spraying the Brink's armored car messenger in the face. Howling in agony, the man's head snapped back, his hands clawed at his burning eyes.

As he grabbed the canvas bags of cash, Anthony prayed, *God, I know you don't like what I'm doing, so I won't ask you for your help. But please do what's best for my family and take care of them.*

God was listening, but He had His own plan.

Anthony dashed away from the bank toward his getaway, but he felt as if he was running in slow motion. *Am I being followed?* He risked glancing back, but no one was there. *Are they trying to figure out if the other landscapers are part of the robbery?* He turned his attention back to trying to get out of sight. The bank bags were terribly heavy and he realized he couldn't carry both, so he dropped the small bag while crossing Old Owen Road. Still, the larger bag with most of the loot was heavy and bulky; it was putting him off his stride. It wasn't as easy as making for the end zone with a football. Although there wasn't an opposing team he could see, he knew they were out there—and soon there would be helicopters and police cars.

By his calculations, he was off all of the cameras, but it was hard to concentrate with the terror of the robbery, coming off his high and trying to get out of there. *What's my next step?* His mental fog cleared a bit: *Right. Down this way next.* He crossed Old Owen Road, raced down a gravel road, past a lumber yard and headed into the park. He stopped and looked back, but still didn't see anybody. That's when he realized he was gasping for air and needed a hit. *I'm not the high school all star wide receiver anymore.*

It seemed safe to ditch his disguise now. He removed the painter's mask and sucked down deep gulps of pine-scented air. Then he took off his hat, wig and goggles in one quick swipe and chucked them on to the dirt road. Anthony knew all the police reports would say that the suspect was wearing a blue landscaper's outfit—but he'd made sure the area was filled with suspects. He'd placed a Craigslist ad for landscapers that got over a dozen guys to come to the bank parking lot, all dressed in blue shirts and pants, as cover for his move. But he'd been wearing a special tear-away outfit. Unfortunately, the pants had come off when he jumped the guard, revealing his shorts. He still had on the Velcro shirt with long sleeves sewn in. Once he ripped it off there was one less landscaper suspect. Anthony knew he'd left no prints on the radio, pepper spray canister or other tools he'd left at the scene. This wasn't just from careful planning. He was good at not leaving prints at this point in his criminal career. Even today he finds himself avoiding leaving prints on things that no longer matter, although he's slowly trying to cure himself of these habits.

He was aware he was leaving DNA evidence behind in the painter's mask, but since he had never been a felon, there were no DNA matches for the authorities to link back to him. In his extensive research on the Internet, he couldn't find evidence of a robbery ever being solved using DNA in Washington State anyway.

Finally unencumbered by his disguise, Anthony "opened her up," as they say with cars, and made for the far side of the park. He felt as he had back in college when he ran a 4.5 second 40-yard dash. Of course, with the sack of money, and his college days far behind him, he was quite a bit slower. But at that moment, he felt like the fastest man on the planet. The great Jamaican sprinter, Usain Bolt, couldn't have caught up to him this day.

He scrambled down the embankment to Woods Creek. Anthony quickly found the markers he'd left in the shallow water course leading right to the brightly-colored yellow inner tube waiting for him. When he had first started to develop his plan, he'd discovered the hard way that the creek bed was lined with slippery rocks, and fallen into the freezing water in street clothes. If the slimy stones had caught *him* unaware, it would certainly do the same to his pursuers. As Anthony reached the inner tube, he threw the fifty pound bag of shrink-wrapped money onto it and jumped on top. Then he reached up and located the cable he'd strung over the creek the week before. Quickly, he pulled the inner tube, himself and the money down the lazy creek.

Once Anthony got to the bend in the creek, he dropped the clothing and the radio on the inner tube, grabbed the plastic-wrapped cash and walked up the embankment under the train trestle to the street level next to Al Borlin Park off of Highway 2. Sirens were going on in the near-distance. Two black sedans with flashing lights roared past him.

> "I had just robbed an armored truck for nearly a half a million dollars, not even two football fields away, and the cops were everywhere but where I was."
>
> —Anthony

He walked confidently to the waiting newer four-door Ford sedan. Anthony gave the driver a thin-lipped smile and asked him to pop the trunk. He tossed the money into the back and climbed in after it. Pulling the trunk shut from the inside, he hollered "Let's go!"

In the cramped space, Anthony pulled out a small flashlight and stuck it between his teeth. He went to work ripping apart the bag. Carefully, he sifted each stack looking for the GPS locator he knew the armored car company installed in each bag of money. It had to be there.

As he searched, Anthony could hear the driver talking to himself. The man was getting louder as Anthony started to go through the stack again. Finally he shouted: "I can't do this! You gotta get out now!"

"Listen, just drive, it's all fine," Anthony reassured him calmly.

"No, bro'! We're gonna get caught. I can't get in trouble. . . this is your fucking deal!" the driver yelled. Anthony felt the car slow to a stop, and assumed the car was readying to turn left onto Main Street. "They're everywhere! They're fucking everywhere! Oh my God! They see me! They are looking right at me!" screamed the driver.

Anthony took a deep breath and said, "Dude, turn up the music. Smile and rock out. *Sing!* Trust me, just sing. It's all good."

The driver didn't reply. Anthony froze and listened hard. He could hear the sirens much closer now. He couldn't hear any cars nearby. Were they as close as the driver said, or was he just tripping? He heard a vehicle pass. Then another. Were they cop cars, or just some passers-by? *Shit, I have a fifty-fifty chance of getting out of here if this guy doesn't lose it.*

"You gotta get out now! I'm popping the trunk," the driver shouted.

Anthony heard the *thunk* of the trunk latch releasing. "I'm not crawling out of a Taurus trunk in the middle of Main Street!" he retorted. He fought down his anger. He needed the driver to hang on for just a little longer, then his part would be through. In a calm voice, Anthony said, "Okay, turn left onto the next street and I'll get out and you can drive away."

The car started down the busy road. Anthony hoped the guy would complete his mission. Then the driver shouted, "No! Now! Get out now!"

Anthony tried to imagine how he could get out of a moving car with the loot in the middle of a town searching for him. He had to get the driver to calm down. "If I get out now we'll be caught. *We will go to jail.* Listen to me: in thirty-seconds this will all be over safely for you, and you can go see your girl and have a beer. But right now *you need to drive!*"

The driver didn't respond. The car kept moving. Anthony felt the car make a left. Then the car stopped with a jerk, making the trunk pop open.

"Get out!" the driver shouted." I mean it! Get out now!"

Shit! Anthony jumped out. The driver started to leave with the trunk still wide open, money strewn all over the back. Anthony had to jog behind the car to shut the trunk, before it sped off.

Anthony stood still for a moment, totally shocked. All that money he'd planned so carefully to take had just driven away, he was on a side-street in a small town where everyone was searching for him, and his truck was clear across town.

Why did I trust that guy? Where the hell did he go?

Anthony took a deep breath and tried to focus on what was important—because wondering what was going on with his friend wasn't going to solve the immediate problem of what to do next. *Did anyone see me get out of the trunk?* He quickly scanned the area, but he didn't see any one. That didn't mean no one had seen him getting out, though. Noticing the apartment complex beside him, he made a quick decision and jumped the fence. He knew the place well, and made his way to the co-op laundry room inside. The door was locked, so Anthony put a shoulder to it and shoved it open. He found an all-white Polo shirt that was two sizes too small, and swapped it for the shirt he had on.

Casually, he strolled outside, trying to look like a resident who was trying to find out what all the commotion was about. It didn't take long to see that the cops were everywhere. They weren't buzzing around with sirens now. They were creeping the side streets silently. Anthony had to crawl under some bushes and wait it out until one left. He noticed that it was a sheriff's car, not a regular cop car. He realized they must have every available car looking for him—and probably more on the way. He had to reach his truck across town, but he certainly wasn't going to get there on foot. His stomach was sick from all the adrenaline.

Man, I am so out of my league. Although he had committed many crimes by this time, he was well past his comfort zone. Nothing really could have prepared him for this day. As he sat in the bushes, he could hear dogs start barking in the distance and wondered if they were cop dogs.

The D.B. Tuber armored car robbery—a name the media quickly applied to Anthony—was portrayed as a carefully planned out, smooth operation on TV, in magazines, newspapers, and even the police report. It wasn't. Anthony was scrambling, making shit up on the run, one move at a time. All the pre-planning in the world couldn't have prepared him for getting dropped off in the middle of the escape!

Anthony realized that the one place the cops weren't was the police station. It sounded crazy, but that's exactly where he decided to go since it was right around the corner. Ducking and weaving as if he was in a game dodging tacklers, he managed to get to the shared fence of the police station. He leaned up against it to collect his breath. Then the helicopters flew in and started circling the bank.

I need to get to a phone. And I need to get away from these choppers. He looked over and spotted a real estate office where he knew several agents. Smoothing down his hair and straightening the too-tight shirt as best he could, he strode into the place as if it were just an ordinary day. He smiled and started smooth-talking the receptionist: dropping a name, asking a few questions, and got the receptionist to laugh. He looked down while he was chuckling with her. .

. and with a start realized his shoes were soaking wet from the creek. *God, I hope she didn't notice when I walked in.* Yet, he didn't miss a beat when he finally asked, "Hey, can I use your phone?"

"A realtor without a phone? Isn't there some law you guys have to have one glued to your ears at birth?" she joked.

Anthony laughed with her. "Yeah. I have two. And they're both out of juice! And so is my car battery. Wouldn't you know?"

"Bummer of a day for you, huh?" She pointed to the phone on the edge of her desk. "Go ahead. Just don't call China."

He chuckled. "Thanks." He quickly dialed his driver. Anthony tried to act as if nothing was wrong and he didn't want to kill the guy. "Hey, I'm at the real estate office on Main Street. My damn battery went dead. Can you pick me up?"

"Yeah, I'll be right there," his driver told him.

The receptionist gave him some real estate pamphlets to look at while he was waiting, and Anthony continued to joke around with her. He was constantly monitoring her face to get a gauge on her thoughts and kept the conversation open.

Ten minutes went by, but no ride showed up. Anthony called the driver again. "Where are you?"

"Hey, I'll be right there. I'm close," the driver said.

Another few minutes went by. Helicopters continued to circle overhead. A group of agents migrated outside to stare up at the choppers. It was such a commotion that the receptionist headed out there, too.

Anthony called his driver back for a third time. The guy said, "Hey man, I can't," and hung up.

Anthony called back; no answer. He redialed. No answer. *Shit!*

Figuring it would look weird if he was incurious about all the noise, he went outside to join the group. "What happened?" Anthony asked.

"I heard there was a bank robbery just down the street," one man said.

"I hope no one got hurt," another said.

He spent several minutes speculating with the agents about what was going on. He could tell the choppers were focusing their search over the Skykomish River, and was glad he'd ditched the idea of a jet ski. The urge to run swelled in Anthony's chest. It was difficult to remain calm. Another ten minutes went by before the agents and the receptionist got bored and went back inside. Anthony followed them in, trying not to look as anxious as he felt.

"You need to call someone else?" The receptionist smiled and pushed the phone his way.

Anthony called his lookout. "I called Bob, but I guess he can't come. Would you mind swinging by the real estate office and picking me up? My battery died."

The lookout was there in less than five minutes. Anthony got in the car and quickly explained his situation.

"Do I get half his share then?" the lookout said jokingly.

Anthony wasn't in a humorous mood. "I'll double yours!"

The lookout glanced at him. Anthony could see the sweat on his upper lip. During the heist, the lookout had come apart as badly as the driver. But at least he hadn't fed Anthony to the wolves. "Um, thanks, man." They drove in silence.

When Anthony got to his truck, he changed his clothes and drove out of town. He had the lookout follow him.

Anthony called the driver from a prepaid cell. This time, the guy answered. "I hope you're all right," Anthony said.

"Yeah, I'm good," driver answered awkwardly.

"Meet us where we agreed." Anthony instructed.

They all met where they had planned after the robbery. Anthony got out of the car, walked up to his driver, grabbed his coat and pushed him against the car. He looked him in the eyes and said, "I oughta beat the shit out of you."

"I. . . I. . . I'm, I'm so sorry," the driver replied, obviously scared.

Anthony turned his back on the driver. "Whatever," he grumbled. He transferred the cash to the duffle bags he'd brought. "All right [lookout], I'll call you in a few. [Driver], you're coming with me," Anthony ordered.

The sight of all that cash turned the men back into old friends. Besides, they knew Anthony wasn't a violent man. The feeling of a successful crime has a certain forgiving quality to it.

At a Motel 6 in Everett about an hour later, Anthony and the driver counted out the money. Anthony lost count after $330,000. Over $100,000 was in twenties, so it looked like way more. After Anthony gave the driver a cut, he drove him home. Then he went to the YMCA where he had a gym membership and put the money in two separate lockers.

He checked his watch. *Shit.* He knew he wasn't going to make practice. The football coach was his planned alibi. As the assistant coach, Anthony was well-liked and a fixture in the daily drills. He sent a text message to Coach RB telling him he was running late. But he had no intention of trying to go pretend everything was fine.

Anthony went home as if he had just come in from work. He kissed his wife and two little daughters, then he ran upstairs to take a shower.

And just like that, it was over.

Or that's what he thought.

Two

Anthony's dad had been a star wide receiver on the high school football team that earned him a scholarship to play at the University of Idaho. He and the girl who was to be his wife were high school sweethearts. When Anthony's dad went to U of I, his mom transferred to Washington State University from University of Washington to be closer to him. After graduating with degrees in education, they married and started a life in Hood River, Oregon. There they were Special-Ed teachers at the junior high, and his dad coached football. When Anthony's oldest sister was born, they moved back up to the small town of Monroe, near Seattle. They started a successful landscaping business and had Anthony's other sister.

Then, on September 1, 1980, came Anthony Jay Curcio. He arrived on the same day there was a riot at the local prison. His parents hardly noticed the chaos of the wounded inmates and guards wandering the halls and filling up all the beds at the local hospital. They were too excited about the birth of their only son.

> "From Day One I was dressed up in different outfits they would put me in, carried around and mothered by Mom and my two sisters. I'm told I hardly talked, just grunted and pointed at what it was I wanted. My mom tells me that everyone knew when I was up from my nap because they

would hear the 'thud' of me hitting the floor after climbing out of my crib. I didn't like being caged then either."

—Anthony

Anthony went to an elementary school right down the road from the family house, where he met some of his closest friends. Louis and Dave lived a few houses up the road, Ryan lived close by, and in the house across the street were two brothers, Tim and Andy. Nearly every day after school, the group would all get together and pretend to be their favorite baseball and football players. Anthony always pretended to be his second favorite receiver of all-time, Jerry Rice. Of course, his favorite was his dad. You never wanted to start the "my dad's better than your dad" debate with Anthony. It usually ended in a fistfight and someone crying. "He was the best. He was my hero," Anthony says.

Anthony knew all of his dad's statistics by heart, like his forty-yard dash times. He read every thirty year old, yellow-tinted newspaper article. He plied his father with questions about every signature of every player on the signed game balls in his dad's study. His favorite story was when his dad's team ran the "hook and ladder" route at their conference finals his senior year in high school. His dad had run out ten yards, cut in and the ball was there! After the catch, he spun inwards to the center of the field as the corner closed in. But then he waited until the safety also came in to make the tackle. As they were closing in on the halfback—his best friend even to this day—came out of the backfield. The perfect "hook" was set. Anthony's dad pitched the ball to his friend who ran fifty yards for the touchdown. The 5,000 hometown fans went crazy.

His dad went on to earn a full-ride college scholarship to the University of Idaho, and he was a storied receiver there, too. What amazed Anthony was that, as great a receiver as his dad had been, he never talked about it. His dad's humbleness just added to his legend.

Because of that, Anthony always felt he had big shoes to fill. Setting goals and working hard to realize dreams and make them happen was instilled in Anthony from very early. He always knew that someday he would wear Jerry Rice's number 80 jersey and play college football and beyond. He loved sports, and that was basically all he did . . . along with occasionally causing a bit of trouble.

When it snowed, they threw snowballs at cars, with Anthony a bit more daring than the rest. When a car skidded to a stop and the driver screamed, "You damn kids!" all the kids ran. But Anthony would stand his ground and try to hit the driver with another snowball as he got out of the car.

He and his neighbor Andy would dress up in army gear and build booby traps in the yard and sneak around. That lasted until one day when Granny was gardening and fell into one of the holes. She dropped onto a stick that propelled a small boulder at her. She wasn't hurt, but she was mad.

Anthony and his friends also played with fireworks—which also ended abruptly when a smoke bomb got thrown into a daycare. They blamed Louis.

In third grade, Anthony broke his wrist by jumping off the swing at school. The doctor put his arm in a cast, and gave him a bottle of prescription pain pills. For the next few days, he sat on the couch watching cartoons all day—every little kid's dream. The pills made him feel especially good; a memory he carries to this day.

Anthony and his friends played video games and went swimming together. They set up lemonade stands and used the money to buy baseball cards. Their family's landscaping business was successful. His home was on a private lake, and everyone would come over to swim in the summers. His childhood really couldn't have been any better.

Anthony didn't notice girls much until eighth grade. A skinny girl named Emily Chester was the prettiest girl in the entire junior high. Anthony thought she was wonderful, but couldn't summon the courage to speak to her. Plus, she liked the bad boys, which Anthony wasn't. He hadn't thought much about the guys who acted out in school, but now he found himself hating them.

At the end of the school year, before leaving for high school, there was a dance called the Eighth Grade Recognition. Anthony was so nervous, later he couldn't remember if he asked Emily face to face or not, but she said yes. The night of the dance, Emily wore a green dress. Anthony's mom convinced him to give her a rose and to offer it to her on one knee. He followed her advice, and gave Emily the flower at the dance. The other boys laughed and ridiculed him the rest of the night. Anthony was never afraid to take a risk, but the payoff had to be worth it—and Emily was worth it.

Emily and Anthony at the Eighth Grade Dance

> "Eighth Grade graduation was a big deal. I remember shopping for the perfect dress weeks ahead of time. My grandparents came and everything."
>
> —Emily

During the Summer and into their freshman year in high school, Emily reconnected with a friend who took her to parties thrown by older high school students. Because of those parties, she started using alcohol and cigarettes. Anthony wasn't a fan of the new behavior. He never took his eyes off of her, although she seemed to completely forget all about that skinny kid who gave her the rose in front of everyone.

> "My girlfriends and I chased after the senior guys; we didn't pay too much attention to our fellow freshman. Anthony wasn't happy. We call those years 'the hate years.' He was pretty rude to me - which everyone knew just meant he still really liked me. We laughed about it later."
>
> —Emily

Anthony's freshman year, the coaches already knew who and what he was. They assigned him to play on the junior varsity basketball and football teams, instead of the freshman teams.

> "You could tell way before high school athletics that Anthony idolized and respected the older athletes, and not a lot of kids did that. There were other high school guards that were receivers on the football team as well, and he'd pretend he was them. He had a lot of respect for those who came before him, and he looked up to these athletes. He wasn't all about himself."
>
> —Louis, his friend and quarterback

Anthony was also the class clown. During a going-away party for a teacher, he dared a friend, RB, to throw a pie in the teacher's face. When RB said no, Anthony promoted the event, and in ten minutes raised over twenty dollars to sweeten the deal. In the end, RB did throw the pie. There was an awkward pause, but then everyone exploded in laughter—even the teacher. Then she realized the pie was all over her dress, and she got mad at the kids. She'd planned to go to the airport directly after class.

In Spanish class, Anthony borrowed the next day's VHS of "Destinos," the Spanish language teaching tape. At five minutes into it, he spliced in about a second's worth of a porno—a page taken right out of "Fight Club." The next day, Anthony watched the teacher's reaction instead of the tape. Her face registered, "did that really happen?" Then she shut off the tape immediately. The class roared with laughter. Anthony was the prime suspect, but his cover was never blown.

> "Ask anyone. I was the kid parents trusted their kids with. I was the good kid, and I really was. I was always polite and kind—except for the booby trap on Granny. I also loved to talk. I think it was passed down in my genes because my sisters never shut up. I was the class clown and loved to joke around. I was fun, and so were my friends."
>
> —Anthony

By Anthony's sophomore year, he was the starting point guard on one of the league's best basketball teams and Anthony led the league in assists. He hit four three-pointers in the second half of his team's last game in the divisional playoffs with the winner going to the state tournament. Anthony's team lost the game by a last-second shot, and just missed going to the championship game.

> "I will always remember that game because when I was shooting free throws, I caught the eye of the most beautiful cheerleader—it was Emily! The next three-pointer I hit, I held up my shooting hand all the way back down the court. I was the man! Well, I was the man until the huge photo of me in the paper the next day turned up on a wall at school. My armpit was circled in red pen, and everyone could see there wasn't even one hair there. Devastating. I was a late bloomer."
>
> —Anthony

The new notoriety made the upper-class women notice him. It also seemed to give him a get-out-of-anything pass. A natural charmer, Anthony could talk his way out of most situations. When Anthony and a few of his friends suspiciously aced their science test, the teacher wanted to chat with their folks. Anthony swore he hadn't cheated and said, "Can you please let me talk to my parents first? Please?" The next day at lunch, Anthony paid a friend with a deep voice to call the teacher and thank him for his concern. It worked fine until the teacher called his parents back to chat.

The Monroe High School head football coach was old-school. Even though everyone wanted to throw the ball more—especially Anthony—coach loved to run it. Anthony made the most of the rare balls that were thrown his way, and he made sure the defense knew it. He was so cocky in practice, he'd yell out the play they were running to the defense. Anthony wanted everyone to know exactly where he was going—he was calling his shot.

Anthony and Louis ran the same plays for thousands of practice hours for ten years. Most often the plays came in: First down: run. Second down: run. Third down . . . . If for whatever reason they couldn't run on third or fourth downs, Louis and Anthony came to life as the bailout crew. He remembered his dad telling him, "If you can touch it, you should catch it." And he did. The former all-star wide receiver also told his son "You're going to get hit whether you catch the ball or not—so catch it and hold onto it. When the ball is in the air, nothing else matters." Anthony wasn't afraid to get hit and loved going across the middle. He understood that he was going to get killed when he left his feet, but there was no way he was letting go of that ball.

Anthony in his uniform, 1997.

> "I respect the guys in the blooper videos that catch the pass a split second before running into the goal post."
>
> —Anthony

Coach got the last laugh by benching Anthony and his arrogance. Seems calling your plays wasn't the best idea by the coach's standards. People who knew him best knew he was good because he could leap and he was fast, but Anthony was a good receiver because he simply wanted the ball more than anyone.

> "Curcio was a great kid. He was a great athlete, a good-looking kid, and the kind of kid that you would trust your daughter with. He had the whole package." Mark played receiver for WSU in the early to mid-1980's, and is still teaching in the Monroe district today.
>
> — Mark Bircher, Anthony's receiver coach.

Basketball and football weren't the only sports Anthony was good at. He was also a speedy centerfielder—only nobody knew it since he claimed to be horrible. His constant need for action and excitement left him bored with baseball, plus that Spring was drinking season.

Being young on the varsity sports teams and friends with the older classmen, Anthony was invited to every party there was in high school. This was when Anthony realized the power of alcohol.

> "When I first drank and felt that feeling, I knew that there was something different about how it made me feel—invincible and on top of the world. It was the most fun thing to do."
>
> —Anthony

Each Thursday he found a source of alcohol for the upcoming weekend's planned party. Whether he stole from someone's parent's liquor cabinet, or used a fake I.D. in combination with dirty jeans and work boots to look the part of the construction worker buying a few cases from the dirty gas station, he wasn't too picky about his methods. Anthony also befriended a twenty-three-year old loser who still wanted to hang out with high school kids and convinced him to buy some cases of beer. He hit up a homeless guy who needed a few bucks to buy some wine coolers. It didn't matter, and nothing stood in his way. He gathered the money from everyone, kept a ledger on who paid, and distributed it all out of the back of his Explorer. Anthony never lost his integrity or bent his family values until the drinking started.

The first thing Anthony ever stole was beer. He was parked outside a gas station when he noticed a beer distributor loading up cases on his dolly and taking them into the store. No one was watching the truck! Anthony got out of the car.

"What are you doing?" his friend asked.

Anthony grinned. "Watch."

He sprinted over to the truck, slid the door open, grabbed two cases, ran back to the car and threw them into the back.

His friend shouted, "Holy shit! You're nuts! We've got enough for tonight!"

"Not enough for the weekend!" he said. Then he went back and grabbed two more.

His friend laughed nervously. "You're a ballsy little shit!"

That led to other beer thefts. Anthony was grounded over and over again for staying out late, and was forced to get a job. He found work at a company that put on weddings, company parties and such. One day, he was told to take the company truck to pick up two kegs from the warehouse. After going through the hanging plastic separators into the refrigerated room, he about keeled over with a heart attack. There before him was a gym-sized warehouse full of every type of alcohol there was—wine coolers for the girls and every beer you could think of. The rest of that day and the next he planned. On the third day, Anthony organized his first heist. For the rest of the Summer, everyone was drinking Bartles & James wine coolers and Miller Light. He also managed to steal about six cases of non-alcoholic beer, having never heard of such a thing. A decade later, the O'Doul's still sits in a friend's shed.

The heists continued. Anthony paid off every grocery store night-stocker in town. He'd organize trucks to pick up beer and other alcohol from the store loading docks. At about this time, his parents purchased a motor home and kept it at the other end of their property. When there was no house to party in, the motor home became a mini-night club. Eventually his parents caught on to the RV parties from things their friends said about their kids and stopped them. They were still in the dark about Anthony's illegal beer acquiring activities.

Anthony was seventeen when Tim, his close friend and across-the street neighbor, died. It was the first time Anthony faced something so emotional. To deal with it, he decided to drink more. It was a pattern that was to become all too familiar in later life.

> "Anthony has an obsessive personality. He'd get addicted or hooked on random things like chess and be obsessed with whatever it was for a period of time then drop it and move onto something else. He had all of his guy friends and most of the football team playing chess. He'd have everyone over to play. They all just did whatever he was doing, it was crazy."
>
> —Emily

After he quit the job at the party planners, his parents made him go out and look for work. Instead of looking for employment, he started making flyers at a friend's house for landscaping jobs and posting them around town. After the first day, he came home and there were a few messages already. Within the next week, he had so many jobs lined up that he hired all his friends. He charged his clients twelve dollars an hour and paid each friend eight dollars an hour—which was two dollars more an hour than their other jobs and under the table, plus they all got to work together. Within a few weeks Anthony was making about thirty to thirty-five dollars an hour driving around, supervising his jobs and bringing all of his friends beer. His parents were both shocked and proud. All was good until ten $800 Japanese vine plants were pulled mistakenly as weeds.

Anthony went to football camp at the University of Idaho that summer. Loads of teams came from Washington, Idaho, Oregon and Montana. The drill was seven-on-seven scrimmages with no linemen. They played both offense and defense. Anthony's Monroe team played the state powerhouse O'Dea High School of Seattle. O'Dea's wide receiver was future NFL star Nate Burleson, who later played for the Seattle Seahawks (in 2010, he signed a five year, twenty-five million dollar contract as a free agent to play for the Detroit Lions). Nate and Anthony were roughly the same size and stature—six feet, 190 pounds—and it was game time. The university coaches were comparing and contrasting the two young men with egos bigger than their statures.

Every ball Louis threw was dead-on. It was like when they were kids and Anthony pretended he was Jerry Rice. Ten yards out, five yards then turn around and the ball was there—boom!—before the defender could react. Louis went with a pump fake: two defenders bit. He tossed up a fifty-yard pass for Anthony and Nate to fight over. They clashed over and over. Each time was like the first because both of them pulled out all the stops that day.

But then there was the big play: O'Dea marched the ball down the field eighty yards in successive plays. The opposing team's quarterback tossed a bullet at Nate, waiting in the end zone. At the last moment, Anthony leapt over Nate's head, snatched the ball out of the air, and ran the whole length of the field for a Monroe touchdown. "That was my favorite personal performance, and it really made me proud," Anthony said. He was voted top receiver at camp.

> "That football camp was where Anthony got on the map. Colleges were there watching. One thing I remember is I threw up a ball and Nate Burleson flew out of nowhere and intercepted me. He was an incredible athlete. Here we were playing one of the best teams in the state and region, and I was sure half of them didn't know where Monroe even was. Anthony did very well at that camp and got noticed."
>
> —Louis

After camp, letters poured in from tons of schools. Anthony's future looked bright.

As an upper classman, Anthony really liked talking to the younger kids. "I remembered how it was with all the older classman taking all the younger girls, and it really sucked," he told the boys as he gave them rides home from practice. But he was also a good listener and loved to hear about other people's stories asking them questions about their lives.

Emily got a job at a local coffee shop in downtown Monroe, and with cheerleading practices and camp she was a busy girl. Anthony had two-a-day football practices and would run past the coffee shop every day and stop in to talk to Emily. "I kind of liked that, I guess," Emily confesses. Then one day Emily heard rumors that Anthony was hanging out with someone else. That's when she realized how much she actually liked him. "Who knows, maybe that was his plan," she recalls. "After all those years of wanting me, he was giving up? That didn't sit well with me. It wasn't like they were boyfriend-girlfriend or anything; it was really new... so I acted fast." Their first official date was the summer of their sophomore year on August 16th, 1997 at Red Robin. Afterwards, they went to see the movie "Men in Black."

Anthony recalls:

> "I'm not big on the terms 'love at first sight' or 'soul mates,' but if I was, those would be the best way to describe what

> I feel about Emily. Obviously, it was her beauty that I first noticed, and because she was so beautiful it's also what kept my scared, skinny, eighth grade self away and too nervous to talk to her! She is my everything, then and now. Nearly every memory I have, she was part of. My first dance, the first and only girl I had ever given flowers too. She is the only woman, outside of my mom, that I've ever loved. She also may be the only girl that I've really been able to laugh with. She may not know this, but I remember when we were getting class awards for eighth grade, and she was voted Class Clown/Best Sense of Humor. She is funny as hell.
>
> "I took her to every high school and junior high dance she's ever been too. Emily was the straight A, 4.0-student who sat a few seats in front of me. Later that year, I would take the crown of class clown away from her—a title I would hold for the remainder of our school days. While she was busy learning, I was busy drawing little 'I love you' notes with hidden messages that she would have to figure out. Then she would pass them back. I would spend half an hour on a full page of pictograms that she would figure out and then pass back to me with a grin. That smile of hers is the sexiest in the world. We've had our ups and downs, and each day of my life I think how lucky I am to have her. She really is amazing."

Just as everything in Anthony's life, he pursued Emily with full force. He loved her, but Emily couldn't get herself to reciprocate as fast. She was the level-headed part of the relationship that Anthony so desperately needed.

Emily reminisces:

> "Anthony was really popular, outgoing, good looking and athletic, but he was also really kind, genuine, charming and

charismatic – in a good way back then. He was the kind of guy who could bridge the gap between cliques and bring everyone together. He was nice to everybody and always stuck up for the underdog. He didn't care what he looked like or what material possessions he had. He was humble in that way. He was definitely humble as a person, but not so much as an athlete. He was a different person on the court and on the field.

"If he were young today he'd probably be diagnosed with some kind of ADD or something, which is sad and scary because his greatest qualities stem from his energetic, compulsive personality. He's smart and creative and dreams big (he just used those qualities the wrong way, obviously). I can definitely look back and see the signs of an addictive personality, with the obsessive behavior and all of that. It's in his biology. His substance abuse problems started way before we were even aware of them because everyone partied like that, myself included.

"But back then he still had a good, moral head on this shoulders. There even came a point our senior year of high school when Anthony decided he didn't approve of some of the things I was doing. He told me I had to stop or we couldn't be together. He tamed me if you can believe that! And it was the easiest decision I ever made. Of course I chose him. Some of my friends didn't understand why I would change my behavior for a guy but I didn't see any alternative. How could you choose a substance over someone you loved? I realize now how I lucky I was, how lucky I am, that I was able to stop. Now I understand why he couldn't and I can't imagine how excruciating it must've been for him, to want to quit for me, then later for our girls, but not be able to."

Amidst the excitement of being a senior, being in love and partying, Anthony passed the NCAA clearinghouse, which made him eligible for scholarships. To celebrate, he drank all night with his friends, then took his SAT hung over.

Emily and Anthony were voted "Most Romantic Couple" their senior year at Monroe High School. They were together so much, the teachers called Emily "Mrs. Curcio." Anthony left notes in her locker and roses on her windshield. She wore his letterman's jacket to every football game, and, as captain of the basketball cheer squad, made certain she cheered for every one of his games, both home and away.

When Anthony first met Emily's parents, he was very nervous. Emily's parents had been watching Anthony play sports for years, but they didn't know his parents or him. For the first two years, Anthony called them Mr. and Mrs. He loved her parents as he did his own. Emily's mom was one hell of a cook, and Anthony would hang out and chat for hours. He respected Emily's dad, but he was completely intimidated by him.

Once Anthony had Emily, his confidence soared. Everyone wanted him to be in their activities or part of their group. But on the football field, that's where Anthony put on a show. He was fast as hell and couldn't be stopped. As usual, the team didn't throw much, but when Louis threw the ball it was to Anthony. Their last football game

Anthony and Emily in their Senior Year

Louis hit Anthony on a sixty-five yard bomb on the second play of the game.

It hadn't always been that way. At his fifth grade season-ending awards banquet, the coach launched into a description of each of the players. When it was Anthony's turn, the coach went to the four-foot-five-inch boy standing in front of a very crowded banquet hall. He said: "Even if I was this close to Anthony and I threw him the ball he couldn't catch it! He can't catch anything! Ha ha! He's a good kid, but he's not a receiver."

Anthony felt like an empty pop can getting flattened. You could hear his spirit go, *Squish!* From the time he could walk, all he'd wanted to be was a wide receiver, just like his dad. There was nothing he wanted more.

The coach had never actually let Anthony play receiver on this team. He was used as a lineman, and a third string tackle weighing all of eighty pounds. Nobody really knew Anthony was an excellent receiver except for his dad and his friend Louis.

The forty other kids and their families laughed awkwardly at the coach's "joke." Anthony did what he did best when he was hurting—he smiled, although he was crushed inside.

The very second the car doors were shut, Anthony exploded in tears. His dad quietly drove, while his mom tried to console him. He knew she was mad at the coach because she called him a "jerk." Anthony's mom didn't say things like that about people. As Anthony wiped his tears, he felt that everything he'd worked hard for had been a waste. His dad was very quiet all the way home. "I think he just didn't know what to say about that coach and what he said about me." Anthony remembers. Anthony felt he'd let his dad down. How could he ever be like him now after what coach had said at the banquet? Through the tears he said to his folks, "I'm never playing football again, ever!" He was as serious as a ten year old could be.

His dad suddenly stopped the car as they started up their long driveway.

Anthony's mom began to ask, "What. . . ." but stopped when she saw his face.

His dad turned back to look at Anthony in the back seat. It was dark outside and the dome light in the car was off, but Anthony could see the look in his dad's eyes—a look he'll never forget. He said, "Anthony, your coach was wrong. You can catch, and you are a great receiver. You have got to believe this."

Although this made Anthony feel a little better, he still didn't believe it. He didn't play football for years, and he never wanted to play again after what that coach had said. If it weren't for the constant support of his parents, and Louis' continuous begging, Anthony would have never played football again. Three years later in the eighth grade, he decided to try out for the football team again. Right away he was a starter playing alongside Louis. His team didn't throw the ball much like most young football teams, but when they did, Anthony caught it.

> "Coach talking about how Anthony couldn't catch, that surely lit a fire under him. He had something to prove, and that coach's speech just inspired him to be a receiver even more."
>
> —Louis

Even though that fifth grade coach's words didn't faze Anthony any longer, he got a chance to put them to rest. During that final home game, the stadium was packed with high school football fans. It was third down in the fourth quarter; Anthony's team was on the twenty-five yard line at the opponents' end. In the huddle the play came in: "I-Right, seven." It was a post-corner route where the receiver runs a straight line, angles toward the middle of the field and at some point he breaks off and runs to the corner. If the defense had a cover-two zone, they could cover the receiver. But if the receiver ran a good route with man-on-man coverage, he could break to the post for a touchdown pretty easily. Anthony loved this call because there were no other options, no Plan B. It was just Louis and Anthony, and it always worked. No matter how much game film the opponents studied on them, they always got them on the post corner route. Louis and Anthony had been running that play since they were eight years old.

When the ball was snapped, Anthony beat the defensive back off the line and got behind him almost immediately. Anthony ran directly at the safety and did exactly as his dad always told him to do: Right as the gap between them had closed, Anthony planted his left foot cleat hard into the turf and broke inside. That put the safety off balance and made him play catch-up. As the safety was changing directions, Anthony planted his right foot and broke right toward the back corner of the end zone, completing the Post-Corner route. As Anthony looked over his shoulder, there was the ball spiraling right to him without a defender in sight. *Touchdown!* Anthony took a few steps past the goal line, swimming in the adulation.

As he turned to celebrate with his team who were running toward him, Anthony's gaze swept the audience. One of the faces looking back at him was his fifth grade coach who had told him in front of everyone that he couldn't catch a football and couldn't play receiver. Anthony just smiled. *Can't catch? Yeah, right,* he thought.

> "The week before our first game, I got mono and couldn't practice, so I didn't start. Everyone was running everywhere and everybody's timing was off with the backup quarterback. Sometimes the backup QB had trouble even getting the ball from center, so the offense was off. At some point in the first quarter, the team was driving the ball, and it was time to run the first pass play so I got called to go in. It was a post-corner play and a bootleg, so I faked to the running back, then ran out to Anthony's side. He was running the post corner. I threw the worst pass ever. Well, it was on target I guess, but it was a duck and I thought,

> 'Oh my God.' Well, Anthony went up for it and took it for a touchdown and the pass looked just fine. That game I went four-for-four for over 100 yards passing with at least one touchdown, and all four completions went to Anthony that game. We won. It wasn't against a very good team, but the post-corner was mighty for us. Anthony was fast, could jump and was good at getting free."
>
> — Louis

More than a decade later, some of Anthony's records still stand, although high school football teams throw the ball more often than they used to.

High School ended great. Amongst all the activities and sports, Anthony managed to graduate, probably thanks to his coaches. He partied with the rest of the seniors, but only for a short time. Everyone else going off to college didn't leave for another month and a half, but Anthony had to cut out of the Summer parties early and report to football practice. Although he was destined to follow in his father's footsteps and set the world on fire at the pass-heavy University of Idaho, he had actually been more interested in following Louis to the private college of Linfield in Oregon. He knew he was going to miss Louis a lot.

> "Looking back, if he'd gone to Linfield, who knows what might've happened. Linfield was further away and a lot more money, but I think he would've been happier there. He probably would've played football all four years. Then again, he could've ended up on the same path, partying too much and getting into trouble . . . so we might still be where we are today, I don't know."
>
> —Emily

Two

Anthony and Emily at the Senior Prom

Three

Anthony packed up everything and drove to Moscow, Idaho, home of the University of Idaho. Two players were assigned to each dorm room and he got to know his fellow teammates fairly quickly. Three practices a day along with their regular college studies made it seem like a ten hour a day, full-time job. The only good things about practice were all the free gear: cleats, shoes, shorts, all kinds of shirts, plus dining cards allowing them to eat anything they wanted. But it was hot as hell in August.

Football was everything, and this was Division 1 college football. No more simple routes: they had intense passing schemes with different audibles, different hot routes and then once a week a two-minute drill. The coaches brought all the players into the 16,000 seat capacity Kibbie Dome, where Anthony's dad had played. They turned on music so loud over the speakers that you couldn't even think, as practice for the real games where the screaming fans were louder than a 767 taking off.

As a wide receiver, Anthony was not a slot-receiver or flanker and was usually on the line or set a ways out. You can't hear a snap count way out on the side, so you watched the ball. When it lifted you went. Everything was visual, and the quarterback was your guide. Anthony would scan the defense. If the free safety shifted past the hash mark and there was an extra linebacker up, then he was supposed to run a ten-yard "quick" across the middle. But if the safety came over, then he was supposed to run a deep-out designed only to pull two defenders with him. Anthony was a great receiver, but he badly missed Louis. He knew what Louis was going to do almost as soon as he did. All these new signals and reads were confusing. If the QB tapped his left foot twice, he was supposed to execute blocking schemes with a slot crackback. If he lifted his left leg, he was calling for the ball if in a shotgun. On and on the new plays went.

After practice, Anthony would collapse simply due to exhaustion. Athletically, he was there at six feet, 194 pounds; he could bench press 330 pounds and run a 4.5 second 40-yard dash consistently. He could also leap as if he was well over six feet tall. Anthony had worked his entire life for this, but he had no idea what he was getting into, either. He'd figured after attending multiple University of Washington practices with his dad and meeting with coaches that it would be a sure thing that he could play at the University of Idaho, but he wasn't in high school anymore. Anthony had been a big fish in a very small pond, but now he was just another receiver in the 1999 recruiting class at U of I.

There were two receivers in the recruiting class, but in another week when school started there would be another ten receivers trying to walk on. The walk-ons might not have had the ability, but they had a mentality that was scary to Anthony—like that short, practice squad Notre Dame student they made a movie about, called "Rudy."

All the freshmen were set to redshirt. Anthony was a wideout on the third string team. He played on the punt team as a gunner—a receiver who ran down to tackle the returner. He also was on the punt return team as the returner. Had he known he enjoyed returning punts so much, he would have done it more in high school. The coaches told him if he moved to defensive back he'd get playing time, but Anthony didn't enjoy hitting or tackling. He'd rather have the ball in his hands and get hit rather than hit someone else. As a junior in high school, his coaches put him on defense as free safety, and although he led the team in tackles he was totally uninterested in anything but offense. The only thing he liked about playing defense was when a quarterback would try to throw deep on him, and after a few interceptions they would throw to the other side of field where Anthony wasn't. He also knew that more responsibility meant less party time.

As a football player in college, it seems as if all the girls love you and all the guys hate you. The first week after school started, Anthony drank every single night. The frat parties were unbelievable and something he had never seen in rural Monroe. The Sigma Nu's partied more than any other house. It also happened to be the house on campus that the football guys were in. Plus Anthony's future brother-in-law, who was also a football player at U of I and a frat brother, lived off-campus. Since Anthony was at the house all the time, it was natural to join. The other freshmen in the house weren't on the team, so they didn't have practices. Partying for them was just part of the college experience. Anthony not only partied like a new college kid, he instantly zoomed past the point of fun and straight over the party cliff. He was wild—always laughing, joking, and when a few beers went down he lit up like the Vegas Strip. Put Anthony in a room with a 100 people and in one hour he'd have 100 new friends. He remembers taking shots with everyone in the house. The next moment, four people on stools were pouring beer on him trying to make it in his mouth. If you were outside with Anthony chugging beers he'd dare you to hit as many street signs as he could with empties.

His first night living in the Sigma Nu frat house, he yelled to his new housemates that he would be right back with a present for the house. Anthony walked down to another fraternity house and ripped their current composite—a huge photo with all the members—right off the wall and waddled back up the road with it. One complaint later and he was hauled off to jail for the night. The theft charge was later dropped, but the minor in possession (M.I.P.) of alcohol charge stuck.

Emily was visiting with Anthony when he got his first M.I.P. The head coach woke him up the next morning and was not happy. Anthony was sentenced to running after practice every day the next week, and received his first warning. So Anthony tried to get his shit together . . . at least for a few days anyway. Then the weekend came. He started slow with a beer or two, but then a few more and he was off the party cliff again. He received another M.I.P., and the following Monday he was suspended from the football team for the entire season, along with another player who got a D.U.I.

Anthony's parents were devastated. Anthony dealt with it by simply staying drunk. Some high school friends came to visit him the next weekend, and these guys were as wild as Anthony was. The fraternity down the street called the cops on Anthony again for being too loud and obnoxious. To counter this, his friends decided it was a good idea to rip out the offending fraternity's yard sign and throw it in the middle of the road. The cops arrived, but not before the sign had been run over a few times. Anthony's team was getting tired of his antics and pushed him out of the house. He left gladly, since he blamed them for causing him to drink. He and his mom found a nice two bedroom house off- campus with a hot tub and a

Emily and Anthony during their college years

two-car garage. It was on a farmer's back road, but it soon became a freeway for drunk drivers. Emily would stay over from time to time to help keep him in check throughout the school year.

The season ended with rumors swirling around the head coach. He told all the players he wasn't leaving. But later that night on television, it was the reported that Coach Chris Tormey and a huge chunk of his coaching staff left to go to the University of Nevada. Within a few weeks, it was announced that Tom Cable (who ended as the Oakland Raiders head coach years later), would be the new head coach. Anthony got a second chance with a new coaching staff and a clean slate, so he went back to work training to get in shape for his sophomore year.

> "Looking back, this was the beginning of his real substance abuse problems. It had started to affect his life and was apparent to others. Anthony got away with a lot in high school for being talented and a good kid, but in college he was getting reprimanded for the same actions. People no longer put up with his behavior because now he was a small fish. He was pissed at life, but instead of cutting back it simply escalated. I think this ruined his chances of ever being a great athlete."
>
> —Emily

Anthony got serious, changed his ways and played basketball to stay in shape in the off-season when everyone else partied. A friend from home moved from Seattle to live with him, and that helped keep things from getting out of control again. They would play pickup games with the U of I basketball team players and were competitive with them. At six-foot-nothing, Anthony could reverse dunk, do one-eighties and more. Then football practice started again for his sophomore year. Up every day at 4:30 a.m. and at the Kibble Dome at five to start the military-style training at 5:15. The coaching staff ran them so hard, players were throwing up every ten feet—where the coaches had placed garbage cans just for that purpose. The coaches pushed their players past the point endurance to sheer body breakdown—a fellow player lost control of his bowels. Apparently Coach Cable was proving a point and introducing himself his own way. Anthony was ready though with his preparation, and it felt good.

Anthony studied the four-inch-thick playbook while he hung out with Emily. Everything was going good. He had gotten himself in a great position to have a successful year. His ugly freshman year was behind him. A new speed trainer from the NBA's Orlando Magic was hired as their new strength coach and introduced plyometrics to the team. This is the science behind track and field starts and forty-yard dashes. Over the next three weeks, Anthony couldn't tell any difference in his game speed, but it did sharpen his forty-yard dash with new proper form: leaning into the start, arm cocked back and no false step taken. He was now running NFL forty-yard dash times and had quit drinking and partying. He was completely ready to play football at a high collegiate level.

Then it happened.

Anthony was enjoying practice that day on special teams and was practicing punt returns. The punt was a short line drive that took a big bounce and popped back up. Anthony caught it with an over-the-shoulder basket catch. Then he spun around heading upfield. He took a few steps, and measured up the incoming defensive players that were rushing him. *There,* he thought, *I'll go right between those two.* Anthony planted a foot to make a break. . . and then he heard a horrible *Pop* in his left knee. The pain was like a thunderclap and almost made him throw up. Down he went.

His season was over before it started.

Two assistant coaches helped him off the field and into the training room. The team doctor looked him over and did a few tests. "You've torn your ACL—your anterior cruciate ligament. It's one of the four major ligaments of the knee. I don't think it's a bad tear though. Probably won't need surgery, just some physical rehab. We'll get you down to the MRI and have a look at it."

Very shortly thereafter, he went into surgery anyway. The doctors opened up his knee to do arthroscopic surgery on it, but found that it wasn't a complete tear. There was enough intact cartilage for the knee to recover on its own within six to eight months. They put Anthony on a machine that rotated his knee at a very slow speed (a full rotation every twenty minutes or so). After a week or two, he was put on crutches. Painful physical therapy followed.

Anthony knew other guys who'd had torn ACLs and never played again. Between the pain and the fear of not playing football, his face was a mask of misery.

"Pain's pretty bad, huh?" the doctor asked.

Anthony just nodded, afraid to talk.

"Here, take this pill. I'll also numb up the knee some." He wrote a prescription and gave it to Anthony. "These will help in the next couple of days."

His first prescription was for a bottle of twenty 5/500mg hydrocodone tablets—the generic version of Vicodin. Not only did these pills stop the pain, just as when he was a third-grader with a broken wrist, they made him feel very, very good. Anthony talked the team doctor into a second prescription—because the pain was so bad. It was for thirty Vicodins. He told Anthony there wouldn't be any more pain pills from his office. The third time he got a refill, it didn't come so easy. The school doctor was skeptical that Anthony couldn't control the pain with aspirin or ibuprophen. Anthony complained to the coach how uncaring the doctor was about his pain. Coach dialed the school doctor immediately and read him out. Anthony was given a stronger version of Vicodin called Lortab.

As the prescriptions continued, the rest of his life started to come apart. Anthony stopped showing up to practices completely. He sat on the couch playing video games, taking pain killers and drinking. Thoroughly high on pain meds, he quit caring and the phone quit ringing.

> "My dad always told me, don't worry when the coach is yelling at you. Worry when they stop."
>
> —Anthony

The coach quit yelling. Since it was a new coaching staff and they hadn't gotten to know Anthony well yet, they didn't have a connection. But in reality, coaches don't go looking for players on the couch. To make himself "feel better," he started fighting with Emily.

> "The injury was an excuse for missed opportunities. But he'd made mistakes well before that ever happened. Although I didn't know it at the time, hurting his knee justified everything for him, and made getting better and getting clean that much harder to do. Once he started abusing drugs and without football to keep him going, there was no turning back. I thought Anthony was depressed - upset about getting hurt, about getting kicked off the team and about the state of our relationship. Really his behavior (and the trouble in our relationship) was due to his early addiction to pain killers."
>
> —Emily

During Anthony's senior year, he and his parents had gone on a recruiting trip to Washington State University. Each player was shown around campus and treated to a fancy dinner. They were there just in time for a game. Before play began, he and the other ten recruits were announced to the 28,000 people at Martin Stadium. The crowd roared as Anthony and the others walked out of the tunnel. *This is it. This is what it'll be like to be a college football star,* he thought. But he never got much closer to playing college football than that moment.

The more pills he took, the more Anthony was changing. He was unsure what he thought of himself, who he was; he had lost sight of his dream and couldn't remember what the dream was. All he could think about was how to escape the pain. The actual pain from the injury was gone in a month and a half, but the pain of failure and disappointment felt insurmountable. He felt embarrassed. He couldn't escape the depression. Anthony found that the pills helped ease the feeling of disappointment and filled the void in his life without football. Before long, his grades started to suffer. Anthony blamed everybody and everything for his failure: It was the University of Idaho's fault for being too big and not helping him adjust to life in college. The ACL tear had ruined his career—even though with physical therapy he could probably return to his old form. The coaches were at fault for working him too hard and then not caring when he came apart. It was a combination of things, and it was everything. . . . And none of it the truth.

Emily recalls:

> "In high school, Anthony got a free pass most of the time. His basketball coach came down harder on him than his football coach did, but he still got away with a lot. He never got in trouble for being late to practice because he was the star player. I remember I was going to be cheering and his bus was leaving for the game. We were making out and I warned him that we were going to be late. He wasn't concerned though. 'Whatever, they'll wait,' he said. It was partly his hormones talking but it's a good example of his attitude toward authority, teachers and coaches. They all let him slack. I have to admit though that even when a teacher did ride him hard, I was right there to bail him out. But when we went to college, without his family and without me constantly by his side, he wasn't going to get away with anything. He was good but he wasn't special anymore. He

had to follow the rules and Anthony wasn't used to that. Now he had a new addiction to prescription pain medication and wasn't even aware he had a drinking problem. I would eventually ask him to choose me over the drugs and he wouldn't be able to do it. It's an impossible choice for an addict. So he would be plagued by guilt which would only cause him to fall deeper into his depression and, therefore, his addiction. It took more and more to escape from the shame each time."

Four

Anthony decided to call it quits at University of Idaho. He walked away from his athletic dream and transferred to Washington State University with no intention of playing sports again. He wanted a clean start with his future wife, so he transferred to WSU which Emily was attending, just eight miles from University of Idaho. A new semester was starting, and Anthony had loads of old friends on campus. His knee was fully recovered, but his dream of playing football was somehow lost at the U of I.

Anthony and Emily at WSU

One night, he was playing basketball at the college gym against some guys on the football team, who were trying to stay in shape in the football off-season. A WSU assistant football coach—a former NFL player—was there watching the game. He recognized Anthony from his recruiting trip in his senior year. Anthony nodded as he was leaving. The WSU receiving coach stopped him and asked, "You're not playing football?"

Anthony pointed to his knee and explained the situation. He could see the confusion on the coach's face. The guy had just seen Anthony play four straight full-court basketball games against top Division 1 Pac-10 athletes and there was no evidence that Anthony had any sort of physical disability.

Before the conversation ended, he invited Anthony to walk-on and try out for the WSU football team as a receiver. The coach smiled and said, "Come down next week and fill out all the locker room cards and get gear issued."

Anthony thanked the coach profusely. As he walked back to his car, he thought, *I've got a second chance at my dream! No scholarship, but a walk-on. And all because I was playing a pick-up basketball game!* Happy as hell, he got into his Explorer, reached into the passenger seat pocket where he'd hidden a prescription bottle and popped a few Norcos—twice the strength of Vicodin—to celebrate.

But over the next few days, he took enough pills to forget the dream even existed in the first place. He never showed up for the walk-on. It wouldn't be until he was in prison that he would pick up a football again.

Anthony stormed through the hospital waiting room with a scowl. He was sweating and swearing under his breath. People probably assumed he had just heard some horrible news. Perhaps he was dying of cancer or maybe he got a huge bill? Anthony was near tears as he went through the motorized doors to the parking lot. The security guard raised an eyebrow. He'd seen this guy limp in a while ago, and now he was stomping out in a rage. It must be something real bad.

It *was* really bad. Anthony had gone in with an "injury." He'd hoped the doctor would write a prescription for OxyCodone, or Vicodin or something like that. Instead he was prescribed 800mg

Ibuprofen tablets—which are simply four regular strength tablets combined that you can buy in any convenience store. He got in his car and the tears ran down his face.

The feeling was coming on. He turned on the car, ignored his ringing cell phone, turned off the radio and drove back to his little college apartment in Pullman, Washington. His head was heavy and in a fog. He had to turn on the air conditioning full blast—and then he was terribly cold. He switched over to heat, full blast—and then he was sweating buckets. Then back to the air conditioning. Everything in his young life was flashing through his head, but he couldn't actually focus on any one thing. He was in a complete panic—gasping for air and terrified of everything. Anthony drove to his apartment and hustled inside, stopping only to make sure the deadbolt was locked.

Devastated, Anthony dropped into the flowered couch and spread out the contents of his pockets on the coffee table. Just hours ago, suffering from withdrawal and battling the demon of addiction in his mind, he'd come up with what—at the time—seemed like a brilliant plan. He took off his sock and slammed his foot into the solid oak table, over and over. The Monster in his head told him this was a good idea. He kicked the table so hard, the veins split in his foot. He wondered why there wasn't much discoloration or swelling right away. So like a madman, Anthony kicked the heavy table again and again. Eventually he got tired and limped into the bathroom to take a leak. He looked down at his foot, which had a softball-sized lump on the top of it. It hurt like hell, but he thought, *Holy shit! This will do! This is my ticket to some serious painkillers!* His foot started to throb—but that didn't stop him from gimping out to the car and driving to the hospital. He was no quitter when it came to pills.

All that, and what do I have to show for it? A sore-ass foot and I-bu-fucking-profen. He wept a little in frustration.

He knew he had a problem with Vicodin—and really any painkillers. Like a nomad always on the move from place to place looking for food, the first thing Anthony would do when entering a friend's or family's home would be to locate where the medications were kept. They were usually in the master bathroom's medicine cabinet, but every so often they would be in the kitchen cabinets somewhere. As soon as his host would leave the room, Anthony opened and closed cabinets quickly, looking for any little bottles with white lids. He scanned for the drugs he wanted by their brands and equivalent generic names: Vicodin, hydrocodone, Norco, Percocet, Lortab, OxyCodone, and of course the infamous OxyContin, were all his main targets. Finding any of them would be a major victory. An immediate extraction would usually take place next. The amount he took depended on several factors, but the first was how well acquainted was he with the person whose house he was in. If he didn't know them well, then he would take the whole pill bottle. If it was a pal, then he had to be careful. It was similar to raiding your parent's wallet or liquor cabinet. Some people pay attention and some people are clueless.

Another factor that crossed his mind was the date on the prescription. If it was recent, then there was a good chance someone would soon be taking another dose, and notice any loss. The thought of the victim making a discovery before he left the house horrified Anthony, but he was ready for almost anything. He'd practiced a routine so that he would be properly appalled at the news of a drug theft in the house and help his friend search for that "dirty bastard."

The one factor that affected Anthony's decisions whether to steal prescriptions or not was how desperate he was. If he hadn't had a pill in a while, if there was no way he could figure out how to get the drugs in any other way, then he started to feel the painful effects of withdrawal. Many addicts refer to this as *jonesing*. When he was jonesing, Anthony felt he had absolutely no choice but to steal the entire bottle. All concern of getting caught went out the window.

His closest friend in college suspected Anthony of stealing pills from his girlfriend's apartment when she was gone. Anthony denied it until the end—and he actually started to believe he hadn't done it. Truth was, he'd climbed a tree that was very conveniently located in front of their house leading right up to an upstairs window. The fog in his head kept Anthony from having rational thoughts and caring that he was climbing a tree, and breaking and entering, in broad daylight on a busy street where everyone knew him. He had sucked every known resource in his personal life dry. He was becoming *That Guy*—the guy everybody was tired of putting up with.

Often, he would come home so completely drunk and stoned, he could hardly speak. Those were the nights when, after he fell asleep, Emily would check his breathing to make sure he was alive. Many times he wouldn't come home at all and she'd call his friends trying to find him.

Anthony thought this was normal behavior in college. It was what people did to have fun. When everyone around him was making mixed drinks, he was chugging rum out of the bottle and chasing it with Pepto Bismol. He thought jumping out of a third story window, flipping over Volkswagens with friends, stealing sandwiches from people on alumni weekends—things he would have never done sober—were just part of the party. It got to the point that Anthony's wild friends told him he needed help. And he did.

By the time Anthony turned twenty-one, he had accumulated seven charges for underage drinking. He decided to quit drinking, much to the approval of his family. But he'd only quit because it got in the way of the greater feeling of the legal narcotics. Even though Anthony thought he didn't look like one, he was sure he was an alcoholic and had graduated into a drug addict.

There was a Monster in Anthony's head. It roared and demanded to be fed—no matter what it took, no matter who he hurt, no matter what risks he took. He *had* to serve the angry beast of his addiction. And if he didn't—well, then he would feel like right now. . . as if he were going to die. He felt as if his flesh was trying to peel off his body and his guts pour out of him like lava. He had to do something to make it stop. To get back to that wonderful place only the painkillers could take him. Because nothing—not Emily, not football—brought him that kind of feeling, and he *had to have it!*

He sat staring at the useless prescription still lying on the coffee table. He had about two hours until Emily came home. *What can I do? How do I get some pills?* Then it hit him. And that's the moment Anthony's criminal career started.

Anthony wasn't a great student, but he did have good computer skills. Taking the hospital prescription, he went to the computer on the desk. He put it on the scanner bed and downloaded the image into his editing program. Anthony quickly wiped out the words "Ibuprofen 800mg," and with a little research online he was able to replace them with "Vicodin 5/500mg." The line under that read, "Take 1 to 2 tablets orally every 4-6 hours as needed for pain." He left that untouched. Printed off, it looked a little rough, but it would have to do.

Anthony took the homemade prescription down to the nearest pharmacy. As he was waiting his turn in line, he evaluated the forged prescription in his hand. *Man, that looks like shit! What am I doing?* But his fear didn't dissuade him, and when it was his turn, he handed over the bogus scrip. "As an addict I was simply just too stupid to consider the consequences, and it was complete desperation that day," Anthony remembers.

The pharmacist looked at the prescription, then eyed Anthony suspiciously. She said, "One minute, sir," and went to the phone. When she returned, she said, "Sorry, sir, but we won't be able to fill this until tomorrow, so we can verify it."

Anthony didn't look like the typical drug addict or criminal, otherwise he probably would have been arrested. The pharmacist had likely delayed the transaction so they could make sure the prescription was valid. Before she could finish explaining why she couldn't give him the pills, Anthony removed his shoe and sock and said in a sad voice, "Well, do you have anything—anything at all for this? Dr. So-and-so told me whatever that medication is would take away this pain. It hurts sooo bad."

"Oh, my God! You poor thing!" she said. "Let me get this filled right away. You must be in so much pain!"

Really, who would ever suspect that someone with a swollen, badly bruised foot that barely fit in his shoe would have done that to themselves? Anthony was simply amazed at the size of the swelling. It had gotten huge in just a few hours.

Within minutes, he was hobbling out of the automatic doors of the pharmacy with a bottle full of Vicodin. He felt his life had been saved—as if someone had just thrown him a life preserver. As he walked out of the pharmacy, the joy inside of him was nearly impossible to hide. Anthony's limp resembled more of a skip. He got into the car, and the first thing he did was dig into the pill bottle, like a fat kid looking for his cake. He crushed a few of the pills in his mouth. (Patients are specifically cautioned not to chew or break apart Vicodin, as it is a timed-release drug, and doing so releases the entire drug at once.) There was no moment better, no touchdown catch that was more exciting and no Christmas morning more glorious. And once again, Anthony started to cry, but this time with happiness.

Anthony laid back his car seat. He waited for his temperature to return to normal and the emotions to settle down. Slowly he felt every part of his body—which had been yelling for the drug all day—finally shut the fuck up. The Monster was curled up in a corner of his mind, purring contentedly . . . temporarily.

Anthony sat up and turned on the car. He didn't need the air conditioning. He didn't need the heat. The radio was playing an oldies station. The sun was out, and it was t-shirt weather. Everything was perfect. Emily called, and he was so very happy she had! "Hey, honey, do you want to get a movie tonight? Do you want me to pick something up to eat? Okay, love you, too. Bye." Life was good as he sang on the way home. The Monster was asleep. With that many pills, Anthony didn't have to worry about him for a while. He didn't have a clue what he had just done to his life.

These were the beginning phases of Anthony's addiction. He was already really good at covering it up. He kept it hidden from everyone he loved. Everyone who loved him expected him to be great, and he wasn't going to disappoint anyone.

> "The apartment was nice. He had a two bedroom all to himself. I shared an apartment with a roommate one building away so I was at Anthony's a lot. It was like we were playing house in a way. That summer, we barbequed with friends and partied at the river. Anthony was carrying his pills everywhere he went but he always told me they were for anxiety. He hid his early addiction pretty well. I thought he had anxiety because he wasn't playing football and didn't have anywhere to channel his energy. Although it was hard for me to understand what a big deal it was that he wasn't playing anymore. I didn't grow up thinking I was going to play professional softball, but boys like Anthony grow up assuming they're going to be a professional athlete. So without football, he had no drive, no sense of commitment or focus. And now he was addicted to drugs too. So he started to spiral into depression."
>
> —Emily

•

The Center for Problem-Oriented Policing states that in 2000, an estimated 2 million Americans over the age of twelve used prescription pain relievers for the first time, up from 400,000 in the mid-1980s. In 2001, an estimated 11.1 million people used prescription drugs non-medically, and more than 6 million abused pain relievers.

In a recent article in *The New York Times*, Dr. Paul Christopher said, "Prescription drug abuse is America's fastest-growing drug problem. Every nineteen minutes, someone dies from a prescription drug overdose in the United States, triple the rate in 1990. And according to the Center for Disease Control and Prevention, prescription painkillers (like oxycodone) are largely to blame. More people die from ingesting these drugs than from cocaine and heroin combined."

Farther along in the article, he says: "[A] large and ever-growing body of research paints a far more complicated picture of addiction.

"The cognitive concepts that we typically associate with 'willpower' —motivation, resolve and an ability to delay gratification, resist impulses and consider and choose among alternatives—arise from distinct neural pathways in the brain. The characteristic elements of drug abuse—craving, intoxication, dependency and withdrawal—correspond with disruptions in these circuits. A host of genetic or environmental factors serve to reinforce or mitigate these effects. These data underscore the powerful ways in which addiction constrains one's ability to resist."

When asked if he had statistics on prescription drug abuse in the country, David Holtz, founder of Drug Rehab That Works in Florida stated, "I do not have exact statistics, and I think that it would be impossible to get real stats because so many people are unaware of what a drug really is. What I mean is there is an illusion, or really *de*lusion, that if a drug is prescribed by a doctor it is not a drug. Here is an example; a few weeks ago I wanted to hire extra security for our center in Atlanta. We found a nice man in his early thirties with a military background and a college degree. He was very clean-cut and interviewed very well. He stated that he rarely drank alcohol and had no drug history. He also said that he would have no problem passing a drug test. Surprise! He tested positive for Benzodiazepines, specifically Xanax, but since it was prescribed by his doctor he did not consider that it could be a 'drug.'"

Holtz continued, "This is all too common. Powerful opiates like OxyContin, Oxycodone and Hydrocodone (Vicodin) are actually synthetic forms of heroin. They are powerful painkillers, but they create physical dependence very quickly with withdrawals that are painful and messy. Benzos or anti-anxiety drugs like Xanax, Valium, Ativan, and Klonopin also create dependence, but the withdrawals are so dangerous they must be medically supervised. These opiates and Benzos make up about seventy-five percent of all intake into treatment centers today. The majority of heroin addicts that we treat today started on some form of Oxy because it's socially acceptable, and they only transitioned to heroin when they could no longer obtain prescriptions or realized that street heroin was a cheaper way to maintain their habit."

•

Once Anthony figured out he could successfully forge his own prescriptions, and he had the computer skills to do it, he started researching everything. His instruction came from medical universities online. He found articles on "how a prescription should be written" and "effective communication with pharmacies." This required some writing in Greek symbols, which he soon understood. The unknown scribbles on pads now made some sense: "PRN" translated to "as needed for"; "PO" meant "by mouth"; "BID" was "two times daily"; "TID" meant three times daily, etc. He discovered a source for sample prescription pads he could purchase online. He learned what is required on a prescription and why there are two lines to sign. Anthony's research continued throughout the night and into the next day.

Before Emily left the next morning, she asked, "What got you up so early? Your first class doesn't start for another three hours."

"A big research project. I hope I can get it done today," he replied. She wished him luck with it and left.

Anthony was in his third year of college, but he was already on pace to be at least a sixth-year senior. The prescription research was far more important than any study he did for any homework assignment. In fact, Anthony was rarely in class these days unless he was high. He scheduled his classes later in the day since the early classes conflicted with his drinking schedule and the time needed to recuperate in the morning. It didn't matter anyway on this day because he didn't intend to go to class at all.

Later that night, Anthony lay in bed waiting until Emily started breathing heavily. When he was sure she was asleep, he got up out of bed and spent the next few hours creating the finest and most detailed prescription that ever was and could possibly be. He was proud of himself because this prescription was perfect.

Anthony knew that he had a great forgery—all the colors were right on. He pulled out the pills he had from the other day and nearly finished them off. It was a little present to himself. Soon he would never need to worry about finding pills again. The Vicodin entering his bloodstream gave him the confidence that inspired him to devote even more time to his new life-saving hobby. Anthony printed off a few copies and went to work writing out a sloppy version that a doctor would create and sign. He had used the same hospital information, same prescribing doctor and everything the same as the successful prescription just two days before. The prescription had the same info, but the new one was unbelievable looking.

Apparently the pharmacy that he took it to had never seen such a cool prescription either. Within a split second of handing it over, the pharmacist's professional demeanor turned into rage. "I'm calling the police, stay here!" she said.

Ohshitohshitohshit! Anthony flew past the other customers and into his car. As he drove home, he thought: *what the hell went wrong?* He was about to turn into his apartment complex when he realized there were four or five police cars outside the apartment! Not too subtly, he gunned the engine and raced down the road. He wound through backstreets, trying to make sure he wasn't followed before he finally pulled over.

His phone rang over and over again. He knew it was Emily. What could he tell her? He was absolutely terrified about what would happen next. He suddenly felt he was at the end of the line and knew he needed help. Anthony looked down at the prescriptions in his hand. Immediately he saw he'd made several crucial errors—but none was worse than using his real name! He crumpled up the prescriptions. *I hate my life.*

After a few hours, he drove home. The cops had gone. Emily was not happy to see him. She glared at him, and shoved a couple of business cards with detectives' names at him. "They want to talk to you tomorrow. What happened?" she asked.

"I'm so sorry. I fucked up. I really screwed everything up." But he was only really sorry he'd gotten caught. He tried to explain without mentioning the pills or what they meant to him. He thought Emily didn't know what was going on with the Vicodin or prescription pills, and he wanted to keep it that way.

The next morning, Anthony nervously went in to the Pullman campus police department and met with the detective. The officer was nice enough, but he explained that there were some serious consequences. He also explained that prescription forging carried some jail time since it's a felony. Just like all those television shows, there was a good cop and a bad cop who interrogated him. He liked one of them, but hated the other. It was clear to Anthony that they wanted him to admit to what he had done, but he didn't understand why the police didn't just put him in jail if his crime was as serious as they said it was. After nearly an hour, the Bad Cop said, "Listen kid, you might as well just tell us the truth because once we get the tapes it won't really matter."

Tapes? Oh shit! thought Anthony. In retrospect, he'd noticed they had cameras. At that moment, he felt like such an idiot—such an *addict*. All Anthony had cared about was getting the pills, and it clouded his judgment and decision-making ability. He hadn't been thinking about an exit strategy.

The police officer added, "If it wasn't for the fact that you turned in your prescription across state lines we wouldn't have to wait to get those tapes."

Washington State University is about eight miles from the Idaho border, and about nine miles from the store Anthony had tried to get the prescription filled. As deflated as Anthony was, he maintained his innocence, claiming that his wallet had been stolen—including his driver's license. "It must have been someone else. Who would do such a thing?"

"All right, okay," the police officer said. "Keep in touch."

Anthony agreed on the surface as he was escorted to the doors. When he got to his car, he thought, *What should I do now?* Soon enough they would have those tapes, and he would be a felon, kicked out of school and probably go to jail for a while. He berated himself for how stupid he was acting. *Shit!* he thought, *If only I had those tapes!* Then an idea occurred to him.

Posing as a student reporter doing a story on security and surveillance in business, Anthony met with the drugstore manager. He could tell that being interviewed meant a lot to him.

Anthony wrote a lot of notes and pretended to be interested as best he could. The manager walked Anthony around the store, pointing out the surveillance system, of which he was very proud. They stopped right in front of the pharmacy as the manager pointed to a camera. Anthony saw the pharmacist and realized it was the same woman at the counter who had nailed him—she was only fifteen feet away! His adrenaline really started to pump in, and he couldn't pay attention to anything the manager was saying. He turned away from the counter so she wouldn't see him—even though he was wearing a baseball cap and fake glasses.

"Come with me. I'll show you the whole system," said the manager.

Anthony gladly followed him to the back of the store.

The manager led Anthony into the back room by the bathrooms. They both slid sideways through those long-hanging, head-banging plastic strip things that separate the warehouse storage area from the main grocery store. Right by boxes of what Anthony presumed was stale food or something was a little painted black wooden door where the overweight manager took out a little key to his office. Anthony had imagined walking into some CIA surveillance or Vegas casino equivalent operation, but they were staring at two dusty little monitors. One monitor was showing the parking lot, and the other had smaller squares, but only a few of them were actually on.

The manager said, "We don't technically have a security department or anything like that. We only have eight cameras throughout the entire store and one pointing out into the parking lot. Each camera sends feedback to a recording device, but it's really just a VCR recorder. We don't have the kind of money like a mall security camera system does. Those can zoom in after recording even. It's that new digital stuff, you know?"

Anthony was amused that he was referring to a mall security system as if that was the top-dog stuff.

"We don't have too many issues here anyway. Between you and me," as the manager leaned over and whispered, the reek of coffee almost made Anthony sick, "almost all of our theft is from our employees."

The manager pointed to a box of unorganized VCR cassettes. Anthony could see that the labels had different dates and times written and crossed out. "These are all the tapes I keep, and I start re-recording after they're full, which is about fifteen days or so. It's kind of a pain in the ass, but I do change the tapes. These ones we just got can record eight hours of footage, so that makes it nice."

"What's with the black boxes on your monitor?" Anthony asked. In the display, several of the camera views were blank.

"Yeah, a couple of the cameras have been down for a while. I've just been so busy that I haven't had time to get them up and going again." He added, "Like I said out there, the one viewing the pharmacy was the first to go, and within two days these other two went. I'm not sure what the deal is. Talk about bad timing too, the only time there's a need for the tapes they don't work."

Anthony instantly knew that he was referring to the incident with him, so he changed the subject. "So how long has it been out?"

"Geez, at least a month or a month and a half," said the manager.

Anthony experienced a wave of relief so profound, he almost passed out. He'd gone into the store prepared to steal those tapes or destroy whatever evidence would send him to jail. But he'd gotten lucky.

The manager gave Anthony his card. Anthony was so emotional at this point that all he wanted to do was to hug this man, but he settled for a handshake and a quiet walk out. *I'm not going to jail! The police don't have any tapes and no proof it was me—and never will!* He hopped into his car and drove home, elated. But his hands were clammy and his heart was starting to race. The Monster was coming on.

Watching television with Emily, Anthony could hardly sit still. She knew something was up, but he was blowing it off. There was still the possibility the police were going to make trouble. But that wasn't really the source of his anxiety. Anthony couldn't even eat dinner—and it was his favorite, lasagna. He was tired, but he couldn't sit still for longer than a few seconds. He was agitated and uncomfortable. Emily tried to help but Anthony was instantly irritated with her. He picked a fight that eventually ended with him shouting, "Leave me the hell alone!"

Anthony hadn't known what having high blood pressure meant, until he felt as if his blood was boiling. He was afraid he couldn't keep the withdrawal symptoms under wraps. Anthony drank a tiny bit of Nyquil, thinking that it would clear up the flu-like symptoms at least. His mind was racing and his nose was running, and snot was dripping down his face. He was freezing but sweating like crazy. His skin was pale, clammy and blotchy. He felt weak and disgusting as hell. He kept telling himself, *I just need to get through one night of this. When I wake up it'll all be good.* Anthony drank another clear plastic cup of Nyquil and tried to lie down. To Emily it must have felt as if she was lying in one of those sleazy, vibrating beds in an hourly-rate motel, Anthony was shaking so hard. The more he tried to stop it, the worse it got. He got up to go to the living room.

Emily asked, "Are you all right?"

Anthony replied, "Yeah, I just can't sleep." He could hardly spit out the words, he was so fucked up. He went to the couch and lay down. Anthony thought this must be the feeling that an animal gets when it picks a spot before it dies.

The Monster was awake and in a rage. It screamed at him, "Listen you little shit, get me some God-damn pills!"

Anthony started to convulse, and slipped in and out of consciousness. His mind was filled with horrible images and things that couldn't possibly be real. Anthony wanted to shimmy up his throat, get his hands on each side of his mouth and pull himself up and out of his body. He had to get away from the Monster!

Then his stomach started, and Anthony ran to the bathroom. The toilet seat was cold, and instantly fluids started running out of his body. *Oh, thank God it's gone.* Before the next spasm hit him, he ran to the medicine cabinet and took anti-diarrhea medicine and some Tums. Then back he went. At times, he could make it all the way back to the couch and cover himself with a sweat-soaked blanket. But then he'd find himself staggering to the bathroom, pee running down his leg. Anthony took more medicine and prayed they would put a dent in the symptoms, but they didn't. For a minute, he was able to get a small break from the torture by dozing against the wall. Trying to blunt the Monster's rage, he chugged the contents of the Nyquil bottle like a beer and finished it, but it just made him exhausted. The Monster didn't want Nyquil. It wanted Vicodin, Norcos, Oxycodone—NOW! He dozed off, but he woke to the smell of vomit on his skin. It was burning his throat. He feared he would die from choking on his own puke, but he could hardly summon the energy to sit up.

"That's when I gave up," Anthony says.

When he next opened his eyes, he saw that Emily was up. Anthony thought she must be disgusted with him. He wondered what she was thinking as she kissed him on the forehead. Just a couple of years ago, she was courtside in her cheerleading uniform and her pompoms rallying the crowd for Anthony while he was sinking three-pointers and throwing behind-the-back passes—always smiling for the crowds. She had to know that this life was very different now— that "her Anthony" had been exchanged for something else. Perhaps she could see the Monster?

As she left for work, she said, "Call your mom or I will."

Anthony was beaten down. He felt he'd lost. He called his mom.

Anthony was sure about one thing: moms never quit loving their babies. As pissed off as he had made his mom over the years, and as much as he thought she hated him at the time, Anthony knew that when one of her cubs were in trouble, Mama Bear would come running.

His mother could hear in his voice: the confusion of admitting defeat, the shakiness, his disillusion. "I feel like I'm in the middle of an ocean, away from all shipping routes, treading water," he said.

"If you hang in there, we can get you help," she replied.

"Nah, I don't need any help," Anthony said. "I just, well, Emily really just wanted me to let you know what's going on."

His mom told him she was going to finish what she had going on and try to come out there within the next few days.

Four

Washington State University is about a five hour drive from his parent's home in Monroe, near Seattle—that's if you speed ninety percent of the trip through the farm lands of Eastern Washington. That's why Anthony was very surprised to find his mom at the door a mere four hours after they'd gotten off the phone.

She gave him a long, long hug, then told him to go lie down. Mothers always comment on their son's appearance: "Your hair is long" or "you've been working out" or "you're so skinny, have you been eating?" But Anthony's mother didn't say anything, and he found the silence loud. She turned back toward the door, but not before Anthony saw a tear running down her cheek. Her voice cracked as she said, "I'm just going to get my stuff out of the car."

Anthony lay down on the flowered couch and watched her bring in a suitcase, a makeup and shower bag and then several trips worth of grocery bags. He looked at the clock on the cable box above the television: 3:33 pm. Then he flipped open his phone to see his outgoing calls with one that read, "Mom 11:16 am." He wondered how she'd had time to shop and pack and somehow get there in four hours. *Maybe she's Superwoman?* he thought tiredly.

When she finished unpacking, she sat on the couch next to Anthony. She handed him a print-out about drug addiction, opiate addiction, their withdrawals and what "we" should expect. "I'll help you through this, if you'll try and get better." With a lump in his throat, he could only nod. "I got you a doctor's appointment at four tomorrow. I had to beg them to see you. We're still waiting to hear back about bed space in the Yakima facility. We won't know until Jerry calls back."

So much information so fast! Anthony had a hard time grasping everything that was going on. *My mom is the most amazing, caring person I've ever met. I love her so much!* But seconds later, the Monster stirred. *Why doesn't she mind her own damned business?* "Doctor's appointment? And what do you mean *bed space?*" he demanded.

"Anthony, you're going to rehab," she said in a forthright tone.

I hate her, he thought to himself.

The Monster sprang into self-defense: "I don't need treatment. This isn't a big deal." Suddenly, he saw his mother as an evil woman who had come to ruin his life. "This is bullshit!" he shouted. Anthony ranted, raged and raved at her for over an hour.

Finally, his mom burst into tears—but she wasn't sad. She was *angry*—as only someone who has given birth and raised a child for twenty-two years can be. She launched into a speech that she seemed to have been practicing for years. To this day, Anthony can't recall exactly what she said. But it was *powerful.* And he knew she wasn't taking no for an answer. Her love and determination were so forceful, the Monster had no choice but to shut up for a second. Anthony realized that only Jesus and his mom had the power to cast out demons.

"I guess I'm going to rehab," he said.

Five

The doctor prescribed Lorazepam—a Benzodiazepine similar to Valium—and Clonidine— to lower his blood pressure. Anthony could feel the Monster was still there, but the drugs made it take a seat. Even with the new medication, the withdrawal symptoms came and went for another three days. He felt like a walking corpse, but he was just enough alive to feel a tremendous amount of shame. Each day, Emily and Anthony's mom chatted away as if nothing was wrong and made him meals. He loved them both, but felt totally removed from them.

Anthony was scheduled to enter treatment on the afternoon of the fourth day. Emily and Anthony's mom told him to drive himself to the treatment center since everything was all lined up and they had to get back to their lives. After all, everything was going to be all right since they had done their jobs. Anthony wasn't experiencing withdrawal symptoms that day, and they felt they'd successfully nursed Anthony back to decent health.

Anthony's mom had left on the third night. Emily wanted to take Anthony to rehab, but she needed to get to school and then to work. She cried as she hugged him. "I love you so much, and I miss you already. I'll come and see you as soon as I can." They were both crying when she left.

Anthony started to pack. He couldn't believe all that had happened over the past week and how much hell he had gone through.

The withdrawal was horrible, but the depression and guilt were just as bad. He said to himself, *Never again will I go through that,* never.

Not two minutes later, the mental addict took Anthony over again. The terribly hard week he'd just gone through turned into a distant, fuzzy memory. All he could remember was how incredibly good he felt after taking those pills. He recalled how every worry in his life left and only confidence remained. The pills made him feel at peace with the world— no sadness, no guilt, no depression and no insecurities. They let him forget the pain of being alive.

Anthony sat down at his computer desk and made another prescription. It was a very basic one this time for ten 7.5/500 mg Lortabs. On the way to treatment, he went into a pharmacy and got the fake prescription filled with no problem. *I deserve one last good feeling*, he thought to himself. He'd taken them all by the time he arrived at Sundown M. Ranch in Yakima, about two-and-a-half hours away from his apartment. "I wasn't nervous at all. I felt everything was just going to be fine," Anthony remembers. That was how the pills always made him feel after a long absence.

For the next few years, Anthony would see these patterns repeat themselves over and over in himself and in others, but he never could truly understand it. There was the physical addiction, but then there was the mental addiction as well. To recover—to have any shot at fighting this thing—you could never just cut off the bad part of the worm (the physical aspect of drug addiction) and expect it not to grow back (the mental addiction that demanded the drug).

Anthony had no worries about pulling into the Sundown M. Ranch's long driveway. At first, the place looked very peaceful to him. But then the happy glow of the pills dissipated and he thought it looked a lot like the pictures he'd seen of that religious cult's compound in Waco, Texas—the one led by that psychotic David Koresh. Heart pounding, Anthony parked his car and turned over his keys to the person in the main lobby. He was instructed to sign a bunch of papers regarding treatment, insurance, the rules, and the like.

Five

Anthony was surprised that there were no gates, fences or watchtowers around the complex at all. He kept thinking of that scene from "One Flew Over the Cuckoo's Nest," when Jack Nicholson tried to escape. Perhaps they had security cameras everywhere. If you decided to run for it they would shout two warning commands at you before tasing you from three different angles. The camouflaged guys would come out of the bushes that lined the long driveway and take you down.

But then Anthony read the rules: *A patient may leave the premises at any time, but will not be allowed to return for treatment.* Myth Number One was busted: the treatment center wasn't a heavily armed psych ward.

Groups of men and women walked past him dressed in normal clothes. Myth number two was busted: patients weren't forced to wear medical gowns.

He was surprised to see that it was a co-ed facility. Myth number three was busted: he'd thought he'd be in treatment with a bunch of addicted guys.

He stopped to look at the copy of the rules he'd been given. *If you are seen looking frequently at a member of the opposite sex, you will be warned. . . . If any communication exists between patients of the opposite sex, you may have your treatment ended immediately and will be asked to leave.* Anthony thought that was pretty harsh and wondered why they needed such a rule. Just then a girl walked by, glanced over at Anthony and smiled. As Anthony smiled back, the entire group of girls laughed, and he could tell she became excited. Later, it would be explained to him that the opposite sex can fill a void within just like the Vicodin. Having interaction with fellow patients not only wouldn't help his addiction, it would harm his treatment—and hers.

No phone calls were allowed for the first five days. No cell phones or other communication devices were allowed. All the focus was geared toward the treatment and the recovery without outside influence. As Anthony continued to read the rules, he was becoming more and more nervous and questioning what he had gotten himself into.

The number one rule *was Absolutely no drug or alcohol use will be tolerated.* They wanted their patients to hit the ground running and be past their withdrawal symptoms when they entered the facility. Anthony felt a twinge of regret at taking those pills on the drive there.

He was led into a plain room with twin beds and shown where he could put his stuff. Then he was introduced to his roommate, who had also just arrived. He was a 400-pound African man who said he was a minister from Zimbabwe. He had gotten addicted to cocaine. "See," as he pointed to his huge nose. The flap between his nostrils wasn't visible any longer. Feeling overwhelmed, Anthony lay down on his bed and almost immediately fell asleep.

The next morning: "It's 6:55 a.m." announced the loud speaker Anthony hadn't known was there. Then: "It's 7:00 a.m."

Okay. . . how often does it do this? Anthony wondered. Then he heard noises in the hall. Resigned that he wouldn't get any more sleep, he rolled over, and opened his eyes. Right in front of him stood his roommate, dressed in a tribal beaded wrap-around. Yesterday, the man had been dressed in perfectly ordinary Western-style shirt and pants. Anthony blinked several times at the man's outfit, wondering if he was still dreaming, or perhaps hallucinating.

"Time to eat, young Antonie," his roommate rumbled. Then he went out.

Anthony had no choice but to dress and follow him.

The schedule at the rehab facility was very structured and simple. Each morning after breakfast, all the patients met in a lecture hall for about an hour or so to listen to a speaker. For most, this usually turned into an early morning nap. Then they broke into groups until lunch. After the meal, it was back for another big meeting and then groups again. Evenings were for personal time until 7 p.m., when they were required to watch recovery-based films. They also held an outsiders-welcome Alcoholics Anonymous meeting every Tuesday night, which took the place of the required films.

In Anthony's first ever AA meeting, he had no idea what to expect. He'd been required to attend meetings before by the courts after the seven drinking-related charges he had racked up over the years, but those had been pretty loosely run. This meeting was different right from the start.

Anthony sat down next to his cocaine-fueled roommate and watched everything. There must have been 150 people in the room. They started out reading out of the Big Book, a copy of which Anthony had been given earlier. He had already been given an assignment to read about an old guy named Bill. There were weird chants and sayings that people kept shouting. Thankfully, he had the big guy by him to give him some feeling of comfort, because it was really starting to feel awkward. He wondered if they were going to pass out Styrofoam cups and tell them to drink the Kool-Aid. *Just drink it, no questions!* But it was just coffee. He wondered if they stopped chugging so much caffeine, maybe they wouldn't shout all that weird shit? It sounded like Tourette Syndrome to Anthony.

"Easy does it," shouted many.

An old lady with no teeth repeated, "One day at a time," over and over.

Even the normal-looking guy murmured, "It works, if you work it."

Faker, Anthony thought. *He's no addict.*

After the basic introduction and some reading about Step One—which was "admitting to ourselves we are powerless"— the woman who was chairing the meeting, shared her story. It was her third week of treatment. She was going home in a few days and she told the group she was scared.

"Why the hell would you be scared to leave this place?" Anthony asked his roommate. He just shrugged.

The woman talked about her several failed marriages. She told them how she'd left her kids locked in the car with the windows up outside of meth houses while she got high. Then she shocked Anthony. She told the group that she and her husband sold their newborn baby on the black market to raise cash for drugs. She had been searching for months to track the baby down. She blamed "the disease" for making her do all of that.

Anthony hated the woman. All that "disease" stuff sounded like a cop-out to him. He felt that she wanted something to blame so she didn't have to accept responsibility for her actions. *Fucking loser. God, just kill yourself, please.* Anthony got up in disgust to try to leave, but realized leaving would have created a commotion, so he slumped back in his seat. Thankfully, the lady sat down. The room was silent. Anthony couldn't figure out why people weren't throwing things at her.

Then a normal-looking guy in a business suit—which seemed odd for treatment—stood up and thanked her for what she'd shared. He spoke softly, while looking around at everyone. Somehow he commanded respect. He explained the beauty of what AA is and how the courage of one inspires us all to have it. He started to explain how he'd wanted to get his wife help, and he'd thought things would get better if she had just attended some AA meetings. He didn't realize she was so sick. He said the disease took his family from him, and now he leaned on them to be his family.

Anthony blocked out most of it. The crying and the blaming and the nonsense stories—and no one was telling these people how awful they were. He glared down at his shoes, wishing this guy would shut up.

After the meeting was over, Anthony went directly to his room. He didn't feel like talking to anyone. He'd just crawled into bed when his huge roommate came in.

"Antonie," his roommate began in his heavily accented English, "did you know that man who spoke this evening was married wit three young children? He worked for Boeing—they build airplanes in the sky, you know? Anyways, his wife was drunk an' went for a drive wit her little children in the back. She killed them all. So sad this dying. Good night, young Antonie. So sad," he murmured to himself as he lay down on his bed.

The lights went out, and Anthony realized his anger was pointed at all the sadness from this thing they were calling a disease.

Anthony would later describe these feelings in treatment as he opened up to the group: "All my problems, all my negative feelings about myself, and even insecurities I have, are like a bunch of holes in me. When I take drugs, every one of those holes is filled and covered up. But as the drugs wear off, the holes reopen and there's always another one there. One more hole to fill in the next time. So I threw it all away again."

The next morning at the lecture hall, there was a very charismatic speaker named Clay—who turned out to be the director of the entire treatment facility. He told them he'd been twenty years sober. Clay asked everyone to pull out their required notebooks, they were about to play his favorite game. He asked everyone to rank the five most important things in their lives, with number one being the most. A few minutes later, he called up five people to come to the front with their papers. He grabbed the first paper from a woman.

"Oh, nice," Clay said with a big smile. "Your boys, how old are they?"

"Three and five," she replied with a big smile.

"Number two is providing a good education and home for them. Okay. Number three is caring for your mom. Number four is your relationship with God; and number five is being a good person. A heart of gold," Clay said.

The woman beamed.

Then Clay's demeanor completely changed. He practically snarled at her as and tore up the paper and aggressively threw it to the ground. "Pick up the pieces and go sit down," he almost yelled.

Several people gasped.

Wow, this guy is a real dickhead, Anthony thought.

"Next," Clay said, as he reached for the next list of five. He scanned it and quickly tore it up and basically said the same. Then he did another. By the time that he got to the last guy, people were damn near booing him.

The last kid nearly wouldn't hand over his sheet. Clay went through his list and ripped it up. He said, "You all have written on your papers what are the most important things to you, but you haven't put what was most important first. If sobriety is not number one in your life, you will lose all of these things you love."

He may be a dickhead, but he's right, thought Anthony as he looked down at his list and realized sobriety wasn't important to him either. Anthony definitely got the point of Clay's game.

On Day Twenty-One, Anthony was discharged from the Sundown M. Ranch in Yakima. He was given a coin and his sobriety, with instructions on how to keep both. To keep the coin, newly sober addicts needed to keep driving past the bar up the road that would take the coin in exchange for a pitcher of beer. Then he gave his exit speech and rang the little bell outside the complex, as all those who'd been treated did. As Emily drove Anthony away, they followed a van that had left the treatment facility just before them. Anthony watched as the van pulled right into the bar parking lot.

Anthony told Emily, "Everyone in treatment should be serious about recovery. Many of the newly released addicts faked the whole thing to please the courts and avoid jail. That van was full of fakers." He felt no urge to stop as they drove by the bar.

Anthony's instructions were: "Ninety in ninety," meaning he should attend ninety AA meetings in his first ninety days. Relapse is something not quite understood by the addict new to recovery. He felt cured, healed, and his nightmare was behind him. In his mind, he wasn't like the people at the meetings. He was different.

He wasn't the guy in the van trading in his coin, and as long as he could find someone else whose addiction was worse, his didn't seem that bad. What he didn't understand was that relapse is real. Just as the diabetic must take his disease seriously and take insulin and monitor his condition, the addict must constantly monitor his disease as well.

> "I did drag myself to a few meetings, but I immediately noticed differences between myself and them. They planned activities to stay sober like Frisbee golf. *Pussies*, is all I thought. I never played Frisbee golf until ten years later in prison."
>
> —Anthony.

Not a week out of treatment, he was told to follow up with a doctor. He was diagnosed with bipolar disorder, depression and severe anxiety. He was put on Zoloft, then later Paxil, and also given a sleep-aid similar to Lunesta. It seemed to level him out.

> "One thing about addiction is that it creates illnesses and the presence of disorders that aren't really there. Therefore freshly sober addicts or ones early in their recovery will get diagnosed with something that they don't actually have. This is a major problem, and also one of the reasons why anti-depressants and anti-anxiety medicines do so well."
>
> —Anthony

Anthony went back to his college classes. He also picked up new hobbies, including learning how to play poker. He loved the game so much that he went out and bought a Texas Hold'em table for about $100—this was when Texas Hold'em poker was gaining in popularity. He decided to put on some small poker games when he went home for Spring Break. Just as with sports, Anthony attacked his new hobby obsessively. The gas was either fully open or he was on the brakes—there was no coasting for Anthony in anything he did.

One of his friends fell in love with the table and offered him $1,000 for it. That's when his entrepreneurial spirit kicked in. He figured all of the people his age in the fraternities were into this new fad. He knew he could sell poker tables. He knew they'd started construction of a casino in Pullman, but decided that company needed a little competition.

> "Just like when we were young, he wanted nothing to do with rules. Even after Sundown, he wasn't following the rules. He totally disregarded and disobeyed what they told him to do at the treatment center. I knew nothing about addiction back then, but I still knew he had to go to those AA meetings! Well, he didn't, and so here he was right back in the same environment partying harder than before. I was confused and still pretty naïve –he can't take the pills but he can still drink?"
>
> —Emily

Emily had finished her undergraduate program at WSU, but since Anthony still had over a year's worth of classes left, she decided to stay on and attend the MBA graduate program and help Anthony complete his undergraduate degree. She was a full-time graduate student while working as a student teacher that paid for her tuition, so she was super busy. Anthony didn't enjoy how busy Emily was, but her absence also made it easy to keep a lot of his personal life from her.

Anthony kept going to what he called "lame" AA meetings as he continued his research of how to get to a source of poker tables. It turned out there were many manufacturers, and they made a lot of these tables—and they were in many ways disposable. Hundreds of Blackjack, Roulette, Poker and Craps tables were made with foldable legs and basic markings on the felt. They were created from the cheapest materials to withstand constant two-week use by casinos for training conferences. All the tables had drop slots for pushing money through with a paddle that dropped into a cheap, metal, removable drop box. To someone in the gaming industry, these tables were basically garbage. But to college kids all over the country wanting to have their own poker nights with the right table, they were the coolest thing ever.

It wasn't long before Anthony had worked out a plan. He could acquire a table for about $100, pay for bulk shipping of a few and turn them around for $750 to $1,200 all day long. Very quickly, his personal eBay account turned into Tony's Gaming Supply. Orders started pouring in. He couldn't get his hands on tables fast enough.

Anthony was doing so well, he decided to open a store in downtown Pullman. Tony's Gaming shared a building with a lock and safe company, a hair salon, a restaurant and a phone store. The pace of business kept him so busy, he ran out of time to attend school. He hired a good friend from back in Monroe to move to Pullman and manage the new store for him. Anthony found everything about his new business cool, even the business cards, on which he spent much time making them just perfect. Anthony's parents were proud of him as they took pictures of his storefront. The owner of the building approved all of the remodeling plans he submitted, so Anthony hired five college students to work on the build-out. He created a Vegas theme, with murals of the Strip painted all around. The back of the store had stockpiles of tables. He found a custom poker chip maker that would print custom graphics. Anthony was also able to find someone to make custom playing cards as well. He had custom logo playing cards from Atlantic City as giveaways. For $100 you could buy a carved oak table box that had blackjack on one side of the lid, then you could flip the table over and play roulette with a removable wheel. Right before his grand opening, he even stocked neon signs and poker dealer hats. He posted a list of tables for sale and started pre-selling them on eBay prior to the store opening. Orders came flooding in. Things were going good. The real estate company he was leasing from brought their friends over to observe the store, and there was quite a buzz around town.

Anthony's entire adult life had been spent playing a game. Before, it had been football, but the gambling supply company seemed to fill that need for him. People who loved Anthony, and people he loved, seemed to be proud of him again—and he was proud of himself. The money was coming in, and to celebrate he drove home that weekend and bought a brand new $40,000 Tahoe with every cool option on it, to the dismay of Emily.

> "He was obsessed with buying that car. I fought him so hard on that stupid Tahoe. Here we were, broke college students, with a $600 a month car payment! Don't get me wrong. I like nice things—but not when you can't afford them. I rarely bought anything that wasn't on sale and my idea of 'nice things' was a new pair of jeans from The Gap. When Anthony started abusing drugs, he also became extremely materialistic. It was like he was also addicted to material things. He bought me a purse and a pair of Seven jeans for my twentieth birthday. At the time, I'd never even heard of these things. He made a big show of it and made me open them in front of all our friends. He even had to explain to me how 'expensive' they were. The jeans were $150 and the purse was $400. I was pretty shocked considering I'd never paid more than $60 for purse or a pair of jeans! Of course they were nice and I loved them but I didn't live and die by stuff like that and neither, I thought, did Anthony."
>
> —Emily

The following week, Anthony was in class when his phone wouldn't stop vibrating. It was his manager calling over and over again. He walked outside to take the call, and his manager said, "They pulled guns on me and cops were everywhere!"

"What? Who?" Anthony replied. He hurried to the store, to discover the same two men who had visited the previous month. "What's this about?" he asked

The men identified themselves as special agents for the Washington State Gambling Commission. They told Anthony they were confiscating his entire inventory. Every question he asked was countered with an invitation to go to jail. They seemed unfamiliar with gambling equipment; one of the police officers even confused a dealer rake for a gun from the other side of the store. The rake was used in a set-up display for marketing pictures for eBay auctions. Things were very tense until Anthony explained what it was and the agent examined it.

They loaded table after table in their trucks. One of the agents said, "You needed a wholesaler's permit to sell this stuff. The application costs $5,000—but you'd never be approved."

Anthony said, "But don't I have a chance to fight this? What did I do?" They cited a host of "infractions," which included the illegality of selling anything with markings on the felt.

Anthony started yelling at the people loading up his tables in cars and box vans. "If I was doing something illegal, why didn't you tell me when you were here over a month ago?"

"Sorry, kid," was all he got for an explanation.

Anthony sat on the curb outside of the store and watched as one by one the trucks left. He decided to call a few lawyers in town, but none would see him after he explained the situation.

It took one compassionate police officer to explain to him what had really happened. Tony's Gaming sat directly across the street from the fire department. One night late—because Anthony was still trying to attend college during the day—he and his manager were moving computers, furniture and inventory around the store. This drew the attention of a firefighter, who figured they were running an online casino. He told his good buddy the real estate agent—who had a financial interest in the only casino within seventy miles. The guy had thought Anthony was competing for his revenue and called in the Gaming Commission.

The policeman explained that the town was setting an example by shutting down a student running an underground casino with elaborate tables and devices. He confirmed that it was against the law in the state of Washington to sell any gambling felt with any kind of markings on it. However, he acknowledged that you could go into Wal-Mart or Target and find the exact same things for sale with gambling boxes and different felt markings.

Anthony understood the situation finally, but he couldn't understand why they hadn't just told him months ago. And why make an example of him?

"Luck of the draw, kid" the cop said, trying to be funny.

Then the phone started to ring. Call after call came in from buyers who had paid for the tables that had just been confiscated. After Anthony tried to explain it once to a buyer, he discovered that it sounded like a scam to them. They wanted their tables or they wanted their money, and he had neither. He called around to see how much he could get for his new Tahoe with less than 800 miles on it—he'd have to take a $10,000 loss. Anthony was instantly broke.

The day after Pullman's first casino had its grand opening—the one the real estate agent owned—Anthony went out and got wasted with his ex-manager. While Anthony's friend slept off his hangover the next day, he went back to filling bogus prescriptions. He felt the drugs helped him with his problems, but that is the lure of drugs.

Emily says:

> "A little while after Sundown, Anthony was back taking the pills. Then he would stop again, using me to help wean him off, asking me to ration his pills. Of course I was happy to

help. He always told me that he wanted to stop, that he was going to stop—and I believed him every time. Every time he said it was his last. We had fight after fight about him quitting. I begged him to stop, I was so worried he would overdose or do something stupid.

"I remember waking up in the middle of the night to make sure he was still alive. I'd put my finger under his nose or watch for his chest to rise and fall then lay there just watching him breathe. One night, I woke up and he wasn't there. He'd never come home. It was the dead of winter and there I was, walking up and down Stadium Way in my slippers, calling his name, calling everyone I knew. I was sure something bad had happened; that he was in trouble or passed out in a ditch somewhere. I couldn't find him so I went back to my apartment, showered and got dressed for the day. I was administering an exam that morning for the class I was teaching. On my way to class, I made one last stop at his friend's apartment and banged on the door. No one answered, so I finally just went inside. Anthony and about ten other guys were passed out on the floor. I was stepping over them in my suit and heels. It was then I realized how insane this was. The dichotomy of it all! I was in graduate school, a teacher, a grown-up. Yet here I was picking through bodies looking for my boyfriend. But still I believed that he would stop. One day, he would just stop—right? I screamed, I threatened, I begged some more. But obviously, he never stopped."

"One thing about addiction is before you can ever have any control over it you need to first say goodbye to it, then nev-

> er greet it again. I never formally said goodbye, so it wasn't much surprise when I'd picked it up again."
>
> —Anthony

Anthony decided to go face the real estate agent. It didn't go well. In fact, Anthony still had five months left on his lease, and the owner wanted every penny.

> "Part of business is having a Plan B. Every business deal is potentially a risk, and the best you can do is to honor your commitments even to heartless, greedy bullies. I had a new commitment that day. From that moment on, I became a criminal."
>
> —Anthony

He didn't want to be any criminal. He wanted to be *the best* criminal. Of course, the drugs helped him make that commitment. Anthony would soon prefer an illegal fifty cents to a legitimate dollar. He respected it more. His new attitude toward business was, if you're not cheating you're not winning.

Screw those guys who stole my tables. Screw the real estate owner—who was a big fish in a little pond—and screw that guy's friends in high positions in the city who facilitated the whole thing. Anthony had gotten professionally robbed, and he was damned well going to make the man pay.

A few days later, every computer was stolen from the real estate office. The following day, the front page of the newspaper reported that the real estate company couldn't run their business. Every file—including lease agreements for a ton of college kids—was gone. They'd never backed-up their information. The reward money for information about the robbery went from $1,500 to $5,000 that first week. The following week, the Pullman police department issued a statement that no arrests would be made if the computers were returned. A few days after that, the university police issued a similar statement.

After a week of guarantees, Anthony decided it was time to return the computers. He asked a friend, who was a student at WSU and struggling to stay in school, to help him return the computers and split the reward money. He didn't have to ask twice. The friend decided to call to set up the meeting. The cops traced the line and were at his apartment within an hour. Anthony dropped off the computers at the real estate office one night, hoping that the trouble he had gotten his friend in would disappear. But his friend never got credit for the return of the computers and wasn't given a dime of the reward money. Although no charges were filed, the arrest gave the university police enough reason to kick him out of school.

Anthony felt responsible—not just for paying back the buyers of the tables—but also for his out-of-work manager and his out-of-school friend. He cleaned out his phone messages, simply because they were mostly a mixture of pissed off buyers ready to call the police. Too cowardly to return the calls, he sent out a bulk email saying that he was sorry for the delay; he'd recently gone out of business and would issue a full refund via PayPal shortly.

Anthony had been through a lot—a relapse, a failed business, getting his friend in trouble and he still owed a lot of money. He knew it wouldn't be long until he was arrested for selling the gambling equipment, taking money for the stuff and never shipping them to customers. Yet he still struggled to maintain his studies. One of the classes, Anthropology, was in a brand new building that was still under construction, but it did have a computer lab and a coffee shop up and running. One day, while he was watching workers move everything around, he noticed fifty or more sets of the nice, modern Italian leather furniture. There were three- and four-person leather sofas, recliner-style love seats, wrap-around u-shaped connect sets, and the finest coffee tables, end tables and ottomans. It was all on the first floor, probably waiting for construction to finish before it was distributed to the other floors. He thought: *Everything this university has is mine. They owe me for their part in taking my tables and ruining my business.* After taking some pictures, Anthony used a fictitious account to run a test eBay ad to see what would draw the most buyers. Then he started plotting.

For less than twenty dollars, Anthony purchased three sets of white, paper cloth painter's outfits, a stack of invoice forms to carry on a clipboard and some WSU hats he found in a clearance rack that made the disguises look perfect. Anthony bought a tape measure and got measurements from the furniture. Then he found an all-white, old-as-hell milkman style delivery truck. He stole a faculty parking pass from a car with an open window.

On the morning of the planned heist, Anthony popped a lot of pills for confidence. He recruited two friends to help him with the lifting. They parked in the neighboring staff parking lot—and it felt like it was a mile away. They sat in the huge, rusty milk truck, each too terrified to get out and swipe the furniture. When someone walked past, they were sure the person knew exactly what they were up to.

"This is freaking me out, man," said one of his friends. "I don't want to do this."

"Me neither," the other guy said in a shaky voice.

Anthony didn't argue with them, and started up the milk truck.

The next morning, Anthony reminded himself that stealing the furniture was the answer to his current financial issues and his not-so-distant future legal issues as well. From the responses he got on the auctions, he knew he could sell the furniture. He talked his friends into going back to the building with him. He had them go in and sit on the couches for a while and check out the scene. If they'd been paranoid in the milk truck, the three rookies were a mess as they sat on the furniture. Everything caused near-panic.

"Don't look, she sees us."

"Oh, my God, he's on the phone."

Or the heart attack they had when a group of teachers walked by.

Anthony decided to try and at least move the couch they were sitting on nearer to the door. That went well, so he had them move the couch outside. Once it was out, they decided to go for it—and ran with the sofa toward the milk truck. Anthony realized it's the stupid criminal who gets himself caught—and they looked like participants in a TV show called "The World's Dumbest Criminals."

In a moment of panic, Anthony yelled, "Bring it back!"

The others slowed to a walk. In that moment, he decided real university movers making $6.25 an hour wouldn't be sprinting with a couch over their heads. They'd be moving slowly and acting like they didn't give a shit. They set the couch down on the ground. Anthony went and got the truck and parked it on the sidewalk, like real movers would. They placed a couple of cones in front of the bumper to make it look legit. Anthony took a new look around and realized they were within sight of everyone and right next door to the campus police. This is the way to do it! So obvious nobody'll notice. Anthony and his crew moved couch after couch and end table after end table until the milk truck was full.

Then he thought to himself, *Where do we store all this stuff?* He'd never thought about what to do if they actually pulled it off.

Anthony and his boys took the milk truck back for a total of four trips to nab more furniture. Every time they left was a rush. They filled up three local apartments and still had to rent a storage unit the next day in nearby Moscow.

He used eBay auctions to sell the furniture one piece at a time. Anthony discovered he could sell more furniture offline to the bidders who didn't win—and in the process avoid listing fees and records of the sales. He had to drive to Spokane several times that month to ship off furniture.

The whole escapade was sloppy as hell, but it accomplished all Anthony set out to do, with a satisfied feeling of revenge on the WSU police that supported the raid of his poker business.

He was also able to refund every single person who had purchased a table from him. He would have refunded the money even sooner had PayPal not temporarily suspended the new account due to the amount of money flooding in. Anthony ended up with some personal cash in the end, and none of his friends ever needed any furniture again.

It took nearly a week before anyone at the University figured out they'd been robbed. The little newspaper put the theft on its front page. Everyone had seen Anthony and his crew, but nobody had actually noticed them. Not one witness. Luckily for Anthony, the cops didn't cross-reference the missing furniture with pieces available on eBay,

Afterwards, Anthony reveled in the glow of pulling off a successful crime. He had a feeling of honor and success, mixed with an adrenaline-rush, heightened by opiates. He'd enjoyed the camaraderie of his team, his growing bank account, and the respect others showed him. Anthony was getting criminally savvy, and so he decided to pursue more jobs. An idea would hit him, and he'd go do the research, calculate the odds and the payout and start the planning, including the recruiting. Within a year, he had his hands in all kinds of jobs. His friends would come to him and ask, "You got anything?" Sometimes they were referring to new capers, and sometimes they were referring to pills. The disease had spread.

Anthony stopped attending AA meetings. He'd found his therapy.

Anthony decided it was time to ask Emily to marry him. He was absolutely in love with Emily—even more so than when he'd first fallen for her in Eighth grade. Even when Emily drove him nuts, he knew she was always trying to make him a better person.

He started to plot the perfect marriage proposal with the same attention to detail he had planned his gambling company. He wanted to wait several months to plan out the most special way to pop the question, but only a few days after getting the ring, he found himself at Emily's house for one afternoon back in Monroe.

Emily's family and Anthony were around the island in the kitchen talking and joking. Her dad started heading outside. It hit Anthony he had to go now. No waiting. In the middle of the family conversation, Anthony stuttered to Emily's dad, "Will you, um, I, um, will you take a look at my car. It isn't sounding right."

Anthony followed him outside like a little puppy. He respected and liked the man, who he secretly called Charles Ingalls, from the show "Little House on the Prairie," since he always seemed to be helping everyone. When it started pouring down rain in the middle of his sister's outdoor wedding, Emily's dad had once again saved the day. There were shade tents set up, but they were no match for the deluge. Everybody—two hundred-fifty men and women—ran inside to get away from the dumping buckets of water. Anthony's sister—one of the bubbliest and most cheerful people anywhere—was close to tears. In full suit and tie, he somehow dragged a huge 1,000 square foot tent to cover the caterer's table and all the food all by himself. Water from the tent rolled down his back. His glasses fogged up. Finally, some men joined him. Then women pushed their men out to help. Before you knew it, he was directing traffic and had set up a new area for seating, formed rows of chairs and organized the caterers to temporarily set up shop in the open garage bays. Fifteen minutes later, somehow it was all ready to go again. The pastor started to speak, and everyone was seated. Anthony looked for Emily's Father, and discovered him standing in the back watching. Of course, he had given up his seat for someone else. He never said anything and never wanted thank yous.

They walked to the Tahoe, and Anthony was sure that her dad was wondering how a new car wasn't running right.

> "I got ready to ask him for permission to marry his daughter. Holy shit, my heart was pumping. Adrenaline was flying, but as much as I wanted to hurry up and ask him, I couldn't. Her dad kept asking me troubleshooting questions about the car. I even went along with answering his questions, but I don't remember what he was asking me because I was so nervous. I popped the hood and took his orders and gave it some gas. I was sitting in the driver's seat with the window down. He asked me to push the pedal again, but I was already out of the car and around the front standing in front of the most intimidating man I'd ever met, my future father-in-law. I bet men have been afraid of their father-in-laws for thousands of years. Somehow I managed to stammer out, "The real reason I asked you out here was I wanted to talk to you. . . ." When my eyes met his, I was paralyzed both physically and mentally. He asked me a few questions in a really serious tone that I'd never heard before. The last question that he asked was, 'When are you planning on doing this?' Right now! I said."
>
> —Anthony

Anthony walked into the house with his future father-in-law shadowing him. Conversation stopped as Emily and the others saw the look on his face. To Anthony, everyone around Emily faded away. He began to tell her how much he loved her in front of her family. He was sure that the people standing around were guessing what was coming next. Anthony dropped down to one knee, just like when he followed his mom's advice when he asked Emily to their Eighth grade dance. Except this time Anthony didn't have a rose—he had a ring that had been burning a hole through his pocket.

Emily said yes, and they hugged. They were engaged! The family joined in the hug.

> "It was the perfect proposal, right there in front of the family I loved so much. It was adorable and genuine. Not fancy or fake. It was real (or so I thought). He told me I was his best friend, that he'd always loved me and that he'd always wanted to spend the rest of his life with me. Of course I said yes. I accepted him in spite of his addiction to drugs because I loved him more than anything, in sickness and in health—even though we weren't married yet! But there was a lot I didn't know back then. I knew nothing about his 'other' addictions, or that he had relapsed again."
>
> —Emily

Anthony was a fraud. He was pretending to believe he could live with his addiction. He was about to bring Emily and her family deeper into his world of chaos.

Anthony and Emily's engagement portrait

Six

Anthony and Emily chose a date for the wedding and also decided to buy a house. They decided to build a small custom home in a new development and put down a large deposit. They both found planning the wedding fun, but it was almost overwhelming to do that and all the choices they had to make for the new house.

After the ridiculous furniture thefts ended, Anthony needed a new way to make money, and eBay was the big thing. It was like a giant garage sale. Anthony had a friend who was involved with baseball cards, and Anthony tracked the eBay auctions for them. He watched other auctions, as well. He discovered that older men who were kids in the Fifties and Sixties and grew up idolizing Mickey Mantle or Joe DiMaggio bid on cards that ranged in quality and sold anywhere from $10,000 to well over $100,000. There were cards that sold for over a million dollars! No matter what happened in the economy or stock market, the collectors bought cards. Anyone who could afford a $50,000 baseball card wasn't going hungry anytime soon. The idea that an old piece of cardboard that had been printed to sell with tobacco or bubble gum packages decades ago could be worth that much blew him away.

He scanned in his personal collection and sold the cards on the website. The results were astounding. His Fleer #57 1986-87 Michael Jordan rookie card went for $850. A 1984 Star XRC Michael Jordan rookie card sold for $740. Anthony didn't understand the trading card system, but he decided to learn everything there was to know about it. For instance, why were there two different rookie cards?

His study of the sports trading cards business at first focused on familiarizing himself with the different valuable time eras in each sport and the many different card makers. New cards weren't of any interest to him. Vintage cards were where the money was. But as Anthony learned more, he discovered that the most important thing wasn't the card's make, year or player—it was the "grading" that mattered. It determined everything. Grading a card determines the worth of the card based on the centering, edges, surface condition and the corners. Each criterion was given a point value on a one to ten scale. The point value determined the worth of the card. It was a cutting edge field and less than a handful of companies were doing it. After working hard to understand all the ins and outs, he filled out an application and paid a fifteen dollar fee. Just like that, Anthony owned a card grading company he called VGS, for Vintage Grading Service.

Anyone familiar with eBay understands the importance of "feedback." Its numbers and ratings have a direct impact on sales you can make from each auction—good feedback means the better buyers will participate in your auction; bad feedback drives them away. Anthony had 100 percent positive feedback and was a power seller.

He purchased large quantities of cards, pulled out the best for selling individually and gave them a good grade, then resold the remainder at one price. He bought ungraded and sold graded. He scoured the country for sources of card collections: the grandma who discovered her husband's collection in their attic collecting dust; a guy in California selling his Willie Mays rookie card to pay the bills; the small card shop going out of business in Utah. He found a 1933 Goudey Babe Ruth off a Yahoo auction (back when they had auctions) for $500. He graded it, then resold it the next day for $1,500. He picked up an ungraded Mantle for $1,500, and turned it around after grading it, for $4,000.

People sought Anthony out so they didn't have to pay the higher grading fees from the bigger card grading companies. His website advertised a fee of just six dollars per card. He was doing well and grading as fairly and honestly as possible. After some research, Anthony learned that the major grading companies typically under-graded as much as possible to keep their names valued and respected. Meanwhile, the companies' employees were buying, regrading and selling on the side differently and making big cash. It was a trend he learned to identify.

Anthony would sit up in his apartment for days running eBay auctions and grading cards. He was still passing classes because he was paying a friend to attend for him. Even though he wanted to go, he could no longer sit still and pay attention. His pill addiction, ADD and OCD, alongside his growing anxiety, made going to class overwhelming. Anthony got a student I.D. with his pal's picture on his WSU I.D. From that point on, Anthony stopped flunking classes due to poor attendance. In fact, the guy who was substituting for Anthony felt it was good enough money that he actually put pride and effort into his "job." Once, he invited Anthony over to show him "our class project." But one day, the friend had to go home to Seattle for a week. Anthony attended—and discovered to his horror that there was a quiz. He struggled through it. When he went to turn in his paper to the teacher's assistant, the man looked at him puzzled and said, "Wait, you're not Anthony." He left quickly after some excuse, then later dropped the 150-person class online.

Anthony was so busy, he even tried hiring someone to buy his pills for him. The problem with teaching someone how to forge prescriptions was that sooner or later it would go to hell since they eventually got addicted themselves and disappeared. Or the pharmacist receiving the scrips would start to question the amount of pills being dispensed. He didn't really mind going out and getting the pills himself. It gave him a break in the action and got him out of the apartment for a while. The one thing that Anthony had going for him was his appearance. He didn't look like a drug addict, and it made him wonder what a real drug addict looked like.

> "Prescription drug users are your judges, your police officers, your professional athletes, your bosses, your coworkers, entertainers, your pastor, his wife, your wife, your kid's school teacher and even you. The only thing worse than you being a drug addict is when your child is a drug addict."
>
> —Anthony

Anthony would typically drive to Spokane or Seattle in an all-day trip, with his route to various pharmacies pre-planned and set up on MapQuest. He turned in fictitious prescriptions from doctors or dentists to drugstore chains, a major wholesaler and even a mom and pop pharmacy. He often submitted the scrips sporting a pair of crutches, a cast, or cotton balls for the pulled wisdom tooth. Later, he'd circle back to the first one for the pickup and follow the same route. If the pharmacy had some reason such as, "We didn't have time to fill it just yet," or "we're almost done, just wait one minute," then he simply left—although that rarely happened. After numerous trial and error situations, he discovered that no cop would wait five hours hiding in the parking lot for a prescription-forging addict to return. Usually if he dropped off ten prescriptions, he'd get ten filled, and on a good day he'd be driving to Pullman with 500-plus pills. The problem was that was less than a two-week supply.

There were phases where he was reckless and almost wanting to get caught. He'd see how many famous names he could use to fill prescriptions, and it got to the point where it would piss him off how careless the pharmacies were. He'd use names like Bill Clinton and George Clooney, but the scrip would be filled all the same. The worst that would happen was the counter person joking, "You probably get this all the time, but I've never filled for someone famous before." Then they would laugh together. Anthony always noticed the signs posted all around the pharmacy stating: "We verify all controlled substances," and "Must show valid I.D." His I.D. was never verified. Anthony would think to himself *They should add: "We check, but only if you look like a drug addict."*

Just as the gambling tables started with a bang, so did the cards. Anthony was making fairly good money, and to a college kid, he was making "killer cash" and loving it. But it wouldn't last much longer.

Anthony purchased a nice, under-graded in his opinion, PSA-5 '52 Mantle for $12,000. The money was transferred out of his PayPal account to the seller, who sent him the card. It was, indeed, under-graded. Anthony re-graded the Mantle to a VGS 6.5, and put it up for auction starting at $15,000. It didn't sell. He relisted the card over and over, dropping the price each time, but still no sale. After a few weeks, the auctions ran out.

That's when he got an email from a supposedly wealthy Canadian businessman saying, "Hey, you still got that '52 VGS 6.5? I'll give you $18,000 for it. That's $3,000 more than asking, but I need it shipped before I leave."

Anthony replied, "Still got it. Send me the money and it's yours. I'll mail it out tomorrow."

The next day, he checked his account and found the expected $18,000. The buyer description didn't have an address since it was in Canada. The account was listed as unconfirmed. That usually meant the credit card used in PayPal was different than the shipping address. There are risks when sending to unconfirmed addresses, but Anthony had $18,000 just sitting in his account that had cleared PayPal. He mailed out the card as promised and sent a message, "Mailed her out, and here is the tracking number." Within minutes he received a thank you reply.

Anthony tracked the card as it left the United States. Just as it cleared customs, he checked his PayPal account. The money had disappeared. The transfer had been cancelled and reversed. He called the buyer—who didn't answer—the Post Office and PayPal, to no avail. After some research and a few more calls, he found that the "buyer" had found a way to steal nearly half a million dollars worth of eBay auctions in less than seven days. eBay wouldn't help since Anthony had sold the card outside of their auction. The internet seemed like a different country to local police. He felt it was outrageous that PayPal would allow this sort of behavior, but they didn't help. The Canadian authorities didn't seem to care either. His only option was to leave a complaint on some stupid FBI website. He received an automated response.

Anthony became obsessed with getting his money back. That $12,000 was most of his bankroll. Anthony figured the guy could resell or dump the card somewhere later for $6,000, so he looked for it online. It didn't turn up. Stressed out, he took enough pain killers in that week to put him into a mild overdose several times each day. Most of the other people the fraudster stole from were all selling relatively small in size but high dollar items—like baseball cards. Anthony tried to get the other victims to band together so they could find a way to get the guy. But nobody seemed to care as much as Anthony. They all seemed to get over it. He had trouble getting over anything. The fraudster had gotten Anthony, but he had underestimated his victim.

Anthony used another student's debit card and address, and set up new eBay and PayPal accounts at the college student library. Using an unlinked email account, he set up a fake auction for a PSA-8 '52 Mantle for sale with a bottom price of one cent. He didn't think anyone would believe it, since his new seller account and his fake grading company didn't have any feedback. The following morning he checked the auction, and sure enough there were bids of $4,000 in the morning and $8,000 by noon. Two days later, he emailed the high-dollar bidders offline and said, "Trying to sell this thing offline to save on eBay fees. Still protected through PayPal. Let me know if you're interested." By the end of the week, $20,000 had cleared PayPal. Anthony hired a friend to walk into the bank and withdraw his money. He drove to a Moscow Post Office, bought insurance for $20,000 on a shitty baseball card worth fifty cents and put the card in the mail. He split the loot with his friend. He was pleased that he'd made back the money he had lost and placed the "victim" tag on someone else. No one came after him about the card, so he never got caught. He really only cared about himself, and nobody else mattered in his addicted mind.

Anthony continued to grade cards, but it was never the same. That $20,000 made in less than one week changed everything. Seeing the crisp bills on his coffee table, was enough to change his attitude toward his business. Anthony lost all respect for the value of the dollar.

That's when he took his card business to a whole new level. He started trimming cards for better centering. Then he learned how to improve color-fixing without detection. Using coffee grounds, he yellowed the card, making it appear aged. All of these methods allowed him to improve the grade on quite ordinary, cheap cards. He discovered how to open sealed card cases and reseal them without any outward appearance of tampering. That allowed him to change the grade of other, well-known, companies' cards. He could re-grade a PSA-4 Mantle to a PSA-7. He would make the barcode reflect the change while trimming.

Right in the middle of modifying some cards Anthony got an email:

"Hey, you still got that PSA-rated Mantle? I'll give you $12,000 for it. That's $2,000 more than asking but need it shipped before I leave."

Holy shit! Anthony knew it was the fraudster. He could also see that the guy was bidding on roughly $400,000 worth of auctions. This time, his address was posted with a suite number. Anthony knew he had a chance to catch the guy before he split again. He carefully crafted a three-line email that would convince this ghost that Anthony was on to him. He offered a one-time "make this right before I do" deal. It was a shot in the dark, but it hit the target.

The guy sent Anthony an AOL instant message saying, "What do you want?"

Anthony replied, "The money you took from me."

"I'll send the card back," he replied, "and I'll put in other stuff. Trust me, it will be worth it."

Sure enough, a few days later there was a package in Anthony's P.O. box that contained the '52 Mantle, but there were also '52 Topps Mantle rookie cards that were all identical. They were the finest counterfeits Anthony could imagine.

Over the next few months, Anthony sold the exact same card over and over, using many different accounts. In this time, Anthony contributed heavily to flooding the market with what was called the "Reprint Mickey Mantle." But the same scam was going on with the Fleer Jordan Rookie that he had nothing to do with. The fraudster sent more identical Mantles every month. Eventually, he explained that he had in his possession an old printing press that had been taken from a baseball card printing company in the Eighties. The printing wasn't a problem—it was finding the card stock sheets. He also needed to acquire the highly graded cards to replicate.

Then Detective Carl Bell showed up at Anthony's doorstep. He'd been sent to investigate a replica baseball card that someone purchased from Anthony. They weren't happy with the grade that VGS gave the card. Apparently, they'd gotten suspicious and had sent it to PSA for a re-grade. PSA saw the fraud and returned it to the owner with an explanation. Detective Bell had been told what to look for, but it was clear to Anthony that he didn't know much. To the untrained eye, it's very difficult to detect a counterfeit.

Anthony sat Detective Bell down and showed him the finest in sports memorabilia, his license and explained his legal process. Bell left seemingly convinced VGS was a legitimate sports memorabilia dealer. Anthony was reminded of one thing that day: never to do anything in his own name again.

He had avoided prosecution, but it wasn't long before every eBay and PayPal account was shutdown. He received a letter signed by eBay president Meg Whitman banning Anthony from their website for life. Any computer he had ever used to access those programs was shut down. His mom's account, Emily's brother's account and Emily's account were all shut down . . . . And of course he had an explanation for all of it.

They shut down his accounts, but not before he took his money and spread it into all kinds of illegal activities where there were no rules and no regulations to shut him out. He "invested" in financing drug dealers and selling stolen merchandise. Things quickly got way out of control. Anthony had a gun pointed in his face more than once. He made retribution on a drug dealer when his investments weren't repaid. He wasn't a tough guy, but he was acting crazy. This intimidated even the tough guys he was dealing with. Mixing drugs and very illegal activities doesn't usually end well, and Anthony was high and spending money as if it were free. Meanwhile, his skin was turning a yellowish-green as if his body was dying from the inside out. He didn't care for his life. He needed help again.

> "Most of Anthony's free time was spent watching 'The Sopranos' and movies like 'Casino' or 'Blow.' I watched them too and thought, 'Wow that was depressing. Their lives sucked.' I didn't know it at the time but instead of feeling disgusted or sad, Anthony wanted to emulate what he saw. It's like he was in another universe. His drug-addicted perception of reality was very different than that of a sober person."
>
> —Emily

People he'd taught his illegal techniques to started getting busted. A friend was arrested for turning in a fake prescription. When the police went to his house, they found he'd been growing weed. Another friend was arrested in Spokane for internet crimes stemming from Anthony's card reprints. He kept calling Anthony wanting to talk and demanding money. Anthony turned his back on him after seeing him meeting with agents in an unmarked car in downtown. He was afraid the rats would bring the dogs.

Anthony felt he was going to die if he didn't get off the pills. Figuring he could just stay drunk for a few days to keep the withdrawal symptoms and shaking away, he decided to go to Vegas with a few friends. What a perfect place to get clean. *I'll distract myself with the most exciting place on Earth, Sin City, with all the booze I could ever need.* On the second night there, Anthony was kicked out of a nightclub. When his friends woke him up the following afternoon, he was confused to find himself in a recliner at Cheetah's strip club, his clothes soaked through with sweat.

They took him back to their top floor hotel room. He discovered a basketball-sized hole in one of the windows.

"Don't you remember, man?" his friend said with a laugh. "You threw a chair at it."

"You OK? You don't look so good," said the other.

Anthony realized he'd blacked out the last twelve hours. The shakes were so bad that he wanted to die. His friends knew something was wrong but didn't know the extent of his problem. He felt as if his body was dead and couldn't move, but his mind was wide awake. Then the feeling reversed: he felt that his mind was dead but his body was wide awake. Everything he didn't want to feel, he felt. Nothing was still. It was the polar opposite of peace.

Anthony flew home deep in withdrawal. He sat in the narrow airline seat involuntarily crying, and breaking into full sweats. He demanded that his friends bundle him up in their jackets, then the next moment he threw everything off because he felt his blood was boiling hot. He was scaring the other passengers and was moved to the back of the plane. The stewards thought he was on drugs, so they wouldn't serve him any alcohol. To say his friends were embarrassed to know him was an understatement.

When Anthony got home, he immediately took some pills. Within the hour, he appeared normal. Better than normal. He was ready to tackle the world . . . or at least go to dinner.

> "When the addict's body cries for the drug, there is no substitute. I thought, *Thank God I'm back on drugs!* As soon as they entered my system after any long absence the addiction Monster immediately began talking to me, reassuring me. It told me I didn't have any problems. 'Look, you just quit for three days. It wasn't so bad. You can quit anytime.' And I believed the Monster. I believed I could control it. This time I'll only take pills in the morning. Then it was, 'Starting tomorrow . . . .' The problem was, tomorrow never came, or it came and the symptoms would change. Things got worse on a daily basis. Whatever stage of addiction I was at when I quit, that was the stage I came back to when I started back up. A progressive disease, they call it. The addiction helps you be selective with your memory, only remembering the good feelings they cause and not the bad ones. When I was high, I couldn't remember the withdrawals or destruction, not the pain and not the way the pills robbed me of my life."
>
> —Anthony

Anthony decided to end his criminal enterprises. He had a lot of his friends on his payroll, and they were paid well. But some of them were stealing from him. There was also the little matter of a paper trail leading to jail for him. He closed down his operations, told everyone he was going legit and opened a fresh bank account.

Christmas morning found Anthony in his parent's house, looking like he'd been up for days. His eyes were bulging out of his head and his skin was an unnerving yellowish light-green.

His parents confronted him on another matter. While they were moving things around in his old room, they found a brand new

AR-15 assault rifle with .223 caliber magazines—a gun nearly identical to Scarface's—hidden under the headboard of his bed. Anthony's family knew he didn't hunt and didn't have an interest in guns. Here he was, supposedly a broke college kid with a new SUV and an automatic rifle, along with having a history of substance abuse. The message seemed clear.

Anthony's mother asked, "Do you need help again?"

Anthony said, "Yes. I think I do." He reflected that he hadn't made the signs of his relapse too hard to spot.

> "You always want to think that a relapse isn't possible. One trip to rehab is enough, and one night in jail should be enough to teach the lesson. Sometimes it is enough. Sometimes the speech at the high school assembly is enough or the brochures that are handed out make a difference. Sadly though, addiction is a disease, and like any disease it requires ongoing treatment. There is no quick cure, and the truth that isn't told enough is that relapse is part of the process—at least my process."
>
> —Anthony

Anthony had left treatment at Yakima feeling strong, knowledgeable about abuse and with a desire to stay clean. But when daily life started becoming routine, the pain of addiction was slowly forgotten. He started to believe he was "Doing fine"—when he was the most vulnerable. Anthony relapsed, got clean, relapsed, got clean. But this relapse had gone on for long enough, he knew he was in bad trouble. It was time for Anthony to go back to rehab, even he knew that, and he didn't put up a fight.

Addiction is a disease that makes users and their families absolutely desperate to control it. Anthony's folks looked around and researched different treatment centers. His family considered recovery rates, success percentages and what the chances were that not only would Anthony get clean but stay clean.

Anthony was skeptical at this point of any treatment center's stated recovery rates. After all, the Yakima center still considered him sober. He felt his parents were just hearing sales tactics designed to fill up bed space, rather than speaking the truth about addiction and its suspect recovery record.

Enter the Waismann Institute for rapid detox—the quick-fix to drug addiction. Their treatment plan was to put the patient under anesthesia and give them a chemical called naltrexone that is an opiate antagonist. It goes into the system and reduces the physical withdrawal symptoms from seven to ten days to about three hours. Just a short nap, then the patient is clean. Anthony's mom made the appointment.

His mom and he flew down to California. Anthony was taking over thirty Norcos a day (10mg hydrocodone) and had been for several months. By the time they got to the treatment facility, he had been without anything for sixteen hours and was very agitated. They took Anthony directly to a room for intake.

The nurse glanced at him, and grabbed his hand, felt the sweat and coldness, and then looked into his eyes. "Turn around and pull down your pants," said the nurse.

What the hell? But Anthony looked at his mom, obediently turned around and dropped his pants. *Awkward.*

The nurse gave Anthony a shot in the butt and told him, "I just gave you morphine, and you will stay on morphine until we bring you back. Okay?"

Anthony could hardly put up an argument. Suddenly, he felt great and loved his mom. Everything was just all right. Anthony answered some questions, met more of the staff, and was given more morphine. The doctor explained that the plan was the next morning he would go under. "It's basically a complete oil change," he joked. Anthony was nervous about the idea of just going to sleep addicted and waking up completely sober, but both the doctor and nurse promised that was just what would happen.

Anthony's mom asked about side effects. The doctor said the biggest concern was that "Some patients, while under anesthesia, shake and have convulsions. Occasionally, someone will lose control of their bowels."

They shit themselves? Anthony didn't want to embarrass himself like that!

The next day, Anthony was taken into a treatment room and asked to lie down. He was told to start counting backwards from twenty. He got to eighteen and he was gone.

Anthony woke up completely clean. His body had not a trace or symptom of withdrawals.

The first thing Anthony asked when he awoke was, "Did I shit myself?"

"Congratulations," the doctor and nurse said, as if he was cured.

All Anthony could think was, *Can it really be this easy?* Then he remembered that it cost his mom another $10,000. He'd had money enough to buy a new car, a machine gun, and a trip to Vegas, but he didn't have the cash for treatment.

> "It seemed that my recovery was always more important to my parents and Emily than it was to me, and that was the problem."
>
> —Anthony

Sitting with his mom, eating cookies and waiting for his flight home, Anthony began to have some old feelings. He was shaky and feeling out of control, as if he were having an anxiety attack. But it only lasted for a second or two, and then he'd be fine again. His mom went to call the facility and came back with, "Completely normal. They said to tell you you're fine."

It was hard for Anthony to fathom how it could take years to escalate to his high level of drug use, and become physically and mentally addicted with all the baggage that comes with addiction, and somehow get clean overnight. He was realizing the true affect of the mental addiction that he would have trouble defeating. This was his first formal introduction to the true craziness of mental withdrawal. Anthony no longer had the shakes, the fevers, the hot and cold, the sweats, but he also had zero control over his emotions. He was a complete basket case. From the time his flight landed to when he arrived at his house, he crossed from one extreme to the other crying and laughing and crying, over and over. Anthony was way off and he knew it.

Everybody was telling him that everything would work out, but nothing felt right. He was feeling a huge amount of guilt and failure for this relapse. Anthony felt weak for not being able to beat this like everyone else did—or so he thought. He just felt completely worthless.

His emotions kept roller coasting up: down, then up, then down. One second he felt excitement and full of adrenaline as if he'd won the lottery, but that was followed immediately by a deep sadness as if he'd lost his grandma. He suffered from a deep depression, feeling there was no point to living. He wasn't sure, but he thought he might be going insane. Anthony couldn't figure out what was going on, but he also knew he couldn't live like this either. He called the people at the facility and explained what was happening.

"It's perfectly normal behavior," the nurse said.

He thought, *You have to be kidding me! I want to die, and this is normal? A million hammers are hitting at my head and tormenting me from the inside of my skull. And this is normal?*

> "When Anthony got back, all I saw was a shell of a person. He was miserable and extremely depressed. This didn't seem like a miracle cure. He'd had suicidal thoughts before, but not to this degree. He'd never told me about those thoughts at the exact time he was thinking them. He always told me later when he no longer felt that way. He tried

> to play it off when he realized how scared I was, but stuff like that is hard to take back. I was freaking out. The Waismann Institute offered nothing in terms of counseling. He was physically sober but how was he supposed to face the psychological part of his addiction? How could this possibly work long term?"
>
> —Emily

Anthony felt the need to be alone, so he went into his parent's computer room. He could hear his family talking behind the closed door, but slowly the noise faded away. Anthony started to cry again, but he couldn't understand why because he wasn't sad. He needed a switch that could turn off his emotions. His whole world and everything he had known had changed. As he looked around the room, everything seemed to suggest itself as a way to kill himself. He spotted a power cord that was no longer attached to anything; it could be used to send 120 volts of electricity through his body. That phone cord over there could be used to hang himself. Anthony pressed a dull envelope cutter deep into his stomach without piercing his skin, wanting to feel something. He craved pain and wanted to hurt physically in order to shut down his mind. He started banging his head against the table. He heard concerned exclamations and footsteps coming toward the door. He stopped.

Anthony thought of the 9 mm handgun in his car. The idea sounded like a simple way to end it. He wrote an emotionless note quickly and left it on the table. Anthony opened the computer room door, smiled at his parents and walked outside to his Tahoe. *Ahh, new car smell,* he thought to himself. Nice. He drove to the lake and parked. Anthony grabbed the 9 mm from the glove box, ejected the clip, popped it back in. Click. He liked the power the sound represented— life-ending and real. There was still no emotion. Anthony slowly pulled the slide back to chamber the gold 9 mm hollow-point round load into the firing position. Then he slid the top slide forward, fully engaging the bullet. Anthony felt the steel of the gun in his hands as he gripped it tightly. Overlooking the lake he had grown up in, swam in as a little kid, he still didn't feel any emotion. He focused on the inside of the car: the smell of fresh leather, the beautiful gray and black interior. It was warming. Anthony stared at the OnStar button and wondered if there was someone on the other end who would save him. What would they say to some lunatic who said he was going to kill himself? There was still no emotion, but the thought created a little smile.

Anthony sat there waiting for God to appear in a bright light to explain what all this meant. He needed enlightenment for his life, but nothing happened. "Fine, God, I'll do this," he yelled. Anthony opened the door and started walking toward the water. He didn't really have control of his legs. He didn't know he was at the shore until he heard the splash and realized his feet were drenched. He stepped back, seeing he'd gone too far.

Anthony raised the gun and fired a shot into the lake, thinking that the noise and slight kick of the gun would wake him up and lift the fog. Still nothing. The smell of the discharged bullet just made him feel more at ease. He raised the gun and placed the barrel against his temple, but it was still hot and he yanked the burning metal away. He stood there for a long moment, soaking in the sights and smells of the surrounding woods. It was dead quiet, as if nature was still recovering from the unnatural sound of the gunshot.

Then he placed the barrel back against the side of his head and just held it there. His finger was not yet on the trigger. Anthony decided it was time to die. His index finger moved over the trigger. Suddenly, he became concerned and wanted to make sure to do the job right. The realness was setting in, and with it, some fear crept in. He told himself it was going to be over soon. He needed to feel better, and this was the only way. If he lived, he'd only let his family down when he relapsed again. All the treatment was supposed to fix him, but he could see that it never would.

Anthony tilted his head, twisted the barrel and pulled the trigger.

Pop!

The sound was deafening and kept going. Anthony thought to himself, *Fuck! I'm awake. I'm not dead. What happened?* To this day he is still uncertain as to what happened.

He realized he didn't want to kill himself. He knew it would have been awful for his parents to lose a son, his sisters to lose a brother and Emily to lose a life partner. Having these thoughts made Anthony feel again. It was over.

Anthony relapsed a few hours later.

Seven

Anthony was sure if he could get rid of the bad surroundings in his life, he could finally kick the pills. He decided that the root of his problem was WSU and the town of Pullman—filled as it was with the distraction of school, friends who took drugs, and the remains of his criminal activities.

Anthony moved back home and decided to finish up his college classes online with Emily's help. He wanted a clean slate. It was time to start a normal life.

However, what Anthony didn't understand was while being a drug addict he was incapable of having a normal life, so he soon decided to go back to work selling sports memorabilia. He had a relationship with some illegal I.D. makers in California, so with a money transfer, a head shot and the information all sent in an email, Anthony had a new license in his P.O. box in a week. In fact, he made multiple licenses and had so many names he nearly forgot his own. It felt like he was starting all over again, since the market for vintage baseball cards had changed. There were too many fakes, and there wasn't one for sale worth over $1,000. The market was flooded and the value had dropped considerably for cards over a two year period. Things were different since everyone was skeptical, but it made buyers who were searching even hungrier for a legitimate deal.

> "A very well known collector contacted me off the internet and arranged a meeting in a large store in Seattle because

he was worried about getting robbed. I handed over a PSA Mantle that I had broken into and resealed and watched him inspect it. Then he makes a call—which I thought at first was to the police. A friend of his appeared, who had apparently been standing only a few feet from us. He handed the man an envelope of cash. The collector told me how happy he was, then gave me his business card and the envelope."

—Anthony

Anthony was borderline broke with the house and no bank roll, so instead of looking for a legitimate job he decided to put this new scheme into place. In order to close the trust gap with buyers online, Anthony decided to start an escrow company that would insure high-dollar transactions. He used a law firm name that was on the Better Business Bureau website. At that time, many companies listed on the BBB's website didn't have any contact information, which made it easy for criminals like Anthony to piggyback on their reputation. It looked for all the world as if Anthony's new escrow company was owned and operated by two of Seattle's finest attorneys. For a small fee, they could be hired by the buyer after the auction had ended to insure the purchase and remove the risk. They would refund your money if you were not satisfied. Considering there were no escrow companies active online, he purchased some key words to make the company come up at the top of all the search engines. Then he'd recommend to his buyers that they look for an escrow company online. All the websites and internet payments were completed with new bank cards and accounts in the names of his newly hired attorneys Ken Williams and Jeff Thomas. Anthony used two different pictures of himself to create their identities. He even had their legal history available on the website. Anthony thought he was pretty cutting edge.

Anthony knew the scheme was a temporary fix to his financial troubles. He was worried about staying one step ahead of the inevitable complaints, but the payments took five days to process electronically. Good customer service would help to cushion the timeline. But it was only so long until people wised up to the game. About half of the twenty or so payments came in before the bank started getting fraud complaints. As one of the attorneys, Anthony went in to the bank to make a withdrawal, but the accounts had been frozen.

There were a sizeable number of checks that still needed to be cashed, so he decided it was worth the risk to at least try to collect the money. Dressed in a business suit and a tieless colored dress shirt, he headed to another bank. The clerks were behind one-inch-thick bullet-proof glass that ran countertop to ceiling. There were quite a few people inside. When it was Anthony's turn, he submitted the checks to the nice-looking brunette clerk. After tapping at her computer for a moment, she looked up at him, smiled shyly, and said, "Would you hold on for just a moment? I'm new and I have to have the manager look at all my transactions."

"Sure," he said, beginning to worry.

She went over to the manager and showed him the checks. He looked at Anthony for a moment, then turned back to talk to the clerk. He picked up the phone and dialed. It was taking rather longer than a simple check cashing should take, and Anthony wondered if he should leave.

Out of the corner of his eye, Anthony saw a police officer hop off his bike and walk into the building. The manager came out to the lobby and greeted the policeman. Anthony couldn't hear what the manager said, but the officer mumbled something into his radio and started walking toward Anthony.

This can't be good, he thought.

The officer said, "Excuse me sir, but would you mind stepping over here?" He motioned toward the back of the lobby.

"No problem. What's the issue? Is something going on?" Anthony asked innocently.

Before Anthony could even finish his sentence the police officer was back on his radio saying the words "theft" and "suspect" in the same sentence.

"Am I in some kind of trouble?" Anthony asked, allowing his worry to show.

The officer gave him a tough-guy look. With one hand, he reached behind him to unlatch his black circular pouch holding a pair of handcuffs. The other hand hovered above his gun. "You are if your name is Jeff Thomas," the cop replied.

Anthony gave him his best look of shock. "Who? My name is Ken Williams. What the hell is going on?"

This set the oversized officer back. The bank manager looked startled.

Anthony decided to play it for all it was worth and looked the officer directly in the eyes. "My name is Ken Williams. I work right down the street at the mall. I'm on my lunch break." Anthony started to reach for his wallet, but the cop made him move slowly.

Anthony pulled out the Williams driver's license, which was right next to the Jeff Thomas fake I.D. Just as he handed it to the cop, he noticed flashing police car lights reflected in the tellers' glass wall.

The officer studied the I.D., and then looked around at the other customers—many of whom looked a lot more suspicious than Anthony. The officer handed him the I.D. back. Clearly distracted, he mumbled, "Could you please wait right here for a moment." The cop and the manager headed back into the manager's office.

Anthony decided it was time to leave. As he was walking out the front door, another officer ran in to the bank and gave Anthony a quick scan, then went right past him. It only lasted a split second, but that moment of brief eye contact seemed to last forever. Another police car raced into the lot and parked sideways. Two more bicycle cops arrived, and stood by the door, their helmets unclipped and their hands on their guns.

He walked calmly around the building, looking into the window to see inside the bank. Anthony's heart was racing: his body was on full alert; his palms were sweaty; all his muscles were taut. He saw the manager pointing at him through the glass separation, clearly trying to communicate to the police. All the cops turned to look at him.

Gotta fly!

Sprinting as fast as he could, even in nice business dress shoes, he turned a corner and slowed to look back. That part of town was generally busy, but at first he didn't see anyone. A second later, he saw two cops riding toward him on bicycles, one without his helmet. A million cups of coffee entered Anthony's system all at once, and he took off through an alley and circled to the left, back to the street-front. A cop in a car spotted him and flashed his lights to show himself. Anthony circled back toward the alley, just as the bicycle cop was turning in. They passed each other about ten yards away—close enough to see the cop's frustrated face as he struggled to turn around. He saw a fat cop chasing him on foot. *That one's not going to be a problem*, he thought.

The sound of the sirens echoing through the town was unnerving him. Anthony crossed another road. A quick check showed he'd probably ditched the bike cop. But then he saw the police car paralleling his movements from the other road. His adrenaline was still keeping him going, but he was getting tired. There seemed to be no way he could get to his car, so he simply had to keep going. Anthony walked quickly into a nearby store. He saw the cop pull in to the parking lot. The employee at the cash register didn't even look up. He strode through the store, pulled off his suit jacket and tucked it into a nearby garbage can as he exited the store through the back door.

Seemingly unnoticed, he crossed the street near the mall entrance. He could hear the police yelling, they were so close. He did the math and it didn't look good: there were three cops in the parking lot of the store he'd just left; a bicycle cop somewhere; and one on foot (probably breathing hard); which meant at least six cops after him. Although Anthony was an extremely fast runner, he still couldn't outrun the radio. He slipped through some bushes, scrapping up his leg. He dashed into the bottom level of the parking garage and emerged between two parked SUVs. A group of people started up to the concrete stairs, and Anthony joined them. In a panic, he wanted to mow the slow-moving people over to get out of there. But he matched his pace to theirs and tried to look as if he was part of the group. Finally, he reached the fourth level landing where he could cross the exterior foot bridge to the mall. He stopped to see if he'd shaken the police, only to see a congregation of officers staring up at him only a football field away.

He walked into the mall quickly. Anthony pulled out the prepaid phone from his pocket, then realized any call from the phone would be traced back to the escrow company. Suddenly, the phone started ringing. He yanked the battery out, un-tucked his dress shirt and did his best to wipe the prints off the phone before dumping it in a garbage can. Feeling like a rat in a maze, he knew he had to get out of the mall before every entrance was blocked off and every mall cop was on his tail as well. He went into a store, stood in a line that seemed to take forever although there were only two people in line. Finally he stepped up to the cashier and purchased a rocker t-shirt and baseball cap. Once he left the store, he quickly put on his new clothes, then worked his way through the mall and out an exit with his head down. He couldn't believe there was no cop at the door. *Did I make it?*

Right then, he saw a police cruiser parked in the fire lane, looking as if it was waiting to pick someone up. Anthony's heart was jacked again, but he kept walking normally, like any other shopper returning to his car. He ducked away between two pick-ups and then zigged and zagged his way back to his Tahoe. He didn't get right in immediately, fearing that his pimped-out SUV was being watched. After half-an-hour, the last police car left for good. Before he got into his truck, he searched the vehicle high and low, thinking there might be a GPS tracker or something, but there was nothing. He got in, drove off slowly and drifted right into rush hour traffic. He'd never felt so relieved to be stuck in traffic.

> "I was totally unaware of Anthony's crimes during this time. It's embarrassing but every time I felt that something didn't add up and I asked him if something was wrong, he never hesitated—he had an immediate explanation and could spin all kinds of stories. My brain just didn't work like his. I never in my wildest nightmares would've believed he was doing the things he was. I didn't realize back then how irrational I was or how affected I was by his addiction, but his stories made more sense to me than the truth would have because I was in denial. I never stopped believing in who he was before the drugs, I don't think I could accept who he'd become."
>
> —Emily

You would assume that the escrow business meltdown would have been a wakeup call—even for a drug addict. But as Anthony sat in traffic on his way back home, he was planning his next caper. The run-ins with the law didn't deter him from crime. In fact, the adrenaline rushes made it all the more fun.

Every day, Anthony woke up with withdrawal symptoms at around ten a.m. He'd drag himself to his stash of drugs, and have just enough energy to open the child-proof prescription bottle. Anthony took six to twelve at a time. His tongue pushed them back in his mouth so his back molars could crush them down into a powder all at the same time. His saliva would make them into a paste. The taste of those pills were enough to make a grown man gag or throw up, but for Anthony it reminded his body of what was soon to come—the answer to everything. He was Pavlov's dog, and the taste of the disgusting chalky pills was his bell. After the first swallow and the clearing gulp that pushed the paste down his throat, he would collapse, breathing but looking for all the world like a corpse. Then it happened. Like a sped-up and fast-forwarded video of a lifeless flower that had just been given water again and put in the sunlight, he slowly came to life. Color returned to Anthony's face, his blood pressure regulated itself, the sweating stopped and his mind stopped panicking. Everything turned beautiful and peaceful. This feeling would last over four hours when he first started his addiction, but now the pure euphoria of the pills would only last about fifteen to twenty minutes, maximum. He would feel it in the morning and continue to chase the feeling all day long, but it would rarely come a second time in a day... if it ever did. Sometimes the pursuit of the high sent him into overdose, or even the ER. Sometimes the feeling would come the following day, but he just hadn't realized he had woken again, taken pills again or even slept in the first place. At the start of each day, the bottle would be three-quarters full of white, yellow or blue pills. By ten p.m., the same bottle would be completely empty. Most days the empty bottle would fly out the car window on his way to meet friends at the bar. This was Anthony's life, again.

A few days after being chased around town, Anthony got the call that Dave, one of his best friends growing up, had passed away. It hit Anthony like a ton of bricks.

> "Dave was the good one of the group. He was the friend who was kind, the one that didn't drink, didn't smoke and didn't even cuss. Dave was the friend that I could call at two a.m. and say I needed to talk, and three hours later we would be laughing and forgetting why we were on the phone in the middle of the night. Dave was so many peo-

ple's best friend. I played sports and went to school with Dave since the first grade. He had unswayable integrity. He was an unreal friend. Dave knew what I was involved with, and he was concerned and wanted to help, but also never judged me. I think anyone who truly knew Dave wished they could switch places with him. I felt guilty to be alive. It never should have been him. I honestly didn't get it. I didn't get God, and I didn't get the meaning of life that I had been struggling with for so long. At this point, life really made no sense. I could have never prepared for this type of thing in my life. Grandparents pass away, not your twenty-three-year-old best friend. I loved Dave."

—Anthony

Anthony carried Dave's casket, spoke at his funeral and even got a tattoo of his initials, but he doesn't remember any of it. He'd put himself into a purposeful drug-induced coma, or the best he could anyway. After Dave's death, many old friends got back in touch at his funeral, and the group started going to the bar all the time. Anthony was also on an assortment of anti-depressants, anti-anxiety and blood pressure medicine to accompany the pain medicine and enough alcohol to get a rugby team drunk. Emily was very close with Dave and his girlfriend, and she did her best to hold it together and get ready for their wedding. Everyone seemed to deal with the loss differently, but Anthony didn't deal with it at all. He decided to just keep doing what he had been doing since college—escape reality and run from it all. He ran directly into the arms of the chemicals.

Anthony was sure that most friends knew he was using again, but perhaps they tolerated it because they knew how close he had been to Dave. He thought he didn't care, but then his upcoming nuptials changed his mind. He wanted to be able to say his vows to Emily sober, so that she would know he meant them. He felt he owed this to Emily and to Dave, who didn't have a chance at living. And he owed it to his future family. It was time to get clean again.

But Anthony wasn't getting sober for himself. The trouble is that an addict must get sober for themselves. The fear of jail or death really isn't enough.

> "Just as the fear of hell isn't enough to force people to do the right thing, a person has to do the right thing because it's the right thing and not out of fear."
>
> —Anthony

His plan was to use his forgery skills and, using an assortment of medicines, taper his withdrawal symptoms. He told everyone he was deathly sick. It wasn't easy, but he had been through withdrawal many times and knew what to expect. He called all his friends who took pills and warned them that he would be calling and begging for pills. He also told them that if they gave him anything that they wouldn't be friends any longer. He destroyed all of his fraudulent prescription paraphernalia: the computer templates that he cherished, removed his printers, threw away his special prescription cutters and disabled his internet. He planned to visit every pharmacy around the area, show his face and say, "Do not give me anything," but he only managed to warn the nearest store where he had filled the Lorazepam and clonidine, detox and withdrawal medicines.

> "It was awkward. It was like no one dealing in the dispensing of these drugs could ever imagine someone abusing them. I tried to explain that I had filled there multiple times, but finally I just left. I didn't want to be arrested explaining."
>
> —Anthony

Day two through five were the climax of hell for Anthony. By day seven, the extreme physical reaction had gone. His next biggest hurdle was not to get dependent on the detox meds, but he accomplished his temporary goal. Anthony was clean, and he made it with about a week-and-a-half to spare.

May 22nd, 2004 was Anthony's and Emily's wedding day. Anthony was sober and happy. He could feel real life again. More than three hundred people gathered in a nice place in Bellevue. Family and friends danced and laughed late into the night. Anthony didn't have a drop of alcohol, and the next day they left for Cabo San Lucas on a two week honeymoon.

The happy couple.

Once back from their honeymoon, the happy couple moved into an apartment in Kirkland for a few weeks until their new house was finished. On document signing day, the builder's agent asked if the Curcios had an agent. Anthony asked why it mattered. The agent said it had to do with who was to receive the commission check. The loan was the same regardless. Anthony called the only friend who he knew in real estate and told him he was listing him as the agent. The house was over $300,000, his friend collected a check for $10,000. When Anthony saw this he realized real estate was to be his "next thing."

When they moved into the house his real estate friend purchased them a $200 barbecue. Anthony told him sarcastically, "You shouldn't have."

After being sober for two months, Anthony finished up his undergraduate degree from WSU, majoring in Social Sciences and a minor in business. He and Emily threw a big dinner with a poker game after dessert.

> "I remember making an honest joke in front of everyone, namely my grandparents, about how Emily did most of my work and really was the one who received the degrees only in my name, and my mom shot a death stare across the dinner table at me before I could deliver my punch line."
>
> —Anthony

He now had two framed degrees to hang in his office, but like an athlete whose accomplishments are achieved dubiously, Anthony felt they had asterisks on them.

The Washington State University graduate

Even as he and Emily were finishing up his undergraduate degree, he started studying for his real estate license. After he passed the exam, it was "go time." Just as with the gambling adventure and the sports memorabilia, Anthony was like a sponge on a spill studying all the aspects of real estate: being an agent, a broker, an inspector and the importance of an appraiser. Every morning he watched all the new listings that came on the market, and tried to understand why this house was higher in price than another just the same across town.

Week after week, he made and dropped off thousands of flyers and mailers advertising his new real estate "expertise." The phone started ringing and he quickly had all kinds of clients who really wanted homes. Even though he found great houses for these first-time homebuyers and wrote up contracts, none of them were getting approved. Some needed "more cash in reserves," or if they had cash, the mortgage broker would say the client needed to have "seasoned reserves," meaning they had to have savings in the bank for six months. If his clients had savings for six months, then they would need twelve. Anthony would be told the clients needed to have a credit score of 650, so he'd help them boost it to 670, just to get to a safe margin. Then the bank would come back and want 720. No matter what he did, he couldn't close a sale.

Anthony found out later that many of his clients would find a house through him, then call another agent, who somehow would be able to make it happen for them. Anthony decided to just buy his own house, fix it and flip it, as so many were doing. He paired up with John, a friend who had been a mortgage broker. They went in together on a fixer-upper without knowing a thing except the place had potential. They took out a mortgage for $220,000, but then realized how expensive it was going to be to fix up. The new place's mortgage was on top of Anthony's own mortgage payments, and he worried about the debt load. But he was also curious how John had gotten him the new mortgage, which was in Emily's name, since Anthony's credit wasn't as good. He asked his friend, "How did you get Emily approved when we already have a mortgage?"

John said, "Just add some zeros here and there, fudge this information, bump the income, reduce the debt, you know . . . ." He laughed. "Everyone does it."

It's all a series of big white lies! Anthony thought. *So this is why I've lost every deal I've ever had? This was how they were able to buy a house right away with another agent?* He quickly realized that without fraud there would be a lot less deals in real estate. Everything he'd learned while studying for the real estate license no longer mattered, it simply didn't apply. It all started to make sense.

Anthony went back to showing homes with a new attitude. But then it all fell apart again.

He was showing a house to a couple about two miles from his house. As the husband and wife were inspecting the bathroom, the wife opened up the medicine cabinet. It was lined with pinkish and orange prescription bottles with white labels. The part of his brain that had been dormant for over two months, that Anthony thought was totally gone, came alive right there again, like fireworks going off in his head.

He started talking to himself: *Leave it alone. Forget it. You're doing great.* Then the bargaining started: *There's probably nothing in them anyway.* But the Monster whispered: "There might be. There could be." He concluded the house tour with the couple, drove them back to the real estate office and sent them on their way.

In minutes, Anthony drove back to the house and sat in the driveway staring at the home trying to stop the inevitable. His palms were sweaty. He didn't want to, but he had to. Anthony thought to himself: *Just go in there, look through the bottles so you know that there isn't anything there and never come back.* But when he tapped in his code and ran up the stairs, he discovered the bottles were marked "Oxycodone," and they rattled when he picked them up. He threw three pills in his mouth and left.

He had four hours of euphoria and remembered why he'd taken the drugs in the first place. All the annoying things, the depressing things, the sad things, they were all okay, welcomed and enjoyed. The trouble was that it no longer took three weeks to grab him and make him its slave. All it took was one time.

The Monster was back.

He returned to the house eight more times in the next two days. After the fourth time he went into the house through the electronic key box holder, he got a call from the listing agent. Then he started to go through a window. For about a week, Anthony was able to function at the top of his game, but after that he no longer was returning calls, no longer helping with the fixer-upper and no longer doing anything except thinking about getting more pills. His business partner kept calling. Anthony's sister was selling her house and wanted to add his name as the agent so he could collect the commission. Nothing was enough for Anthony to return a call. Thankfully, Emily took care of most of the social explanation along with everything else.

> "After we were married, I assumed the role of sobriety manager. I was monitoring his doses of Naltrexone like a hawk (or so I thought). The medication was prescribed to him by the Waismann Institute. It was an opiate blocker that was supposed to make him sick if he took pain pills. I didn't realize until later that he was taking the capsules apart and filling them with powdered sugar! He'd relapsed way before that."
>
> —Emily

One day when Emily was at work, John showed up and told him they were out of money, but still needed appliances to finish the house. He was also pissed because Anthony wasn't helping anymore.

Anthony went and visited the house with John. They discussed what was needed. Three days later, Anthony pulled in with a trailer full of everything they needed to finish the house and the next. The brand new, high-end appliances Anthony brought were nice.

John shouted, "You saved the day!"

The two other laborers working on the home smiled at Anthony and seemed excited. He felt that he'd redeemed himself.

The house sold about a month later for $285,000. Minus the closing costs, they each pocketed about $20,000. It was the closest thing to legitimate money Anthony had ever made.

> "I suspected that he wasn't being honest, so I asked him: 'Where did you get all of these nice, new, really cheap appliances all of a sudden?' Of course he had another perfectly logical and irrefutable explanation, so I let it go and blamed his friend instead. I told Anthony 'If we ever flip another house, I want your word that it's going to be completely legit –that means no business partner –no John.' I wanted nothing to do with him."
>
> —Emily

John wanted to stay partners and flip another house, but Anthony just wanted to do his own thing, answer to no one and for the most part just be left alone and do drugs. But then calls started to come in, "Hey, can you get me some nice appliances?" A buddy constructing homes asked, "Can you get me ten rolls of 14-2 gauge, four rolls of 12-gauge, one roll of 8 gauge wire?" Others called asking for gas fireplaces, tankless water heaters, etc. Anthony knew where to get those items and more.

Anthony organized small groups of guys—that included soldiers back from Iraq who needed quick money and the excitement at the same time. He educated his new recruits on what quality appliances to steal from vacant, bank-foreclosed, high-end homes. Anthony's teams used radios and had an organized approach. People kept coming back to him for cheap, stolen goods. Anthony also sold the excess merchandise on the internet through other people's accounts on Craigslist and eBay again. He daringly returned stolen electrical wire to the big home improvement stores—since that's where it was originally obtained. He had more gift cards from the returns than he knew what to do with.

This line of work somehow morphed into Anthony becoming a criminal consultant and right back into real estate—more specifically, illegal real estate.

With help from a friend in an escrow company, Anthony gathered all the templates he needed. On two separate laptops, he created different documents for use in applications for different loans. He explained how they could just update and input new names, amounts and account numbers using his documents. Anthony again put obsessive hours into perfecting his system with P.O. boxes and separate mailing addresses everywhere. He used fake employers, prepaid phones for numbers to call and confirm employment, and used names listed in the Better Business Bureau, similar to the Jeff Thomas escrow scam. The escrow company created an account with $30,000 in it and added many clients to the account, where their name was on the account but they didn't have permission to remove funds, but it was enough to show "seasoned" assets and get the escrow and lending clients approved. With a few stolen notary stamps, Anthony was able to create counterfeit documents that were better than the real ones. Nobody seemed to care. If the lenders had a problem with the scam, they never mentioned it, because it would have taken money out of their pockets.

> "I was working with these professionals in organized crime, and they still weren't as dirty as the successful brokers and agents in real estate. These criminals had more morals and ethics than the real estate guys. I had been involved in a wide variety of criminal activities at this point for many years, but I never met a real criminal until I got involved in real estate. Some of these mortgage brokers would eat their own young,"
>
> —Anthony

The key to the big money was the appraiser, though. The appraiser was trusted by the potential lender to go out and be the bank's eyes. They put a value on the property based on its year, size, quality, extras and factor in the location, comparative house values and current market trends. If for some reason the appraiser priced a house above the offer, then the banks would jump at the idea of lending money and the real estate agent, the escrow agent, the broker and the appraiser all got paid.

An example of how the scam worked was this: If a deal was negotiated where the seller would accept $500,000, the appraisal could come back at $800,000, the bank would jump at the idea of lending on the home. In fact, if everyone was involved, all these players would have access to that extra $300,000. A straw buyer got paid $30,000 for intentionally ruining their credit by not paying the mortgage payments, but she or he lived free in a $500,000 house for up to two years before being evicted. The seller of the house got their price plus a tip. The real estate agent turned in an inflated Purchase and Sale agreement to the Mortgage Broker for an $800,000 loan, and legitimate P&S to the escrow company for $500,000 without the bank's knowledge. The lending bank would be tricked into overpaying so all the parties would walk away with their take of the overage. Anthony's people would make one mortgage payment to keep any suspicion of liability off the mortgage broker. It was a smooth system that even worked with subpar credit, which only required a larger down payment. It was modern day bank robbery where the bank was writing them a check willingly.

But Anthony and his partners weren't the only ones running the scam. There were lots of cases of this documented later where escrow companies used false Social Security numbers for the occupants, and this scheme turned the "creative financing" into plain old fraud.

None of it was legitimate, and none of it would last. Soon the entire market would crash and lots of examples of mortgage fraud schemes surfaced with big fines and jail time.

Emily recalls:

"Anthony found this 3,600 square foot, rat-infested house in south Seattle that he was hell-bent on flipping. He took me to see it and I was immediately against the idea. It would be an enormous undertaking and the place was disgusting –the cabinet drawers were filled with rodent feces! But once again, he was obsessed and wouldn't take no for an answer. We argued and argued about that house. Anthony told me that I 'didn't believe in him' and that I 'didn't have any faith in him.' That was the hand he'd always play. Once again, it was his way or the highway, so I had to get on board. Another battle lost. The tie always went to Anthony. We were getting into yet another project that I didn't want. Then, a month later, we found out I was pregnant with our first daughter. It was a lot to handle.

"We paid two mortgages for six months and it took a real toll on our finances. Anthony didn't seem to be bringing home any money from his job as a real estate agent, so I thought we were broke. I hated to admit it but our only option at that point was to sell our home in Mill Creek. It was August of 2006 and the market was at an all-time high. The house sold in a week for $120,000 more than we had purchased it for exactly two years earlier. We had to be out by the end of the month. I packed everything up by myself because Anthony was putting in long days at the fixer in Seattle. He promised to help me with the move, but the night before the movers were scheduled to show up, Anthony didn't come home. I called and called and called, wondering where the hell he was. Finally, around one in the morning, my phone rang. It was a collect call from the King County jail. I was fuming! His story was that he'd gotten into a confrontation with some people who were storing things in the shed at the Seattle

> house (they'd been given permission to do so by the previous owner). Anthony told us he felt threatened and had showed them his gun; they left and called the cops. I was skeptical of his story, but I asked my mom to call my uncle, an attorney, and ask him for advice. He told us to get him a lawyer, and gave us a referral. Anthony's parents hired her on the spot and she did what she was paid to do. While I was busy with the movers at our house in Seattle, Anthony was released on a small bail (not the $250,000 originally requested by the DA) and the charges were eventually dropped. Turns out the people pressing the charges had extensive criminal histories and no credibility. Go figure."

Anthony's quarterback friend, Louis, and his wife moved in a block away from Emily and Anthony's Mill Creek home.

> "I would be walking my dog past his house, and we would see each other. It would be just like it was back in the day, and we would catch up. It was completely normal, although there was this elephant in the room. I had all these questions, and he could tell I had questions." Louis continued, "I remember back in '03 when I graduated college, and that year in June I had my bachelor party. All of us friends met in northern California at Lake Shasta, and I drove down with Anthony in his Tahoe with a couple other friends. I remember looking back and seeing the effects of what he was on. He wasn't super bad, but I could see some of the things he did on that trip and how under the influence he was. When we were on the boat on the lake we docked, but then he left for a couple hours and came back. Anthony had some excuse why he was gone, but I'm sure he was out trying to fill a prescription somewhere."
>
> —Louis

Louis moved down to Portland, Oregon a few years later and is now a Portland Police Officer. Here are his thoughts about Anthony becoming an addict and committing crimes, whereas Louis went into criminal justice:

Louis says:

> "I hope that Anthony separated from me out of respect or a bit of embarrassment. In my career, I've gotten to see people with drug issues, people who have gone through it and survived. I know what he was doing back then wasn't him. I knew it, but I also didn't understand it. I know the real Anthony, and that is really all I know. I never really got to know the Anthony on drugs. I know what he is capable of and where he can go. Anthony is willing to take his troubled past and make it better for other people. He reminds me of Chris Herren, the guy who played for the Boston Celtics and became a heroin addict. He turned his life around and now speaks to children about addiction. I can see Anthony doing that with his life. I truly believe that the best of Anthony is yet to come. He's not some piece of shit trying to better himself monetarily. If he were, I wouldn't have responded to him after all the years. I know he can get better and I want to help.
>
> "Some of the people I come in contact with as a police officer have drug problems, and a lot are addicted to heroin. They wake up every morning and look for their fix. They go steal if they don't have the money. Heroin is the next thing they do when their prescriptions run out and they can't get a pill. The drugs are pretty similar. At some point, Anthony would have gotten there because addiction just keeps getting worse. The heroin, for example, mostly comes out of Mexico, and you really don't have any idea of what's in it, who made it, where it really came from, etc. Last year in

Portland and in Oregon there were ninety-three overdose deaths just because they got bad stuff. These were people who were shooting up their normal amounts and it killed them because there are so many variables in the drug from different sources. The last one I went on this boy was twenty-three years old and had a problem for a long time. He got a bad dose, basically. The drug devastates everybody, and Anthony was surely on his way. Now that Anthony has gotten clean, he still has a lot to prove, I think, not just to himself but to the criminal justice world. He has a lot of bridges to rebuild."

Eight

Emily and Anthony were quite busy and had a lot going on: they had just sold their house in Mill Creek and the flipped house in Monroe; they were working on the huge remodel in Seattle; had just put a huge payment on a higher-end, new construction home in Lake Stevens; and were weeks away from building on some waterfront property in the Snohomish/Woodinville area they'd just purchased. They were also having a baby. On top of all the houses and baby news, they took many trips: they went to San Francisco, then to New Jersey for a wedding, sightseeing in Manhattan, and then flew to Galveston for a week-long cruise in the Gulf of Mexico. Traveling to nice places, like Times Square, the Mayan Temples, the Boardwalk and seeing great sunsets, didn't matter because he was an addict with every emotion completely controlled by drugs. It was a good life gone bad.

Anthony enjoyed all the excitement but every morning he was reminded that he had a big problem. The shakes, panic and paranoia never let him think he had a long leash. At this point, Anthony was taking anywhere from thirty to fifty hydrocodone or Oxycodone pills a day. When he traveled, he switched to methadone or Oxycontin—which were both more powerful for their size—so he didn't have to deal with smuggling such a large quantity of pills.

The Seattle house they'd bought was built in 1968, and it hadn't been updated or repaired since it had been built. Anthony decided to teach himself how to do the remodeling. After all, the scams he was running afforded him the time he needed to teach himself. He bought tons of home improvement how-to books and went to work. One of his books was three inches thick just on plumbing alone. If he didn't understand electrical he'd go buy all the books and take them with him everywhere. Mistake after mistake, error after error, he kept at it. Anthony would go buy all the tools that the books showed in the pictures on the way to the house in the morning sometimes not returning home until midnight. He would get to the house and sixteen hours would fly by, but he didn't want to stop. Anthony fixed it all with his own hands from spray texture, putting up gutters at the proper angle, basic framing, using saws, building a deck, laying shingles, concrete work to bathroom tile. He combined his new skills and created a movie room with a motorized remote drop-down screen that popped out of the crown molding with the surround sound wired in. He loved customizing things, adding in shelves and creating cool things with his hands. Just as he had applied the full focus of his life to sports, addiction and his other crimes, he became obsessed with the house renovations. His details had to be perfect. He paid for a lot of the small items with the gift cards from the home improvement stores he'd gotten selling stolen merchandise.

The remodeling became sacred to Anthony, and he felt true passion for all of it. Emily's dad would come by and fill Anthony in on all the gaps of his knowledge that home improvement books didn't cover. It was good bonding time.

When Anthony had quite a bit of labor work he'd hire people. He had two guys who worked for him pretty consistently who knew how to do everything because they'd worked on home construction sites for years. Although these people were friends Anthony could hardly communicate with them in a construction sense. He knew nothing of the language of tools, and they frequently said things that made no sense to him. For instance, one of the guys asked if he had something called a "saw-zaw." Anthony said he hadn't, but sent them off to lunch while he went to the home improvement store. He asked the employee in the power tools section about the mysterious tool and discovered he had three reciprocating saws already. He just hadn't known what they were called. The books taught him a lot of things, but sounding cool in front of contractors wasn't one of them.

One time, he hired some high school kids to take load after truckload of trash to the dump. He gave them money for dump fees. Later in the day, he got a call from some poor guy who owned the property that the kids had dumped the trash on illegally. They had pocketed the dump money and disappeared. The property owner found a business card in the waste pile on his property. He was a lot more careful about hiring kids after that.

With the remodel only partially done, they moved in. Emily recalls:

> "We moved into the big fixer when I was six months pregnant with our first daughter. The top floor was almost done but the rest of the house was a construction zone. I hated that house from Day One, and even more so when we were forced to move into it. Anthony bought it against my wishes, which I resented, but I never thought we'd actually have to live there! I couldn't forget about the dead rats I'd pulled from the walls and the fireplace rocks. I couldn't forget about the seven layers of dirty carpet and linoleum floor I'd pulled up and scraped out myself. I hated that we spent every waking moment working on it and how much we fought about every detail, about every dollar. The only thing I liked about that house was our daughter's nursery. Anthony and I worked especially hard and surprisingly well together on that part of the project. It was perfect and complete by the time she arrived (that is one of my only fond memories of that house)."

The money that funded all of the big renovations and trips came from Anthony's illegal, or at least unethical, business scams. They were the only "jobs" available to a full-blown addict. Anthony would be on drugs for two months, then he'd take a week off to get clean, since he so desperately wanted to be clean and to function like everyone else. He'd be sober for a week or two tops, and then he'd relapse again. This was also exactly why he couldn't keep a real job, since every month and a half or so he needed to take a week off to cry, shake and piss on himself for five days of withdrawal symptoms, then take even more time to recover. Emily got used to this pattern. The insanity was that once he was clean and presented with the thought of a few Vicodin or Oxycotin, he would completely forget the pain caused from the withdrawals just days before. It also didn't help that when he was clean everyone thought he was on drugs, and when he was on drugs everyone thought he was sober.

He continued taking pills up to about a week before their daughter was born, but once again he decided to get clean for a major event in his life. Anthony didn't want to remember he was messed up when his daughter was born, so another horrifying week of withdrawal symptoms ensued.

In December, Emily and Anthony had a baby girl. "She was the most beautiful little baby. It was something I wasn't prepared for. It was every emotion all at once to know I had helped create her," Anthony remembered. His mother-in-law stayed at their house for a week to help them out. Emily was prescribed Percocet that she never took but monitored like a hawk.

Eventually enough was enough, and Anthony broke down and printed off a prescription for a bottle of sixty, 10 mg Norco, or hydrocodone painkillers equivalent to double a Vicodin. In his mind he deserved a treat for making a point of getting sober the week before their baby was born. Since he was able to self-detox successfully, he had confidence that he could quit at any time. He rationalized that he didn't have a problem. He called it in and made a trip down to the pharmacy to pick it up. It seemed to take longer than an hour, but afterwards, he was "rewarded" for his wait by that amazing feeling of ecstasy. This time, he vowed he would keep it under control. He took Suboxone, an opiate blocker used as a detoxing agent, for two days to get clean again. But the Monster would have none of it. The one bottle for celebration turned into a bottle of sixty pills every two days very quickly. He needed the pills just to breathe and function.

> "I didn't answer my phone and watched every DVD there was on how to care for every baby need. As I held her, I would stay up for hours at night and wouldn't move my arm, even though it had fallen asleep, to make sure I wouldn't wake her up. I just watched her and watched her. I changed a few diapers. She was the greatest thing that ever happened to me. When I would stare at her I knew what it meant to love someone so unconditionally. I would gladly give up my life to protect her. . . but no matter how hard I tried, I couldn't seem to be able to stay sober for her.
>
> "No matter how close the rescue boat is, and no matter how many life preservers are thrown down at the struggling swimmer, they still must reach out and grab it and take the help. The problem with me was that I would rather struggle in the waves until I eventually drowned and sank to the bottom. It doesn't matter if an addict is put in twenty treatment centers, they—and no one else—must want to make a change. It must be for them. They must desire a better quality of life."
>
> —Anthony

Because of the baby, Anthony could no longer leave the house unquestioned for hours at a time to feed his habit. He had to limit the field of pharmacies to those he could get to and from quickly. He needed so many pills just to stay normal that it was tiring just keeping up with the demand. He tried his best to wait until the pharmacies had shift changes. This meant he might visit the same pharmacy five to six days in a row. He'd use different patient names and different doctors' names. At 8 p.m. on Saturday he was Ryan from Seattle with major dental work being done. At 11 a.m. on Wednesday at the same place he was Steven from Renton who had chronic back pain associated with a car accident a year ago. But that could only go on for so long.

After turning in nearly 700 fake prescriptions over nearly seven years, and getting out of many close calls, Anthony was eventually arrested. The cops waited this time. The pharmacy agreed with the cops to fill the prescription so Anthony wouldn't think anything was out of the ordinary. When he went to pick up his prescription under his sixth name, sixth birthday, sixth address and sixth phone number that had been different on the sixth consecutive day he'd been to that one shop, he was busted. Anthony later estimated the cops must have been waiting for nearly twelve hours. The ironic part was that he was really trying to quit at the time. He was busted trying to fill two prescriptions that included Lorazepam and Clonidine that were used to come off of narcotic and opiate addiction. But the truth was that he was probably addicted to the Lorazepam on top of the pain killers.

> "Prescription fraud could be nearly eliminated if the system went all-electronic and removed the patient middle-man. The doctor would submit prescriptions electronically to the patient's pharmacy. Instead of new security upgrades to the paper including watermarks, anti-reproduction holograms and required DEA numbers, they could simply just do away with the prescription handed to the patient altogether."
>
> —Anthony

The police questioned him closely and it was clear that they thought he was part of a large drug ring due to the sheer quantity of the prescriptions being filled. He was booked, charged and released from the small but overcrowded jail.

Two narcotics detectives approached Anthony, threatened him and said, "We'll be in touch." And they stayed in touch, all right. They kept calling him and calling him.

Finally, Anthony snapped, "If you have to arrest me then do it, but enough is enough."

After the arrest, and with following a week of throwing up and shaking and going through all the other withdrawal symptoms, Emily took charge and handled everything while Anthony made another attempt to be sober. The Renton arrest was an eye-opener for him in March of 2007. For almost a full month, Anthony put in a deck overlooking Seattle and Mt. Rainier. It took several weeks to get his energy back, and he and his family settled back into life.

> "By early Spring, we were $120,000 into the remodel and desperate for cash. So when Anthony came home one afternoon with a Coach diaper bag, a gift for my first Mother's Day, I was livid! Was he insane? We were borrowing money from his parents to pay the bills, and here he was buying me a $600 diaper bag? 'But I have a receipt!' He proclaimed proudly. To which I responded, 'Thank God! At least you can take it back!' Of course, he refused to return it. He told me I was ungrateful and that I didn't appreciate anything. But it wasn't really about what I wanted. He couldn't have cared less. I liked the diaper bags I already had. He wanted me to have a fancier one. It was the same story with my car. When I decided to upgrade from my Civic to a new Accord (my dream car at the time) he insisted we buy a used Mercedes instead. It didn't matter what I wanted. It wasn't

> about me. It was always about him, about his image and about how he appeared to everyone else."
>
> —Emily

Anthony needed a valuable car, house or other material item since there was no value inside him.

> "I would have been too insecure to step out of a beat-up pickup truck. Actually, I would have been ashamed to step out of a brand new Ford F-150. I remember being embarrassed because the beautiful, newly constructed home we bought didn't have more square footage. When I was in prison and put in solitary, I lived in half the square footage of my old walk-in-closet for six and a half months with another man I hated. Karma. No matter what it was it was never good enough. I couldn't make my hatred for myself go away."
>
> —Anthony

The Vicodin, Percocet, Lortabs and Norcos were all wearing on him. Before the baby, he'd been taking his regular strength Vicodin, which was 5mg of hydrocodone and 500mg Acetaminophen (known by the brand name Tylenol). In his latest relapse, his usual daily amount progressed to thirty to fifty Norco pills a day, which consisted of 10mg of hydrocodone and 325mg of Acetaminophen. Anthony was obviously addicted to the hydrocodone, but the Acetaminophen that came with it was slowly poisoning him. Large amounts of Acetaminophen cause liver damage. A regular Tylenol tablet is 200mg of Acetaminophen. Anthony's daily intake was anywhere from 13,000mg to 25,000mg—the equivalent to taking approximately 125 Tylenol tablets a day for nearly eight years in a row. Anthony realized he was seeing symptoms of liver damage and decided he needed a change. But he didn't quit, he just switched poisons.

May 2007, and against Emily's advice, Anthony decided to attend a birthday party for his friend, John, without his wife and daughter. Even though he told Emily he wouldn't drink, he did. Before long, he was taking beer bongs. Anthony didn't take a single pill, but for the first time in his life he tried cocaine—just what an addict needed.

Anthony was in love again. From that day until the next time he was sent back to treatment, he didn't go without cocaine. It wasn't long before he was also back to thirty to fifty Norcos a day, equivalent to nearly 100 Vicodin a day, on top of all of the cocaine. Relapse after relapse after relapse. He no longer wanted to do cocaine by itself, or pills by themselves, and if he was awake he would be full of both chemicals simultaneously and then some.

The first week, Anthony bought one "Eight-Ball"—that was 3.5 grams. The next week he bought two. Soon he was going through an ounce every week, or about twenty-eight grams. Cocaine wasn't a party drug to Anthony. Again he flew right past fun to snorting a line a half a foot long in a dark shed that would last for only ten minutes. Before he knew it, he wanted more. Many times he'd stay up for three days straight lying to Emily about sleeping on the couch in the front room and faking being tired, when in fact he was wired out of his mind and stuck in the shed. He was in prison with the Monster again and soul-less.

His heart began to hurt badly with chest pains. When he fell asleep, he would sleep for nearly twenty-four hours—only awakened by extreme hunger. Every time he woke, he found that he'd sweated through his clothes, sheets and into the comforter. Anthony smelled like chemicals. His body was working overtime pumping all the shit out of his body. He ground his teeth right through his night guards. Often, he'd completely forget to eat for as many as four days straight. His weight was dropping: ten pounds, then twenty, thirty—fifty!—until he was down to 140 lbs. from 190. Anthony had a greenish/yellow tint to his skin. He couldn't breathe out of his nose. He tried all kinds of things to conceal his new nose problems from Emily and his family, since his nose was bloody half the time. He tried Afrin, decongestants, even a towel over his head over a stove with boiling water trying to breathe again. Nothing helped except for chopping up more lines with razor blades and snorting it in with rolled up bills, straws or whatever he could find. He would attempt to eat, but had to pause to regain his breath since his nasal passages were simply not functional. His nasal thing became repulsive as the draining would come out on the pillow case mixed with blood. Emily called around for ear/nose/throat specialists to see him, although there was no faking this. A doctor would diagnose his problem right away. Then within two weeks he was "cured."

> "Anthony started complaining about having this awful, re-occurring sinus infection. His mom thought he'd suddenly become allergic to our cat—neither of us would've ever imagined he was snorting cocaine! But we'd had the cat for five years so I knew that couldn't be right. It must be a sinus infection. I made him numerous doctor appointments and even tracked down an ENT specialist for him—turns out he never went to any of them."
>
> —Emily

Using Google, Anthony discovered how to smoke cocaine. Instead of quitting the problem, he simply found an alternative way to get the drug into his system. He started free-basing cocaine off of foil using baking soda to extract the pure cocaine, identical to smoking crack. Anthony was a crack-head, but it sounded so much better to tell himself he was just free-basing. Once he started smoking it, his quantity nearly doubled. Anthony was smoking well over half an ounce every thirty-six hours at his peak. Every ounce, every gram he swore was his last. He would say to himself that he had to just finish this one thing and then he'd quit . . . although he no longer could really function. He could hardly go to the bathroom without severe difficulties. The Hydrocodone constipated him while the cocaine made him feel like he had to go, and the combination created problems. He couldn't remember anything people would tell him. Anthony found himself writing himself notes so he wouldn't forget anything—but then he'd lose the notes. He actually wrote himself notes to remember to look at his notes.

When he started doing cocaine, Anthony hated to be around family. Going to Emily's parent's house or his own parents' house was a chore. He had to keep them at a distance to protect his addiction. It was exhausting telling lie after lie, and after it was done he had so many rocks of guilt stacked on his back that it was just another reason to stay out of reality. Anthony loved them and was sick of all the lies, but he felt he had no choice.

> "The addict can't be around people they love or that love them. I hated it. There is so much guilt and shame that constantly reminds them of their short comings and failed lives. It can also be a form of respect where they don't want their loved ones to see them like that."
>
> —Anthony

While Anthony was putting up siding one day, a guy he'd hired for a few days over a year ago showed up at the house and came up to talk to him. He rambled on about the work Anthony was doing. Anthony could tell he was on drugs—surely meth. He noticed the guy picking at the underside of his forearm as they spoke—it was a huge untreated wound. The skin was red, there was blood and Anthony believed he could actually see bone, since he saw a white strip. It almost made him throw up, but luckily he hadn't eaten in days— just a dry heave was all he managed. "You gonna get that checked out?" Anthony asked.

"It's fine. Just bubbles," he replied. Hastily, he covered it up by unraveling his long sleeve and going back to his rapid babble about siding.

Just like that, Anthony's once nice worker turned meth-head. The guy left in a hurry when there was a distant car horn honk. Anthony thought, *I'd be surprised if he lives through the month. Man, he's messed up.* He really felt bad for him. Later, he would realize that as much as he thought at the time they were complete opposites, they were both dying of exactly the same disease.

Thinking that he was always going to quit kept Anthony from buying large quantities of cocaine at a huge discount. Instead, he bought from a local, small-time, addicted dealer. The trouble was, he was pretty unreliable. Anthony decided to put the dealer up in a shitty $400 a month apartment. After that, Anthony could count on him to be available about fifty percent of the time, instead of ten percent of the time. At this point, his cocaine habit was costing him over $10,000 a month. He was spending more on cocaine a month than all three properties, a Range Rover, a Mercedes, food, insurance and every other bill they had.

> "It was in fact my addiction that submarined me and my family, not the crash of the real estate market. However, the market crashing prevented that life from continuing."
>
> —Anthony

Another time, he told the guy who was working for him, "I'll be right back, I have to go get some vice grips." He headed down to the shed and was stuck in there for fifteen straight hours. First, he would freebase some coke, then look for the tool. He found the tool, then went to get high again. Repeat. Then repeat again. At one point, he realized he was in trouble. With a marker, he wrote on the wood table top "I'm sorry that life turned out like this" note to Emily. He thought that any second he would have a heart attack and that would be it. But he couldn't stop.

Ironically, Anthony had watched the guy who worked for him stare down at one of the tenants at the apartment complex down the hill and call him a crack-head, since he drove a shitty car and looked ratty. Meanwhile, his clean-cut boss with a nice car and business was trapped for days in his own shed because of his addiction.

The shed became his own private hell. It was a detached one-car garage with its own driveway veering off from the main drive to the house. No one had done any work on it since it was built in the Sixties on a slope; the whole building was leaning downhill. Anthony had to run separate power down to it because he kept blowing the breakers. He stored all his tools there, as well as, electrical wire, wheelbarrows, table saws, etc. There was a tool bench and table, both with lots of drawers. Anthony stacked the used foils in there. When he ran out of coke, there would be times he would get his hands and arms all nasty digging through the old ones, just to find an unsmoked corner. One drawer must have had over 100 empty pill bottles. Razor blades were everywhere and any hard surface, a notebook, a cd case, whatever, were used to chop up cocaine. Empty baking soda boxes and old water bottles were scattered on the floor. Cell phones, sim cards, laptops, batteries and chargers were everywhere. There were rats at times if he didn't clean out the trash. The only entrance was the garage door and when Anthony pulled it up after he'd been in there for a long time, he'd be nearly blinded.

He would sit on a large cooler for hours, moving back and forth fidgeting with things as he stayed out of reality and spun out on the drugs. Hours flew by. He would sweat profusely and many times cried wondering what happened to his life. Then he'd do some drugs and it would be fine.

One day, Anthony drove home and discovered huge, thousand pound boulders beside his driveway. They had been moved there by an excavator from a construction company at the apartment complex next door. The parking lot was being expanded into an area that Anthony had been assured was his when he bought it. When Anthony called the owners—multi-millionaires who knew real estate—they said they believed the land to be theirs. The disagreement rapidly turned into a dispute over property lines.

Anthony was unnerved. He'd been told the property was a half acre. He and Emily had quite a bit wrapped up in the house. They'd purchased it for $340,000, even though it needed a ton of work. He'd invested about $125,000 with payments, but he expected the finished value would be around $700,000. He was hoping to clear nearly $300,000 at the end of the deal. All of Anthony's other projects depended on the sale of this one big house. The Lake Stevens home had sucked out at least $30,000 of his available capital, and it wasn't yet finished. The waterfront property had its own expenses with zoning costs at the city, permits, plans and septic design and installation coming in. The money was flying out and he had to borrow money from both sets of parents. A property dispute was potentially catastrophic to Anthony's plans.

Anthony purchased a survey of the property at the cost of a couple thousand dollars. The result was as he'd expected: the entire parking lot of the apartment complex belonged to Emily and Anthony.

Anthony decided to ask the couple to pay for the rezoning fee that would legally give them the property so they didn't have to continue to pay the taxes, but nothing. He knew that the driveway property in the city limits could have been valued around $75,000. They didn't respond to his calls and letters. The couple seemed to like the current situation where they used the property and Anthony and Emily paid for it. Emily and Anthony were confused. They were sure that the apartment complex owners would realize how valuable the parking lot was. Without it their tenants had no where to park. Anthony decided to send one last letter, telling them he intended to fence off his property, since the couple hadn't seen fit to resolve the matter.

He never got that far. The couple hit the Curcios with a lawsuit. Anthony hoped that a court date would resolve matters, but they could never get a date in front of a judge. At the end of the year, Anthony and Emily had spent nearly $15,000 on attorneys. They would gladly just have settled, given up and let the apartment complex owners have whatever they wanted. They simply wanted to move on and stop hemorrhaging lawyer's fees.

But the apartment complex owners decided to be vindictive and wouldn't sign off—which meant the dispute continued. The owners kept filing extensions. It was a one-sided battle with nobody fighting back on the Curcios' side.

Anthony had interested buyers for the house, but he knew they'd never get a loan on a place with a property dispute. The house was Anthony's bank, basically holding anywhere from $250,000-$400,000 of their cash flow when it sold, but the account was locked up tight.

Anthony was getting really upset with his neighbors who were keeping his driveway hostage with the property lawsuit. He told himself, *This woman and her husband are keeping me from feeding my family.* In fact it was his drug habit—his new love cocaine, plus his $700 a month prescription narcotic addiction—that was nearly impossible to maintain. He tried to get a loan off of another property, but they were running high credit buying a new home in Lake Stevens and the furniture to furnish it, so the banks were denying any more debt. Borrowing money from family again wasn't an option. He decided to go back to his criminal activities. It seemed the only path open to him.

Anthony had been living two lives for a very long time, and his drug use led to very bad decision-making. In fact, Anthony was becoming an expert in seemingly making all the wrong decisions possible. The worst and most hurtful mistake he made was his need to start seeing other women after he was married.

In his chemically destroyed brain, Anthony's perception of Emily was that she had gone absolutely nuts. She'd get mad if Anthony didn't come home for days and not call. She was furious if he showed up in a new $80,000 automobile—she had the nerve to ask him where he got it! She simply was not minding her own business in the marriage. So what if there were a few plasma televisions all boxed up in the garage? There was a nice big new television in the house that came from nowhere, so what was the big deal? Emily found a bunch of aluminum foils in the garage and he wouldn't tell her what they were used for. On a separate occasion she found a bunch of lighters and was then able to start putting everything together. He couldn't understand why she was getting upset when he would lock himself in the bathroom for three hours at a time with the laptop.

Anthony had different cell phones for everything. He routinely carried several phones and tucked them into his car and various places in the house. They went off at all hours of the day and night.

Anthony felt Emily's constant questions were intrusive. Things like, "Would you like to go to my brother's graduation?" or "Would you watch the baby for an hour while I run to the store?" These stupid requests, along with her nagging, made him believe she was crazy. It wasn't him, it was her.

Anthony was working a different type of job than normal people where he was leaving at 11 p.m. with bolt cutters, power tools and dressed in all black. This confused Emily as well.

> "I was once picked up at 11pm by a semi truck and trailer right outside our cul-de-sac. What I was doing wasn't exactly legal. Some days I went to work in slacks and a tie, and other times I wore jeans, work boots and gloves. Nights like these I just hoped Emily didn't look out the window. Looking back she was upset that I was leaving all the time, and I don't blame her."
>
> —Anthony

Anthony did what every guilty-feeling husband would do, he brought Emily gifts. He didn't bring them every day, but on special occasions he turned up with jewelry and purses. Emily always asked to see the receipts. The gifts were brand new in their boxes, so Anthony couldn't understand why she needed the receipts. He couldn't understand where this ungrateful behavior was coming from since he was working his ass off for her—although he wasn't bringing in actual money for bills.

When he rolled over to go back to bed at 3 p.m., Emily had the nerve to slam the door to the guest bedroom. It was the last straw. Anthony'd had enough of her bad behavior. After all he had done and this was the thanks he got? She just wasn't changing with him. He decided to make a change—not to go to marriage counseling—Anthony was going to have to look for someone else.

Anthony convinced himself that Emily was the problem. He needed someone who really cared about him and wouldn't expect the truth all the time. He needed someone who would love him enough to let him do drugs, one who would be swayed by material things. He needed a girl who thought he was cool for how he acted and the types of businesses he ran. He needed someone new who wouldn't harass him about things.

Sometimes when he would wake up in the morning, before he took his first drugs of the day, he would get really sad at the sight of Emily. She was the most beautiful girl in the world to Anthony, but he couldn't understand why Emily wouldn't treat him as these other women did? Then he would "medicate," cry for thirty minutes and suddenly feel great when the meds kicked in. Anthony found that if he took enough pills, snorted enough cocaine or smoked enough crack, that he could pretty much face any obstacle in his life including the emotional ones. He was an expert at being able to justify his behavior and pretend he was making good choices. . . only his choices were for himself only.

"The real estate market was on its way down the tube and already, the house we'd purchased in Lake Stevens was worth less than what we bought it for just two months before. We weren't living there yet because it wasn't finished—and neither was the Seattle house. Anthony spent all day working on the remodel then left to hang out with his friends at night. I had a nagging feeling that something wasn't right. We both had our ups and downs in college so I'd been insecure about our relationship for a while. We had a new baby and times were rough, but Anthony always assured me I was being ridiculous. That he loved me and would never hurt me like that again. He convinced me I had nothing to worry about and that I was acting like a crazy person. I believed him and decided his weird behavior was due to the financial stress we were under. By this time, we owned three properties: the house in Seattle, the house in Lake Stevens and a piece of vacant lake-front property that Anthony once again, 'just had to have.' I couldn't wait to move into the new house in Lake Stevens. I thought it was the answer to all of our problems. We'd sell the Seattle house, build on and sell the lake property, and everything would be fine. I was in denial again. It's a pattern I wouldn't be able to recognize until years later. I found out after he was sentenced that he'd been lying to me all along. It wasn't financial stress or anxiety or depression, it was drug addiction and everything that goes along with it."

—Emily

It was supposed to be the time of his life. He was in his mid-twenties, good-looking with a beautiful wife and baby, houses, flashy cars, friends and always access to lots of money. . . but it wasn't enough. Anthony test drove a Ferrari with paddle shifters and thought that it was the missing link in his life. Without telling Emily, Anthony and a friend visited dealerships until he found the right car. He decided it wasn't a big deal, considering it was just another payment of $2,000 a month. It was well worth it if it meant feeling great. Buying a Ferrari would make him happy. All of Anthony's success was measured against comparison to others, and he always came up short. He couldn't be the best if the stuff around him wasn't the best. In his mind he was worthless. He dealt with his terrible insecurities by using pain killers, even though they didn't actually kill his pain. They just blanketed his brain.

"Okay, yes I will, don't worry. I'll remember. Love you too," Anthony said as he shut the door. *Thank God she's gone!* he thought. He ran to the window looking out over the driveway and watched Emily's Mercedes pull away. He was finally alone.

Anthony tip-toed down the hallway and slowly turned the door knob to his young daughter's door. Anthony was in such a hurry to get to his love. Just the touch alone made him feel at peace. He opened the door slowly at first, just a crack to peek in. She was sound asleep. Perfect. He shut the door softly and nearly sprinted to the garage. He dug into his toolbox and found his true love—*cocaine.*

Anthony had about seven grams left. His hands were shaking as he tore off the foil, put chopped cocaine on top, mixed it with baking soda and a drop of water, smeared it and lit it. He inhaled, thinking, *Oh, my God!* Somehow, he found himself lying on his back thinking of nothing else but the amazing high for a second. Repeat. Repeat again. Anthony did that until he'd made a stack of empty foils. Then he was finally able to leave the garage. He had to get ready for the wedding.

Anthony grabbed the baby monitor, grabbed his foils, burned and inhaled again. He prepared some foils for when he got out, and then hopped into the shower. His heart was just pounding. He could hardly shower fast enough, looking through the glass doors, keeping his eye on his love, those foils. Shampooing was a dangerous and frustrating task because he had to lose visual contact, though only for a moment. He was done and out of the shower. What a hassle the shower had become. He used the baby monitor to hold down the foil while he ran the lighter underneath. *Ah!*

He looked into the mirror and frowned. The red rash on his face had been getting worse lately. Anthony told Emily they were from all the dust particles in the under-construction house. They'd changed the face soap he was using to no effect, so what else could it be? He turned his face back and forth in the reflection. *Shit, they are bad,* Anthony thought to himself. In just a couple of hours he was going to have to carry his ten-month-old down the aisle at his sister-in-law's wedding while nearly 250 wedding guests—all who knew Anthony—watched. Emily was the maid of honor in the wedding. The only way to hide the insecurities of seeing all of these people with sores and rashes on his face was the dope.

Anthony opened the medicine cabinet. What he was looking for was a cream to cure the rashes and sores associated with a crackhead smoking so many chemicals off of foil right near his face. For some reason, a crackhead rash wasn't listed as a cure on any of the creams. And boy, did they itch! Anthony managed to keep from scratching them, which would have made the mess on his face even worse. He patted the rashes with cold water, rubbed them gently with a cool rag, put ice on them, added some more creams. . . and then took another couple of hits off the foil. With all the attention he'd paid to the rashes, they only got worse. *Why aren't the rashes getting better?*

Then the baby monitor went off, and he could hear his daughter crying. Anthony quickly cleaned up the bathroom and ran toward his child's room . . . but he stopped short, second guessing the idea. He changed course and ran toward the garage so he could make some more "foilies" before he got his daughter out of her crib. Anthony was planning ahead and his priorities were first.

Anthony changed his daughter's diaper and seated her in her high chair. He put out some snacks and turned on her favorite show "My Friends Tigger and Pooh." Then he went off to the garage to burn another foil. He returned to her room to get her clothes and other stuff all together. Back to the garage. Anthony ran to get himself dressed, and looked in the mirror again. *I look like shit!* he thought to himself. Then he ran back to the garage for another foil burn, and back to the mirror. *Oh, it's not that bad.* The perception of his image changed with the flick of a lighter.

His daughter was done and wanted out of the high chair, but Anthony hadn't finished getting ready. He started another show and put out some more Goldfish. The show's theme song was what kept her most distracted. He made a trip to the car with all the baby stuff, and as he closed the car door he paused to look in the mirror at his rashes. *Holy shit, it's horrible!* Anthony thought. *Everyone's going to know I'm smoking crack! Thank God my daughter doesn't judge me.* He burned another foil. All of a sudden the rash wasn't that bad. The effects of the cocaine brought out the euphoria effects of the six Norco pills—it was the greatest feeling of all time. Finally he was good, so it was time to get his daughter in the car and get moving. He took one last glance at his face as he shut the garage door. *No big deal. It's really not near as bad as I thought,* he thought to himself. As long as Anthony was high, all was okay.

Anthony was proud of himself. He was on time, and only had to stop three times—if you counted the first stop where he had to "check the back tire" and fire up a foil. Or the second stop where "the back tire is acting up again," to do one last foil right before they got to the church. They were only twenty minutes late.

Eight

As soon as Anthony pulled into the church parking lot he saw a group of guys he'd gone to high school with, some of them he'd played sports with. "Hey, Curcio!" one called out.

"What's up?" he yelled back.

"Got a cold one for you! Pound one with us," the guy said.

"I quit drinking. Sorry guys," Anthony replied.

Another of the guys said, just loud enough for him to hear, "Yeah right, and started doing what?"

Anthony felt totally self conscious about the comment as he carried his daughter in her car seat past his former classmates and into the church. He found Emily and handed off his baby.

Oh shit, Anthony thought to himself when he spotted his parents. He tried to make a quick exit and sneak back to his car, but then he heard his mother say, "Anthony," in a way that made it impossible not to stop. He had been avoiding his mom for a month or so, but there was no getting away from her here. Anthony was one step ahead of her and pointed to his rashes saying that he needed to get something for it. She dug through her purse and handed him some Nivea cream. As he moved in to give her a quick hug, he knew the look in her eyes. It said that she knew something was seriously wrong again. Anthony was thankful there wasn't time to discuss it. She went back into the church, glancing back sadly at him.

Anthony's decline wasn't just obvious to his mother, it was apparent to everyone. His entire life, he'd been the model of good health. He was extremely fit, not an unnecessary roll anywhere, and he was also good looking. His appearance was causing many people to turn and stare.

As Anthony started walking back to the church, he knew he had to walk past those guys again, so he said to himself, *Fine, I'll have a beer and get these guys off my back.*

"Thought you stopped?" one asked.

"Yeah, I did, but with this rash on my face I need a few drinks." Anthony replied.

He realized that his rash was worse than he thought, because their laughter was more like "Holy shit you let yourself go, and we would be extremely concerned for you if we still hung out" type of laugh.

"Yeah man, you look like shit," one told him. Anthony tried to joke it off and made up some story that only a grandma would believe.

Then Anthony said goodbye and headed back to his car—to his real love, the only one who wouldn't make him feel uncomfortable or judge him. Anthony purposely drove the nicest car in the parking lot only to disguise the loser who smoked cocaine inside of it. His anxiety rose as people followed him to his car and peered in waving and wanting to chat, but Anthony couldn't wait. He hurried the friends away, started the car and drove out of the parking lot. He was finally alone with his love.

By the time he returned, people were seated and ready for the wedding to start. The music had already begun, so Anthony grabbed the baby on a hand-off with Emily and walked her into the seating area. As he entered the chapel, he felt the eyes of the 110 guests on each side staring at him—the once local football and basketball hero, the prince of Monroe. Now his was the face of a beaten-down drug addict who—if you removed the suit and tie—looked like a homeless guy straight off the streets begging for some change. He saw in their faces just one question:

What the hell happened to Anthony Curcio?

Anthony's pace slowed as he stepped up to the altar, trying to hide in plain sight. He looked up at the cross above him—and it was all he could do not to run away forever. The only reason he didn't leave was because that little girl in his hands didn't deserve a daddy like that.

"One thing I thought I'd never fail at was being a father. But I did. Looking back, I realize that my addiction was progressing at an accelerated rate. I was no different from those people I had listened to in treatment so many years before. My addiction was so ruthless. It robbed me of all my morals, all my integrity and really everything that made me human. It nearly robbed me of my entire life."

—Anthony

Nine

Anthony had to turn in paperwork at his real estate office and finish up a few things. He left his house at about 10 p.m. to go to the office, which was in a huge commercial building that his real estate company shared space in. Late at night was the best way to avoid seeing everyone in his condition. Anthony was detoxing, again, and trying to get off the pills. He was using Suboxone—which is an opiate antagonist or blocker that mixed with opiates can make a person extremely sick or even kill them if the addict attempts to take opiates. He was also on a tranquilizer to slow down the process, muscle relaxers to settle his nerves, Xanax for the severe anxiety caused from the detox, Clonidine for his blood pressure, and a half an ounce of cocaine simply to stay awake. Ten minutes before pulling into the office building, he picked up a six-pack of Sparks—which are sixteen-ounce alcohol-infused energy drinks.

At about 10:45 p.m., he pulled into the empty parking lot, pounded two Sparks, popped a Xanax and smoked two foils of crack. He grabbed the packet of papers and headed out. Even with all the drugs trying to blanket his withdrawal symptoms, the Monster still screamed at him. Nothing could replace the pills. He went into the office and threw the agreement on the secretary's desk. That's when he heard a familiar voice in his mind telling him, "All this pain can simply go away. Just print out a prescription." Next thing he knew, he was in front of a computer in the office finding a local doctor's name to forge. Using an old web-based email account that had a prescription template, Anthony printed a scrip, cut it to size and headed to the pharmacy in the next door strip mall.

He dropped off the prescription, but the pharmacist told him that it will be at least an hour wait. There were no issues. She was just backed up. Anthony decided to head back to the office for a while to wait it out. Back in the office, he drank the fifth Sparks, and mixed with everything else, he was very drunk and stoned. He started down the stairwell on his way out to pick up the prescription, when he looked through the windows and saw cop cars everywhere. Anthony froze and slowly stepped back away from the window. He realized that they were looking for a type of criminal and probably wouldn't think they were looking for a businessman in that building. He watched as the cops used their flashlights to see inside in his truck, under and all around his truck. Another officer searched around the outside of the building. Anthony was trapped. There were too many cops to run from. He could see two more parked sheriff cruisers blocking the entrance with their lights off. An hour passed as he sat on the top step of the stairwell and sipped his last Sparks in the darkness, watching the cops. One office light coming on in the office would surely have shown a spotlight on his location to the police outside. He even had to be careful of the flickering lighter he used to free-base. Anthony decided to go back up to the office to use the bathroom to smoke more cocaine.

Fifteen minutes later, Anthony noticed that the cops had parked a car hidden from the street, with another at the other entrance. They seemed to think that he had left the truck there and would be back to get it. *Screw it, I'll wait it out.* More coke. He snorted it with a Xanax. Then he smoked more.

Was it the cocaine or the withdrawal from the painkillers that was making him sweat like an NBA superstar? He couldn't tell, but he also couldn't sit still and stop shaking. Anthony paced back and forth, talking to himself in the darkness.

More coke, and he was beyond gone. Anthony was talking to himself—then screaming. He'd laugh while he was crying at the same time. Then the hallucinations started, which was brand new for him. Something was right behind him! He turned around with a start. *Nothing.* He heard it again, and spun around quickly trying to catch whatever it was. *Still nothing.* He clutched his dress coat under his arm—the better to keep the bag of coke in the pocket safe. His heart beat was so loud it sounded as if it was coming out of his chest, then his head. It seemed as if the Monster had escaped out of his head and was stalking him. It wanted him back on those pills now! He was trapped by both the cops and the Monster, so he ran from room to room with quick sprints, still showing the speed from his youth.

Anthony dashed into the large conference room overlooking the parking lot. He fell to the ground and prayed for everything to go away—the same empty promise that he had now perfected—*God, I'll never do this again if you make it all go away* . . . . Even Anthony knew it was bullshit. But the harder he prayed, the more the room seemed to come alive. Pure evil was oozing up from the drab beige carpet. He heard deep, echoing laughter. Then the Monster started mocking him for being so pathetic as to ask God for help. Suddenly, his arm went dead. He picked himself up and ran to the little kitchen area to splash water on himself at the sink. But every time he bent his head, he caught movement in his peripheral vision. He turned his head to see what it was, but it was gone. Sweat poured down his face, so he put his head under the faucet.

Anthony runs his sweaty hands through his short prison-hair as he recalls:

> "I felt as if I was on fire and breathing so fast, my heart was going boom, boom, boom. Then it was like all the crap that was moving around me, just out of sight, all came right in front of me and screamed. I fell to the ground at the sink

> and had a kitchen knife in my hand. I was beyond paranoid and probably part suicidal—as I always seemed to be. I remember things that couldn't have been possible like conversations and running with that knife everywhere. I'm pretty sure I stressed my heart that night with my arm going numb, and I'm pretty sure I remember the clock read 3:30 a.m."

Anthony heard a vacuum go on in one of the offices somewhere. He squinted at the early morning light coming through the windows. The dried layers of sweat tingled on his body, and he was freezing cold. He didn't have to look into the mirror to know he was pale white. His jacket was lying over his chest, and he still had his dress shoes on. Anthony's mouth was directly on the very thin high-traffic style carpet. The taste in his mouth was indescribable, but it had something to do with blood, carpet fibers and biting on a piece of steel all night. Anthony then started to piece things together. He remembered tipping over the chairs, thinking they were playing merry-go-round around. He recalled falling down. When the hell was that? He grabbed his coat and pulled out his phone— dozens of missed calls from Emily. It was 6:45 a.m. on Saturday morning. The bag of coke was nearly gone. Then it came back to him: the cops, the pills, the prescription and waiting to pick them up, the Monster going for a walk in the halls. Anthony looked out the window and saw his truck in the lot. All the cops had left. There was no imaginary addiction Monster walking around outside his head.

He remembered voices telling him to cut himself. Specifically, he recalled hearing a voice intone a variation of the Bible verse, "If one part of your body causes you to sin, it is better to cut if off and cast it into the fire." *Holy shit.* Then he saw the knife lying in the center of the huge conference table. He put it in his pocket and opened the conference room door.

There stood a man coiling the cord of his vacuum. He looked to be in his late sixties, rather short—no more than five-foot-three—with gray hair, and dressed in a flannel shirt and rough khakis. He paid Anthony no mind as he finished up cleaning. Anthony went to the kitchen to put the knife back. He had to pass the man on his way out and hoped to get by without having to talk.

The man said, "I'm just finishing up here, too. Early bird gets the worm, huh?" He tilted the vacuum back and started to wheel it out.

Anthony smiled and tried to act normal. "Yeah." The last thing he wanted to do was start a conversation with anyone, but to be friendly he asked, "How long have you worked here?"

Next thing he knew, they were engaged in a conversation and all of Anthony's symptoms seemed to disappear. He started feeling as if everything was going to be okay.

The man was the kindest person. He reminded Anthony of his grandfather. And just like Grandpa, he talked about God. He said, "Even during a tough real estate market, when it doesn't seem like anything will ever get better, it always does. But it isn't always the way we think. Remember, He's always with us. He's not concerned with what we have, but who we are. True success is what type of people we are inside." The man gave Anthony a big smile and finished, "You gotta run and I gotta get back to work. Nice talking to you. It was Anthony, right?"

Anthony said, "What do you do here? Are you the janitor for all of these offices?"

"No," he replied, "I work in your same office."

"Oh! Okay, you have a good one," Anthony replied. He went downstairs, got into his car and turned his attention to getting his hands on some pills.

An hour later, it suddenly occurred to him: *How did that guy know my name?* He got home and looked though all the employees featured on the company's website. The man wasn't on the list. He wanted to talk to him again. When Anthony called in to ask the secretary if she'd received his paperwork, he described the man to her. "Do you know him?"

"Nope," the secretary said. "I know all the agents, and no old, small guy with white hair works here. That's for sure."

> "I don't know what this was all about. This guy wasn't the janitor or custodian who worked there or held the contract for the building. He just came out of nowhere. There was no car in the parking lot, no nothing. I'm not saying he was an angel, but it sure seemed like it. I like to think he saved me from something, kept me from a heart attack or kept me safe in some way. I told the story to my parents when I came clean about my cocaine habit and began my outpatient program and drug testing."
>
> —Anthony

The day Anthony told his parents about his cocaine habit, he agreed to start an outpatient and volunteer drug testing arrangement, which would report to Emily and his parents. The deal he made with his family was that he would stay clean or go back to inpatient treatment. He would be accountable to them with no more secrets. Every morning, he had to call the testing facility. If he was chosen at random, he had to go in and provide a urine sample and blow into a breathalyzer, paying out of pocket for the service. The urine sample was taken in a bathroom full of mirrors with a man staring at him. This man had full visual of Anthony—his hands, the cup. . . and the whole thing. Anthony inquired as to the purpose of the scrutiny. He explained that he'd seen several fake penises sold online that stored "clean" urine at body temperature. So he needed an up-close view of the action to make sure there was no cheating. This was Anthony's life for a while.

It was his plan, but after some time he began to hate the process. Anthony was Dr. Jekyll and Mr. Hyde. One personality was addicted and ruthless. The other was sober, loving and kind. Anthony decided he needed a break. He started drinking right after a morning test and drank until 5 p.m. that day. He passed out in the driver's seat of his car and woke up in a parking lot at about 10 p.m., drove home and went to bed. The next morning he was required to go back in to submit to another test. He blew a 0.03—which was bad since it was the next day. A fax went to his dad. Anthony tried to lie his way out of it with something about too much Nyquil. Emily and Anthony's parents knew all his tricks, all his lies and every sign to look for. His dad wasn't fooled.

Anthony couldn't believe he'd gotten that drunk, but he was an alcoholic. He knew that each drink would eventually lead to complete destruction, but he couldn't stop. A sober week would go by, and then a friend turned up, and the next thing he knew, they were drinking, and the coke would come out. The next day, he would test positive for many different types of drugs. One time, five drugs were in his system at one time. Anthony couldn't say "no" even when he knew that a life insurance test was scheduled the next day at his house. Emily was terribly embarrassed when Anthony was declined coverage for failing the drug test.

Anthony went to work for his parents at their landscaping business making good money. But even then, he couldn't put a dent in their financial troubles. So he focused less on the legitimate work and more on the scams in order to just tread water a little longer.

Anthony decided to stop caring. He had life support holding his hand, with his family right at his side cheering him on, but he chose to throw it all away. The cycle of destruction accelerated. He disappeared on a three-day binge. Eventually, his parents tracked him down.

> "I called the outpatient program to request some paperwork I needed to send to drug court as proof that Anthony

was attending rehab. But the person who answered told me Anthony had quit coming several weeks ago—which meant he had been pretending to go all along. It was another devastating letdown; another confrontation. Who knew what else he was lying about? He was supposed to be working for his parents' company, but he had yet to bring home a full forty-hour per week paycheck. I called his parents again and that's when we decided he needed to go back to inpatient rehab. After several hours of research, we determined that Sundown was still our best option. Problem was that Anthony needed a year-long program—minimum. Three weeks was a joke and it was never going to work for Anthony. You don't spend a decade spiraling downward in addiction to turn around and climb out in twenty-one days! But nothing else seemed feasible at the time, considering I was pregnant again and we were in dire straits financially. I didn't know the extent of his problems. I didn't know about the cocaine, or the scams or the infidelity. It took him over a year after he was arrested for robbing the armored car to finally come clean to me about everything."

—Emily

One night, Anthony was up in the ceiling panels of a mom and pop pharmacy, waiting for the store to close so that he could steal some bottles of oxycodone. It occurred to him—just for a moment—that maybe he needed more than outpatient treatment. It certainly didn't seem to be working.

When Emily and both of his parents staged an intervention, Anthony agreed he needed help again. They sent him in for a drug test. He tested positive with what the testing center called an "overwhelming" amount of cocaine, opiates, valium, alcohol and marijuana. Back to treatment.

> "I found out I was pregnant with our second daughter a few weeks after Christmas and about a week before Anthony told us he'd relapsed again. I was freaking out. How was I going to take care of two children under the age of two all by myself? How I knew back then that I'd be alone I have no idea, but I didn't tell Anthony for a month. We'd been fighting so much I didn't see the point. I was preparing for the worst when he came clean about his relapse and started rehab. I blamed our fighting on his using. Money was still tight but we had renters in the Seattle house now which offset some of the mortgage payment. I remember thinking maybe things weren't as bad as they seemed," Emily says. "I decided to tell Anthony about the pregnancy. He didn't freak out. He smiled, held my face in his hands, kissed me and said: 'Everything will be okay.' He could not have been more wrong."
>
> —Emily

When they pulled up to the treatment facility, Anthony knew what to expect. The counselor decided—probably based on his greenish color—that Anthony needed to take a liver panel test. The results were horrible. The doctor told him he should have been dead. Anthony was told that if his drug use continued another month or two, his kidneys and liver would be destroyed. Anthony realized how close he was to completely poisoning himself.

His withdrawal symptoms were bad. Anthony kept trying not to think about how he'd become the guy that seven years ago he thought he would never become, the guy who chose drugs over his family—like that woman Anthony had despised at his first rehab. During that stay, the director made everyone write down the top five most important things in their lives—then he would tear it up if sobriety wasn't on top of the list. Anthony understood what the director had been saying, but now he was too far gone and still not ready to receive the message.

He'd turned in his cell phone when he checked in, but he also hid one so he could conduct "business" while he was inside. He stashed the phone and sim cards in different public areas of the treatment facility to avoid discovery during room shake-downs. During his shower time, he used his cell phone to work out deals.

Emily and Anthony's parents came, as well as Emily's folks, to see him at treatment—it was a three hour drive. His whole family was throwing him life preservers and totally confused as to why Anthony simply wouldn't just get in the boat.

What Anthony later realized was that treatment didn't prepare him well for the actual event of relapse. Relapse is spoken of as if it's a complete failure, when in reality it is just a setback and a common event in an addict's life. But, just like in sports, if you fail, you have to get up and go to the next play. You have to keep trying, since addiction leads to only three things: prison, death and hell on Earth.

> "After Anthony came back from his fifth and final try at rehab, he didn't seem that different to me. He was affectionate, yes, but everything else was the same. He seemed depressed and anxious and withdrawn. A few weeks later, I found some evidence that led me to suspect once again that he'd had, or was having, an affair. He assured me he wasn't and that whatever I had seen was nothing; that the person he was emailing was dating one of his friends and was simply confiding in him. We got in a fight and he immediately used it as an excuse to relapse. He then convinced me I was the one acting crazy and suggested I get some counseling, which I did. I asked him to join me for marriage counseling and he obliged—once. It didn't help, though, because he was on drugs and he wasn't telling the truth about anything."
>
> —Emily

Anthony was dead sober and trying to face his financial woes. *Dead-sober* is a term used by a serial rehabist that means "kind of" sober. The real estate economy had tanked overnight, and as much stuff as he was trying to do to save his family's financial situation, it didn't change the fact that every egg he had was in one basket. The problem was that he wasn't even holding his own basket, and this made him feel absolutely worthless. Their second child was on the way and they were living in their brand new home in an upscale neighborhood in Lake Stevens. The payments on the house were just shy of $3,000. The huge project house cost $4,200 a month. They'd never planned on that house being a rental until the banking industry quit loaning money. They owned the beautiful waterfront property on which they planned to build their dream house; that was costing $2,000 a month. Then if you include the new vehicles, the power bills, the new baby crib, new furnishings for a new house, the $5,000 for a fence, the food to feed the family, insurance, it added up fast.

The money in Anthony's secret bank account had been drained with his very expensive drug habit that included: two "Eight-balls" of cocaine (seven ounces) - $300; forty each 10 mg Vicodin "Norco" tablets - $40; miscellaneous Xanax/Valium/muscle relaxers/tranquilizers - $10, or about $350 a day. That added up to over $127,000 a year. To that point, Anthony had easily spent over a half of a million dollars on feeding his addiction to drugs. His legal fees, gambling habits, state institutions, local police, the federal government, insurance companies and the cost to his family were hard to count in real dollars, much less emotional damage. Anthony was addicted and desperate. "I couldn't come clean. There was so much shit. There was so much pain that I caused. I couldn't face all that destruction."

A normal, rational-thinking person would step back, get an apartment, down-size his life and budget out a change, or at least attempt to. But Anthony with his drug habit was not making good decisions. In fact he was making and thinking the exact opposite of good decisions for himself and his family. The solution to the money problem to Anthony was simple: make more money. The only question was, how?

> "When Anthony started outpatient rehab, I once again assumed the role of sobriety manager. I scheduled everything for him—doctor's appointments, medications, AA meetings and court dates (the prescription forgery arrest from the year before had finally caught up with him). I created color-coded calendars, lists and spreadsheets to keep track of it all. It was exhausting. And it never did any good.
>
> "I found emails insinuating an affair and after he refused to go to marriage counseling, I gave up. I was at the end of my rope and hanging on for dear life. I resigned myself to the fact that I couldn't fix it. I couldn't fix him and so I couldn't fix us. I was sad and scared but I had other things to focus on—I was dealing with a complicated pregnancy (my second daughter was breach until hours before she was born) and I had to take care of the daughter I already had. I stopped monitoring, I stopped questioning, I stopped investigating. I was done."
>
> —Emily

These potential affairs were hugely devastating. Anthony felt that Emily was imploding and behaving erratically. It placed a strain on the family relationship. One night after a fight, Anthony ran off and relapsed yet again. Emily alerted Anthony's parents. They found him wasted, again. The next week he was back on the pills and coke, and this was when life really went downhill in the family.

> "I didn't want to believe that this man was not the boy I knew when we were young. Deep down, I didn't believe him.

> "At the end of July, I made the executive decision to file for bankruptcy. The Seattle home wasn't selling, and the renters were actually a problem. Anthony not once brought home a forty-hour paycheck from working with his parents, but he was totally against filing for bankruptcy. I turned over our vehicles, instituted major spending cutbacks and let the bank foreclose on the big house—even though we would lose a hundred thousand dollars we'd invested over the last year. My parents offered us their vehicles so we had something to drive. But what we needed was a miracle at this point."
>
> —Emily

Drugged and broke, Anthony sat staring at his computer screen in his home office wondering if he had any ideas left. Suddenly, the solution to his money problem seemed simple. Both of Anthony's banks, like Anthony himself, had been doing so well. They had a lot in common, including what they had done in the housing market to achieve their success in the first place. But now they had both reached their lowest point. What the banks and Anthony didn't have in common was that there was talk the banks would soon be loaned billions in interest-free money to get back on their feet—a bail-out. Anthony decided he needed his own bail-out.

And since he was feeling squeezed by the bank, why not target the bank?

Ten

Anthony was sitting in his car eating a Jack in the Box "value menu" lunch and feeling mightily depressed. He had just sold off the last of his tools and deposited the money in the bank across the street. The beautiful Brink's armored truck drove up to the Bank of America, and his mood immediately brightened. He took a bite of his hamburger and kept mental notes of everything. As the all-white truck came rumbling toward him, Anthony felt like a groom waiting for his bride. Only the bride wasn't aware of her groom. It was going to be an arranged marriage.

The clock said 10:58 a.m.

A full hour of observing the ATM showed a customer removing money every two-and-a-half minutes. Figure an average

Anthony's drawing of the Brink's truck—in which he substituted the word "Life" instead of the company's name.

withdrawal of forty bucks—sometimes more, sometimes less. That meant the ATM had twenty-four transactions per hour, from 7 a.m. to 7 p.m., 288 transactions in a twelve hour period: forty dollars a pop is $11,520 a day times seven days a week (although weekdays were likelier busier than weekends), equaled. . . Holy shit! And that was just one of the two ATMs. There were also four or five tellers. The Brink's guard was bringing in a lot of money to fill those machines and tellers' drawers.

Anthony decided he wanted a piece of that.

According to the Brink's website:

> Brink's retrieves prepared cash and check deposits from your business and delivers them to the local bank facility you specify for processing and bank credit. During transportation, your deposits are protected by Brink's, the most trusted name in the security business. At the same time that bank deposits are retrieved, Brink's also delivers any change that you order from your bank. Brink's armored transportation service is a cost-effective cash-handling solution, mitigating your risk of accepting cash and giving you peace of mind, while providing extra time to manage your operations.

Over the next few days, Anthony discovered the truck's route. Every Tuesday, the Brink's truck came into Monroe on Highway 2, heading east. The truck took a left at the four-way stoplight at the corner with the 76 gas station, then took a right into the Ben Franklin and Safeway parking lot. It didn't make any deliveries at businesses in that strip mall, but this route avoided several stoplights. The truck then crossed over Woods Creek Road from the Safeway parking lot to the huge Albertson's that was encircled by businesses, including the Jack in the Box and the Bank of America. It arrived at approximately 11 a.m.—give or take seven minutes on each side. Anthony was there to greet the truck every week for over ten weeks.

Anthony started doing his homework about the armed personnel he was up against. With one call and a lot of observation he found that usually, but not always, there were two Brink's guards in one truck: the driver and the messenger. Brink's employees were mostly ex-military. That was worrisome, as the truck personnel were probably not afraid to shoot someone like Anthony. They were naturally the hero-type, and they stood between Anthony and his treasure.

The driver's responsibility—besides driving—was to keep in constant contact with dispatch. Drivers were not to get out of the truck, no matter what. This was for a good reason. For example, if a criminal pulled a gun on a messenger and the driver got out to help, the criminal's partner could get in the truck and drive away with the entire truck and all the deliveries.

The messenger's responsibility was to safely carry or wheel the money to and from the armored truck. Their mandate was to protect that money at all cost. The messenger didn't count the money or know the exact content of the bags and boxes he delivered. The daily deliveries were set out by Brink's for each truck prior to the truck leaving on their route. The messenger knew the surroundings at each stopping point. He surveyed the location carefully before exiting the truck and was constantly on guard. The messenger was always armed with a hand gun.

Even on a light pick-up or drop-off, the messenger used large, canvas, two-handled bags to hide the contents. This way, people looking on never knew if there were un-cashed checks in there or $50,000 in hundred dollar bills—the bags looked the same, either way. With high-dollar deliveries, say $400,000, the money was first shrink-wrapped and compressed prior to being put in a canvas bag. On a heavy drop-off or pick-up, the messenger used a custom dolly similar to a furniture dolly. The Bank of America stop always required a hand-truck. Anthony learned that there was a specific system to stacking items on the dolly: coin currency stored in long metal containers were at the bottom; paper currency in canvas bags came next (sometimes a couple of them of various sizes), the handles draped around the dolly's handles. The canvas bag handles became a cause for concern for Anthony.

Finally, there was sometimes a third Brink's employee who would almost always be present on city deliveries. With a little research on Google, Anthony found that Brink's did use a third person in the Monroe area. This both concerned and impressed him about their protocol. He also discovered that the third guard he saw in the back of the truck on the fourth and fifth week of observation was there for training purposes. This third man sat in the back of the truck after helping the messenger load up the delivery. Anthony was concerned because he typically carried a shotgun or an assault rifle. The third guard could only see the messenger if the back door was left open or if he stood up to look out the window, but after observing him a few times, Anthony concluded the guard always remained seated.

The plus to an armored truck is that it's, well, armored. The minus is that there aren't many windows and it has low visibility. The driver only has a narrow windshield and door windows that are set up high. The only other ways to see out are the gun portholes, but these are too small to peer through. So the driver would lose sight of the messenger the minute he got out of the truck and shut the door, unless he watched his side mirrors. The third guard couldn't see the messenger unless the back door was open.

Anthony observed that sometimes the driver pulled up to the bank's entrance further than he should have. Part of the building blocked his side window visual of the messenger during his walk into the bank. That one mistake meant the driver would have no idea of a problem unless the messenger alerted him by CB radio, or if the third guard saw the whole thing. Anthony could avoid being seen by the driver by staying in his blind spots, which were really huge.

Anthony thought to himself, *I could do this.*

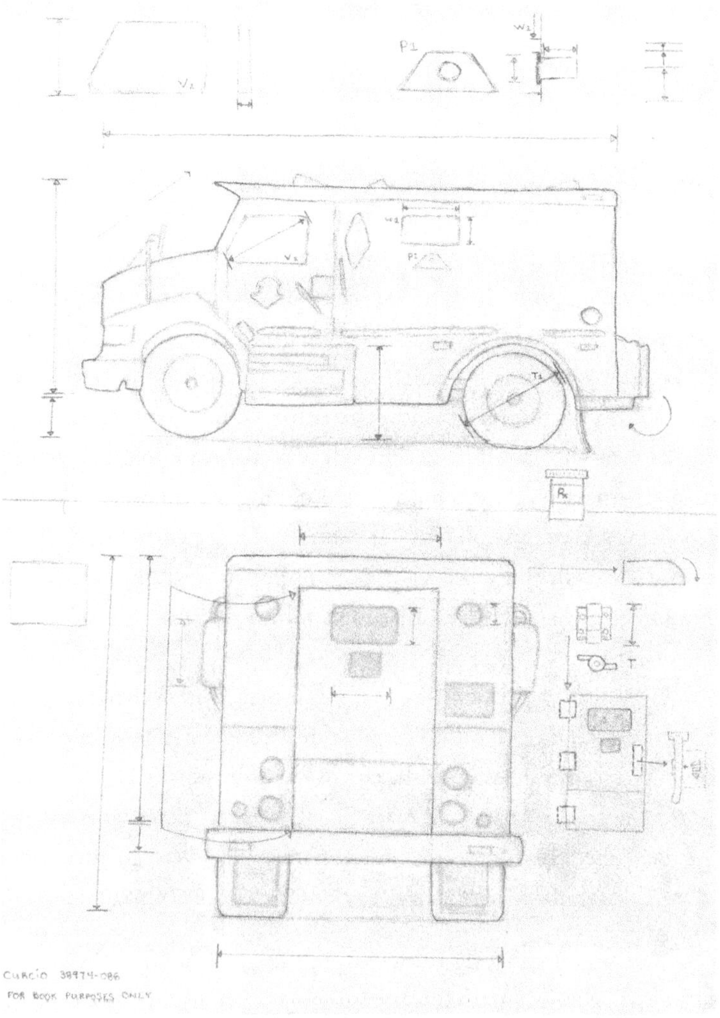

Anthony drew out the details of the Brinks truck

His plan called for him to stay out of view of the cameras at the bank, too. There was a camera facing the entrance and one embedded in the ATM. He was less worried about those, since he planned to be wearing a mask, gloves and hat.

Anthony tried using mortician's wax as a disguise. He molded it to his face, and although he didn't look anything like himself, he resembled Freddy Krueger—in other words he looked creepy, which would be noticeable. He decided the wax wouldn't work. What about a pizza delivery guy? Anthony kept the pizza boxes after dinner one night, but the problem with that plan was it would only work one time. Otherwise the guard would think it odd that the bank employees were ordering pizza every Tuesday at 11 a.m.

Anthony needed to be invisible—which meant he had to be ordinary enough to be ignored. A landscaper's outfit was perfect. Anthony had used this disguise before on smaller crimes. The next week, he sat in his blue shirt, blue-logo hat, reflective safety vest and wig about ten feet behind the Brink's truck scraping gum off the asphalt with a putty knife, a safety cone he'd purchased beside him. The next week, Anthony was sweeping the sidewalk. The following week, he was picking up trash beside the entrance. A Bank of America teller put her Jack in the Box cup in Anthony's trash can. He smiled at her, but she didn't look at him at all.

Perfect.

He had an entire landscaper outfit made with Velcro seams. In seconds he could pull off his disguise, revealing the nice business suit or jogging outfit he wore underneath—he still hadn't decided which outfit was the best to get away in. He planned to carry an insecticide sprayer, since this would give him an excuse to wear goggles and a mask that would cover his face, so cameras wouldn't matter.

> "I was organizing things, trying to get ready for the new baby, and I needed a box to pack some of our daughter's old clothes away. So I went outside to the storage shed in our backyard. I found a bin that was basically empty, except for a small black duffle bag. I reached in to grab it out and that's when I noticed what appeared to be something hairy stuck in the zipper. *Is it a dead animal?* I kicked it, but it wasn't heavy, so I unzipped it and looked inside to find a Thomas Guide and a black wig. *Why does Anthony*

have a wig? I took it inside and asked him what it was for. He flipped out (which wasn't unusual at this point). "Don't snoop around in my stuff!" he yelled. "Leave my shit alone and don't go in the shed!" I just rolled my eyes and walked away. *Whatever*, I thought. *I don't care anymore*."

—Emily

Anthony discovered that the messenger was skittish as hell. His hand dropped to his gun one time when an elderly couple walked too close to the back of the truck while he was getting out. Anthony's original plan was to film the deliveries every week from the back of his Suburban. But he decided it was too stressful to get a good video since the messenger paid too much attention to his surroundings. The driver's side mirror was aimed right in Anthony's direction where he was parked, as well.

Anthony had to get extremely close in his preparation because he had to figure a way to separate the bags from the dolly. It wasn't bad enough the canvas bag handles were over the dolly handles, but the messenger held onto the handles of the dolly, too. He was thinking perhaps he would cut the handle of the bag with a knife or something, but it didn't change the fact he still had the guard with a gun to worry about.

The thought of using a gun was never really an option. Anthony was not a fan of them, since they only tipped the scales in favor of the idiot. The way he thought about it was that if you can't pull off a crime without a gun and substitute creativity, then you were no criminal at all. And Anthony considered himself a criminal at this point in his career.

Anthony needed a quick method. He had a minute-and-a-half at best before the cops arrived. He figured he could increase the time by doing different things to create confusion—like a diversion call to the police. Another possible idea was to somehow stop a train earlier in the day. There happened to be one at 10 a.m. every

Tuesday that would have essentially cut Monroe in half. Something placed on the tracks might do the job. The more he thought about this idea, the more he realized that it was a bigger deal than the actual heist, and gave it up.

He thought for many days on how to get the guard's hands off of those handles and also somehow to buy himself a bit of time so the guard wouldn't shoot him. The riddle took him quite a while to figure out. He wished there was a way the guard couldn't see him afterwards. A smoke screen? That thought led to more thorough research. Then it hit him:

Pepper spray.

The mace would discombobulate the Brink's messenger! He definitely wouldn't be able to see Anthony running away afterwards. The best thing was that no matter how hard people try, they can't keep from rubbing their eyes. This meant that Anthony could easily slip the canvas bags right off of the dolly. He decided he needed to know what getting maced felt like, so he could anticipate the messenger's possible reactions. He purchased a couple of pistol-grip bear mace cans. When he had a few hours at home without Emily, Anthony went into the backyard, sprayed a cloud into the air and walked into the orange-colored mist. Within milliseconds it hit him: his face stung like hell and his eyes were burning pits. *Holy shit!* At first his hands were just shaking at his sides, but that lasted for only a second or two. The next moment, his hands flew to his face and he rubbed his cheeks and eyes, even though he was trying very hard not to. He tried to wash the pepper spray off with the garden hose, but the water only made it worse. He remembered he'd read that mace is acidic and needed to be cooled with a base or an alkaline. *Milk!* He ran into the house and poured milk over his face as he stood over the sink. It seemed to help, but it was hours until the burning stopped.

The bear mace would absolutely work to disable the Brink's armed guard.

On to the critical part: the getaway. Anthony knew that any robbery was incomplete if the robber couldn't get away with whatever he took. From the phone call to 911 to the arrival of the cops, Anthony had only a few minutes at the very most. But he also knew from his previous capers that these minutes always felt like just a few seconds when he was in the heat of the action. The very first thing Anthony had to do was think like the people trying to catch him.

He knew containment would be the very first thing set up. Besides arriving in force at the bank, the police would have cruisers on every major highway, road and intersection within a two mile circle. There would no doubt be at least one helicopter overhead—but that would take a little longer to get there. The major roads leading away from the bank would be an issue as well: specifically Highway 2 would be the highest priority, along with Old Owen Road, Woods Creek Road and Main Street that led to Duvall, most likely in that order.

A K-9 unit would certainly be dispatched, and that one aspect caused him more worry than all of the cops combined. Everywhere Anthony ran, he would be emitting very small odor particles that the dogs could smell. In moments of high stress, humans exude stress hormones and other traces that the police dogs are trained to follow. How could he throw them off his scent?

For a bank robbery—or in this case, a bank truck robbery—the police are never short on man power, so wherever Anthony was going, he had under ten minutes to get there safely before the helicopters were overhead. He needed at least a few minutes alone with the money to search it for a GPS tracking device, which his research showed were included in many deliveries. He calculated that the GPS device had to be located within minutes after the robbery since someone had to contact the Brink's offices to alert them of the crime and then an on-site detective would have to talk to Brink's to pinpoint the location of the GPS device that was on the move. All of these hurdles were tall to Anthony, and he knew it, but he had become obsessed with his planning and there was no turning back. It had become an addiction like other things in his life.

Anthony had photocopies of several Rand McNally maps of the area taped together trying to figure out the getaway dilemma. That was when he noticed that Woods Creek flowed right by the bank. He had lived in the area most of his life, and he'd never really noticed it! The creek ran straight through Al Borlin Park in Monroe and into the Skykomish River. He pulled up the MLS (Multiple Listing Service) maps that real estate agents use to search for properties and checked what was for sale along the river. He found a house a fraction of a mile up the river, and it was listed as vacant.

Immediately, he fastened on to the idea of a jet ski as a means to escape. He could park the jet ski at a spot near the bank, hide it, then when he came back he could throw the money in the front compartment and ride it up to Al Borlin park. There he could stop and search for the tracking device, dump the tear-away clothes and continue on the jet ski into the Skykomish River to the vacant house. He would leave the jet ski there, hop in his car and drive right into town, which was in the opposite direction the cops would expect a bank robber to run. He would go coach the football team and head home. Anthony felt this would take care of all his getaway problems since the scent for the dogs would be left at the entrance to the park. Changing the "venue" of the getaway from street to river would increase his odds dramatically—and everything Anthony did was about increasing his odds. A few things he had going for him was he had the element of surprise and that he knew exactly where he was going. The police would be reacting instead of in control. Just like when Anthony was a receiver, the player covering him didn't have a chance when he was prepared and executed his route correctly. He could lose the police if he ran his route, executed it well and ran the show.

The next day, Anthony could hardly contain himself, he was so excited about putting his escape plan into action. He jumped out of bed, got into the car and drove to the creek. When he got there, he took one look and groaned. "Dammit!" There were branches over nearly half of Woods Creek. If the huge boulders in the water didn't stop the jet ski first, the branches would knock him off. The creek was three feet deep to his left, but only three inches deep to his right. Anthony realized he had a lot of work ahead of him to make the creek navigable.

With his dwindling budget, Anthony went to the store to buy himself a raft, since the slippery rocks made it almost impossible to walk next to the creek. He could only afford the two-person raft and not the more ideal four-person raft he needed. When he returned to the creek, he realized that the two people pictured on the box must have been pygmies, because he had trouble fitting just himself into the raft. But it would have to do.

It took nearly four hours to float the raft down Woods Creek. He must have bottomed out twenty times. Often, he had to get out and carry the raft, and probably walked a third of a mile before he got to the train trestle where he intended to get out of the creek. By the time Anthony got out at the vacant house on the Skykomish River, he had scrapes all over his arms from the branches that slashed at him when he was pushed into the faster river bed. In order to make his idea work, Anthony would have to make a jet ski path double the size of the raft. He also needed a four- to five-foot-wide trough in the creek to give room for turns. But what he really needed was a jet ski.

He decided on a widely used and available model of SeaDoo to plan everything around. He went to one house where a SeaDoo was for sale and talked to the owner while working out the dimensions in his head. The watercraft needed at least twenty inches of depth throughout the creek, less if the large rocks were removed from the creek bed. He also discovered that the water intake would suck up and clog the jets—stalling in the middle of the getaway—unless he cleaned up the watercourse.

Anthony calculated that he would need to average about ten miles per hour traveling up the creek. There were more difficult parts that would force him to slow down to about five miles per hour, but he could speed up to twenty m.p.h. on the straight-aways. If he maintained ten miles an hour, it would give him a six minute mile—that would give him a little extra time. By marking his path in the creek, he could maneuver more easily and increase his chances.

With $1,500 worth of home improvement store gift cards, Anthony purchased the tools he needed to carve the creek path. He purchased about 100 quarter-inch rebar stakes, orange marking spray paint, cordless tools and a reciprocating saw. Every day, from 8 a.m. to 2:30 p.m. before football practice—excluding Tuesdays from 10 a.m. to around 11:15 a.m. when he took a break to study the weekly armored car delivery—he dug out the watercourse. He was popping pills again, but he'd relapsed on purpose. He felt the pills helped him accomplish his task. He figured he would sober up again when the heist was over.

By the second day, Anthony had cut through a foot-and-a-half-thick log that laid across the creek. He used the raft to float along the "good" areas while checking the depth and pounding in rebar stakes and topping them off with orange paint as he went. He did a more thorough evaluation of the creek than the city had ever done.

Several days later, he'd cleared seventy-five yards. Anthony had cut down so many branches, it looked like a thousand beavers had been hard at work. He removed all of the debris he created and that had been collecting for years and put it on the bank. He also found obstacles that were impossible for one man to remove. He made note of them on the map that he kept in his small cooler. The little ice box not only carried some critical tools, but also stood as a prop that made him look like a redneck looking for crawdads.

All of his tools with his raft inflator, change of clothes and many pairs of aqua sox barely fit in the back of his extended Suburban. There were several phones hidden throughout the vehicle.

All of them were of the pre-paid disposable variety. Every day before driving home, he removed the batteries from all the devices. He wanted no traces.

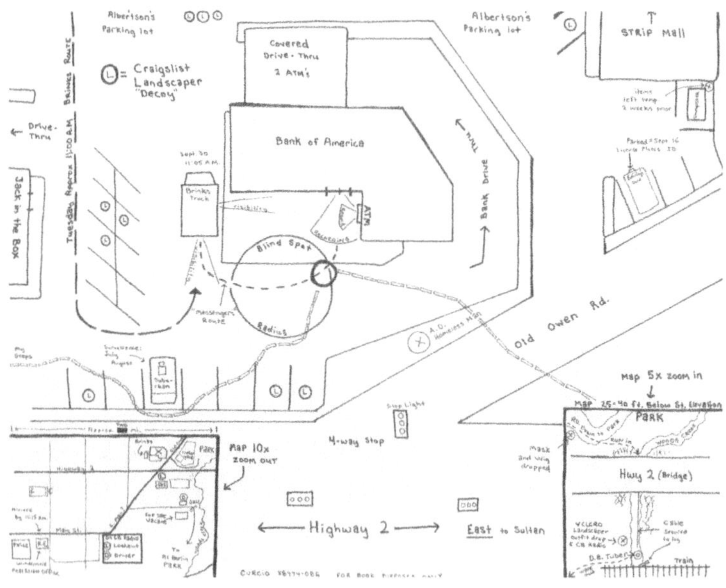

Anthony's plans for the robbery

4:15 p.m.

"Excellent job today, guys. I'm proud of you. We've put three new plays in today out of two different formations. Make sure to study up on what Coach RB is handing out. We'll run them tomorrow," Anthony told the young football team.

Coach RB had been a friend of Anthony's since they were kids. He coached youth football, and asked Anthony to help him coach the team, since coaching and trying to handle the non-football related responsibilities took a lot of his time. Anthony was known as Coach C, the coach who ran with the team. He felt it was important to show that he wouldn't hand out discipline that they couldn't handle themselves.

For as many right reasons as Anthony was coaching the football team, he also had his wrong reasons. He enjoyed teaching kids the joy of the game, and somehow being part of a sport he'd so loved. But the daily sprints around the field were also to make sure that "Coach C" was in shape so he could knock off the armored truck. It would also give him an alibi, when he showed up to run plays right after the robbery.

Coach RB reminded the kids, "Tell your parents that we need waivers back no later than next week. Did everyone get their physicals done?" The team answered mostly in the affirmative. "All right, activity bus leaves at 4:30, so let's get a break."

All the players held their helmets toward the middle of the group.

"Have fun on three. One, two, three . . . ," the coach led them.

"Have fun!" everyone shouted.

The players scattered and headed toward the locker room. Coach RB, Anthony and two other assistant coaches picked up the cones, blocking dummies, skully hats and footballs scattered all over. As Anthony was shutting the storage shed, one of the coaches asked Anthony, "You got any?"

It seemed as if everyone and their mothers took pain killers. He couldn't go a full day without hearing, "You got any?" Anthony replied, "I just gotta pick em' up. Your wife picking up your daughter?"

"Yeah," the coach said.

"All right, let's go get some," Anthony said. "I have to be at Emily's parent's house by 6:30 for dinner. It's her dad's birthday, and everyone's going to be there."

"Do we have enough time?"

"I think so," Anthony replied confidently

Anthony had gotten away with prescription fraud for so long that every couple of months he would start getting lazy. Then he'd and have a run-in with the law, which would improve his focus again. He couldn't remember if this evening's pharmacy technician switched from the day shift where Anthony was Steve and not John.

5:20 p.m.

Oh shit!

Anthony sprinted past one aisle, then past another. He raced past the grandmother pushing her cart, and the parents and their children ambling along. He scanned the store landscape with his heart pumping fast, looking desperately for an aisle that didn't have an officer standing in it. *There!* Like a running back who finds a hole in the defense, he identified an opening and went for it. Whatever fake injury, limp or other ailment the pharmacy had thought Steve or John needed a bottle of oxycodone for seemed to have instantly disappeared. *One last break* . . . . He jumped and cleared an entire row of stacked shopping carts in front of the doors.

ZAP!

The stinging in his right butt cheek felt like a four-pronged grappling hook followed by God-knows-how-many-volts. He was vibrating on the floor tiles, watching the motorized doors of the exit tantalizingly opening automatically in front of him. It wasn't his first time getting shot with a taser gun in a pharmacy, and it probably wasn't going to be the last. He felt as if he'd fumbled the ball right at the one yard line. Game over. All he could think was, *Shit, shit, shit!*

Anthony always sobered up in times like these. The withdrawal symptoms and the depression would happen later that night. He'd have the shaking and cold sweats to look forward to in the county jail later.

They cuffed him and took him outside. "We've been waiting for you, John, if that's your real name," the officer said.

He wondered why they were wasting their time hanging around asking him useless questions. He was angry that they were making him sit handcuffed on the curb in front of the store. Most especially, he felt shame. He replied, "My name is Anthony Curcio. Can we go now?"

"Where are you trying to go?" the officer asked.

"Jail," Anthony said.

Obligingly, they lifted him up and led him to the police car.

Meanwhile the coach was still in the passenger seat of Anthony's car in the JC Penny's parking lot, watching the whole scene. Had the police looked to see where Anthony had walked in from, they would have found it all. In the back of his car was a detailed map, a landscaper's outfit with Velcro pull-off shirt and pants, two-way radios, a wig, a bank map, a river map, a street map, a vacant house map showing houses for sale within an eighth of a mile of the bank, bolt cutters, a deflated raft, cables, multiple cell phones, river depth charts, jet ski specifications and a laptop that put all the puzzle pieces together. They could have stopped an armored truck robbery that was planned to happen in less than three weeks, if they had been in less of a hurry.

7:30pm

Anthony called Emily from the jail to say he wouldn't make it to the birthday dinner. It was just one more call in an endless source of letdowns.

> "Anthony was an hour late for my dad's birthday dinner when the phone rang. My mom answered it and I could tell from the look on her face that something was wrong. She handed the phone to me. It was a collect call from the Snohomish County Jail. Anthony gave me the same sob story he always did and begged me to bail him out saying something about a deal that was set to close in the next few days. He was desperate. 'No way,' I said, 'not this time.' I was due to give birth any day and I didn't want to deal with him anymore. I hung up and took a walk with my dad. I was so emotionally detached that I didn't even

cry. Later that night, on the way home from my parents' house, I got a call from one of Anthony's so-called friends, a fellow addict who was with him when he was arrested earlier. He was calling to let me know that Anthony was busy and wouldn't be able to make it to dinner. Little did he know, Anthony had already called me. I just laughed at him, 'Yeah, no kidding. Nice try.' Anthony had everyone programmed to cover for him (and lie to me). These were guys I grew up with, guys I'd known forever. They were my friends, too, not so long ago—they were in our wedding for crying out loud! Yet they had no respect for me whatsoever. And they didn't care about Anthony, either. They never would've bailed him out if they did. They knew exactly what he was planning to do and they helped him do it. All they ever cared about was themselves; the party, the high, the thrill . . . and ultimately, the payout. The people who really cared about him were the people who wanted him to get clean, not the people who used him to have fun. There is no honor among addicts (or thieves). Anthony learned this the hard way after he was arrested for the robbery—it was a lesson that was long overdue."

—Emily

By 10 p.m., Anthony was in full depression mode and suffering from withdrawal symptoms. He made it through by going over the robbery plans in his mind.

Not long after he got out of jail, Anthony came up from the creek, he ran right into a friend and his brother, who happened to be a police officer in Monroe. They were looking for a kid who stole the cop's daughter's bicycle. Always willing to help a friend, Anthony helped them look for the bike. He was sure the cop knew something was strange, but since Anthony was driving a nice, new car that was parked at the vacant house for sale, he was able to make up an excellent reason for being there.

Life at home was not good during this time. Everyone was worried about the mounting bills and the seemingly short financial future of the family. Emily and Anthony had lost more houses, cars and things than anyone they knew had ever owned. Now they were just barely hanging on. He was so terrified of their financial future, and so obsessed with planning the Brink's that he might as well have been somewhere else completely. Anthony was about to risk everything so he didn't lose anything.

Emily found a specialist who helped her rotate the baby so she didn't have to have a C-section. Anthony watched in dismay as the doctor grabbed the baby like a football in Emily's stomach and simply turned it over.

Shortly thereafter, Emily went into labor. Instead of going to the hospital right away, Anthony left the house to go buy some chew—or at least that was his story. He actually went to the pharmacy to drop off a fake prescription. When he returned, it was time to go to the hospital, so he put Emily in the car and started for the hospital—but again he "had to stop to buy some chew"—this time to pick up the pills. Their second daughter was born September twentieth, ten days before Anthony robbed the Brink's truck. Although Anthony was there, he was extremely distant. They brought the baby home, but the next day he had to go because he said he had shit to do.

Anthony hired a friend to help him move some boulders in the creek. He had to buy another "two-man" raft since the two of them couldn't fit into the tiny raft he already had. Anthony could barely afford it. Later that day, he and his friend hid one of the rafts at the very end of Woods Creek, where it feeds into the Skykomish River, then went to go get the car. By the time they came back, someone had stolen the mini raft. This seemed like karma, since Anthony was planning on returning the raft so he could afford gas for the getaway.

Meanwhile, Anthony looked at different Seadoos that were available. He searched the ads on Craigslist. The ones that didn't include addresses he emailed and called until he got one. Anthony gathered many locations for owners that were selling jet skis: some were parked at docks; some were on trailers or in backyards; some were put away at night; some simply sat in driveways. Anthony would have preferred to purchase the machines and transfer the title legally—only under a fictitious name. But he didn't have any money. Besides, the serial numbers would eventually lead back to the previous owner who could identify Anthony. Since the machine would undoubtedly be found drifting a half mile down the river a few days after the caper, this was something he needed to be careful of. All he needed to do was find a jet ski to steal, but that was turning into a real pain in the ass.

Anthony drove by two older Seadoos that were covered with a tarp on a tandem trailer every single day. They sat in a driveway with no cars ever around. He stopped one day and peeked under the tarp. They were in pretty rough shape. He could imagine the jet ski not starting and getting shot in the back by the half-blinded guard as he struggled to make it go. He decided he needed a nice new one after that, a ski that was dependable.

Anthony asked a friend to help steal a newer jet ski. Involving someone else was risky—and it got worse because of the guy's nervousness. They almost had a newer Seadoo, but when they were about to lower the trailer hitch on the ball of his vehicle, someone walked past and spooked his help who was in the driver's seat. After that, Anthony decided to go it alone. During these thefts Anthony used a set of magnetic dealer plates to cover his real plates in case someone wrote down his license number.

On his own one night, and a bit more desperate, he removed the blocks under the wheel of the old, tandem jet ski trailer, set the hitch down on the ball . . . and scraped the concrete on his way out of the tilted driveway. The huge noise rattled Anthony, so he dropped the trailer back in the driveway and took off. The next day he drove by it again and again, but there was no activity and the owner was obviously not home. But he decided against risking it again.

Anthony was leaving practice one day and looking at all the uniforms. There were no names on the backs of the jerseys, so they all looked exactly the same. On the drive home the idea hit him for the diversion part of the plan: he could become a face in the crowd! He would flood the crime scene with suspects that would confuse and slow down any pursuit by the police, thus increasing his odds. Anthony's next obstacle would be how to get the landscaper decoys to show up wearing exactly what he had been wearing every Tuesday for the past two months. His confidence was growing as he planned this project, and he popped a few Vicodin with a smile. On the way home he drew up the Craigslist ad in his mind.

On a Tuesday trial run, a few weeks before the robbery, Anthony was timing himself to determine how long it would take to make it from the parking lot to the stream. He didn't wear the wig, mask, etc, because it might have looked suspicious. It was also a really nice, sunny day—too hot to have all that stuff on. He was in a little bit of a hurry, so instead of taking the five extra minutes to put his disguise in his car, he stuffed them behind a dumpster about seventy-five yards away from the bank. Anthony thought the risk was low of anyone seeing him. The dumpster was fenced off and even an employee throwing away trash wouldn't have seen it.

After he timed himself, he went to pick the disguise up. A homeless guy ran up the pavement toward him, yelling, "Hey! Hey! I saw that stuff! I'm calling the police!"

Scared, Anthony grabbed the disguise and walked back to his car and drove off as calmly as he could. As he left the parking lot, he slammed his hand on the steering wheel in a fit of rage. He knew he'd jeopardized it all by being lazy. He had magnetic dealer plates with bogus tags sitting on the floor of the car, but they didn't do any good sitting on the floorboard! He had already invested so much time planning and preparing that it was hard for Anthony to fold his plan. He thought to himself, *What are the odds that a homeless guy has anything but a weak description of the make and model of the vehicle—or of me? Besides, I bet he doesn't even have a pen to write down the license plate.*

As it turned out, that was another bad bet. The homeless man had pen and paper very handy because his hobby was doing crossword puzzles in his copious free time. Once he got a look at what was hidden, he was convinced a crime was going to be committed. He had a criminal past and was well aware that a convenient suspect for the cops in any robbery was a homeless person. He told his story to a city worker who didn't really take him seriously, but relayed the tale to the police, a description of the items, along with the homeless man's description of the truck, the license plate number and what Anthony looked like.

Technically, Anthony was caught before he even started.

He made up his mind he had to move forward immediately, which meant that he had to steal the jet skis that were nearby. They hadn't moved, so Anthony backed up the truck once again, hitched them up, hooked up the lights and took off to the boat launch in Monroe. Anthony's skills didn't include backing up a trailer to drop the skis, so he had to ask for help, further exposing himself to risk. Leaving the truck and trailer with his friend made him nervous as hell.

The jet ski started right up, but when he entered Woods Creek the Seadoo started fighting the strong current. He floored it, but lost control and crashed into a boulder. He'd been on the river less than five minutes! Anthony realized that the five-foot width he'd created in the creek just wouldn't be enough. All his hard work had been wasted. He maneuvered the ski back to the dock and slid the cracked fiberglass right up on the shore. Anthony thought about leaving it there, but instead he loaded it up on the trailer, backed it back in the driveway he stole it from—with help—dropped the trailer and got out of there. He was super thankful nobody paid any attention, but he left in shame. Now what?

Anthony decided it was time to lure in the landscaper decoys, so he put an ad out on Craigslist. He set up the account at a Kinko's in Lynnwood, but connected to it via his laptop while sitting in his car in Everett outside of a condo complex that had unprotected wireless. The ad read [Note: this is the exact wording and spelling of the ad]:

> seattle-tacoma > craigslist > snowhomish co > labor gigs
>
> General Cleanup Landscaping for City cleanup project
> $28.50 p/hr (snowhomish)
> Reply to: <redacted>
> Posted 2008-9-27, 3:57 PM PDT
>
> Short term (must be able to work a minimum of 4 days, but prefer the full 9 day project length). Prevailing wage at $28.50 p/hr. Needed immediately starting Tuesday, September 30th, ending Friday, October 10th.
> 15-20 general workers needed for various tasks and general clean up. Must be in excellent physical condition, able to work 8-10 hour days. Must provide valid drivers license or government issued identification card, and have ready 2 personal and 2 work references if asked. Must have some contact number to reach you on. We will provide the tools, however all laborers must purchase safety glasses or equivalent eye protection, ventilator mask, yellow safety vest, long sleeves and no shorts, along with proper foot protection. (all items can be purchased at lowes or home depot for less than $15). Landscaping experience needed. Most importantly must be able to follow directions and work well with others, as you will be in small groups with

> intensive tasks. If interested please respond leaving your name, email address, contact number, work references and any experience you feel would fit well with tasks described. If you receive an email following your inquiry, you will be asked to show up ready to work on tuesday in Monroe and have a short orientation prior to starting the day. You will be paid in person by your supervisor at the end of each friday (10/3 and 10/10) with a company cashiers check, which you can walk into the bank and cash with proper identification. We are sorry we cannot pay you in cash.

In the middle of a recession, the responses poured in. Anthony received a ton of responses—way too many to respond to personally. He wrote to a select group in a mass email:

> You've got the job! Please purchase safety goggles, a painter's mask, and a safety vest. Please wear jeans, a blue shirt and a hat for the first day. Once we are better organized, we will issue uniforms for the team.

Anthony decided to position different groups of people to gather in different spots around the bank's general vicinity. He broke the ad respondents into groups: A, B, C, D and E. Given that the Brink's truck had about a twenty minute window at most, Anthony scheduled Group A to wait for supervision at Position 1 at 10:45 a.m., the next at Position 2 at 11 a.m., etc. That should provide enough cover for a diversion.

Anthony was in full panic mode since the jet ski idea was out. Should he bail on the whole idea or postpone the job? After a few hours of reflection, during which he wallowed in how broke and pathetic he was, he decided he had no choice but to figure out how to make the heist work. That's when the idea of using an inner tube came to him. He could scramble down the hill to the creek and throw the bags of money into the canvas-wrapped inner tube's middle. Then he could climb on, sitting on the money bags. He realized the current would be too slow. He'd have to mount some cables or ropes so he could pull himself quickly downstream. The inner tube would be slower and riskier, but he also thought it might just work.

Anthony found another vacant house to park his car for the get-away, but he also needed someone to drive him between the inner tube and his car. He decided that was the best time to carefully search the bags for the GPS device. Anthony had pulled scams before with the man he recruited to drive for him. This crime-partner would also act as lookout for Anthony, using binoculars from behind the gas station to give him updates, timing issues, tell Anthony when to approach and if the cops were around, via CB radio. But his first choice was a bit undecided whether to help or not. First he was in, then he was out. Just when Anthony thought he had everything covered, something else would pop up. The dependable driver backed out.

Two people now knew about Anthony's plans. They had both helped him with other capers in the past, so they were no saints, but they were still members of the community. Neither of them had agreed to help with the Brink's, understandably. Anthony had two other candidates in mind, since it was important that he have a lookout man and a driver. He offered them a share of the take. Both of these people had worked with Anthony criminally in the past. In fact, most of Anthony's so-called friends in this period in his life had been paid by Anthony at one time or another for something illegal. Both of the two new guys agreed to help. They were each liabilities, though: one had a drinking problem and was known to pop off, the other was a huge gossip.

Anthony met with the guys individually so they didn't know the other was helping. He didn't break down the plan for the robbery until right before the caper. Anthony met with the first one and told him he'd be the lookout. He gave the man binoculars and a CB and explained where the man would hide, where to look, what to look for and how Anthony wanted him to relay what he was observing. Anthony met with the driver, gave him a CB as well and showed him his responsibilities. They each knew what to do, they each knew their payouts, they each knew each other but they didn't know the other was involved.

Anthony's plan included dropping his CB radio on the ground so the cops knew there was more than one person involved. He figured this would keep his partners from talking—and he made sure the driver and lookout understood this. He also put the lookout and driver on different CB frequencies so they could each talk to Anthony, but couldn't hear each other. Anthony would have to scroll back and forth on his radio to chat with one or the other, but he wanted the security of having the lookout and driver isolated from each other.

Anthony drove back to the bank parking lot in his soon-to-be repossessed SUV, and ate another value meal as he ran over the numbers in his mind again. There were four to five tellers. After some research, he discovered that each opened their position with a maximum $15,000 access. One merchant teller window would have a maximum access ranging upwards of $35,000 to $50,000. There was a drive-through ATM, a walk-up ATM and then of course the reserves in the vault. The grand total, best guess, was just south of a million dollars in an average week. There was more business in town that week due to the state fair going on nearby. Anthony figured there should be some serious money shrink-wrapped in those Brink's bags.

As each person entered and left the bank, Anthony thought: *We're nothing but a bunch of sheep living in their system, working for nothing. We're all followers, afraid to take that chance and we are all slaves! To hell with these banks and their behavior with no consequenc-*

es, giving people interest-only loans and their crooked deals. They screw people every day. He felt entitled to every penny he could take.

The last item on the to-do list was to steal the yellow inner tube. It was one of the simplest tasks, but it completed Anthony's preparations. From here on, he was committed to rob the Brink's truck.

On the night before the heist, Anthony sat down and really thought about what he was about to do:

> "This was the day before one of the biggest mistakes of my life. I would say the biggest, but had I never taken drugs none of this would have happened. So taking drugs is and always will be number one. There was a time I wasn't concerned about what the world thought of me, the money I made or the things I had, but that time had gone. I was now ready to risk everything, my life, for some stupid paper. The worst thing that drugs could ever take from me was me. I quit being myself. I had to have all this stupid shit to impress some stupid people. Why I cared can only be because of the drugs and what they robbed me of. There was a progression to it all. I remember when all I needed was some beer and my closest friends in a cold shed laughing with each other. Then we needed girls there, too. Then 'there' wasn't good enough. Then we needed hard alcohol and a warm house. Then we needed weed. Then I needed pills. Then cocaine. No longer was a house or good friends enough. Then elaborate trips and huge money was spent. So many times I've spent over $1,500 at a bar buying everything for no one who cares. All to impress, because I needed someone else's approval of who I was. I was fake, and it all ended where it started, back in that cold shed except with no friends now, only cocaine and pills and a helpless person that I refer to as myself, now fully addicted.

Now money had become my master, and I was its slave. Instead the addiction Monster had taken control. I just didn't know any of this then.

"I had kept myself so preoccupied with the planning, the work, the thinking and the constant stress that it didn't quite set in until the night before.

"Watching my two daughters sleep, I cried realizing I didn't really know them yet and might not ever. I went to bed after setting my alarm. I had completely convinced myself that I was doing this for my family, but it was my family that I would soon be gambling with. I later learned you should never gamble with something you don't want to lose.

"In the morning, I was up before it was light out, and no one else was up. I loaded up a duffel bag that I'd packed the night before. I watched Emily sleep, and I just felt shame for what I'd become. I hated myself. I felt like such a failure, such a loser. I could no longer talk to her because I had become so irrational in my thoughts. I loved her more than anything, and I hated all of this. I wanted it all to be different, but it wouldn't be until I did this."

Eleven

September 30th, 2008

Anthony had been meeting for the past two weeks with the driver and the lookout at a vacant apartment he kept. He held the meetings at different times so they didn't see the other. But today!—it was the day of the robbery and he was scared. Pacing around the empty apartment waiting for the driver's knock on the door couldn't have been any more nerve-wracking. Scared was an understatement. Terrified was more like it. All of the illegal things he'd done up to that point prepared him for this level of crime, but they hadn't prepared him for it emotionally. Nervously, he went over all his preparations in his mind: the inner tube, the disguise and the landscapers, the driver and the lookout. Anthony planned to leave his truck at the apartment, along with a change of clothes, a fresh cell phone and a letter he'd written Emily the night before in case things didn't go as planned. He wondered if he'd left anything out. Then he heard the knock on the door—it was like a ref's starting whistle. Where are my pills?

Game time!

Anthony welcomed the driver into the apartment. He thanked him and told him he was helping Anthony's family. Anthony gave him a hug and they left. The driver dropped Anthony off two intersections away from the bank, on the other side of Safeway. He stepped out of the car wearing the tear-away landscaping outfit over shorts and a t-shirt. The CB radio was connected to his belt with Velcro. He'd strung the microphone and earphone cables up inside the landscaper blue shirt. Anthony put on his wig, the glasses and the hat. He grabbed his mask, pump sprayer, can of mace and took off. As he was walking away, Anthony glanced back at the driver. The guy didn't say anything to Anthony, but he had a look of total disbelief and shock on his face, as if he couldn't believe anyone was capable of actually going through with robbing a Brink's truck.

Anthony understood what the guy was feeling. It was like what he was doing wasn't real. Just as when he was a kid throwing snowballs at cars, Anthony was always willing to take things a step too far. He knew the bank truck heist was a step too far, but he felt he had to do it to get the money and save his family from the financial ruin that he caused.

Anthony walked around a building, wondering if the driver was ever going to go to the next stop on the itinerary. Last he'd looked, the car was just sitting there. He tried not to worry and strolled up to the Albertsons about ten minutes later, at around 10:20 a.m.

Still concerned, Anthony turned on his CB and called the driver. "You all right?" No answer. He said it again.

Finally, a soft voice said, "Yeah. You there yet?"

"Almost," Anthony replied.

"Let me know when you get there."

Anthony put on the safety vest and surveyed the packed parking lot. Then he noticed all of the other "landscapers" who'd answered his ad. The sight should have made him smile, but the adrenaline kept him focused. Then he saw two Monroe police cars had stopped to talk to them. *Holy shit!* Anthony hadn't thought that having so many people turning up at once might make the cops suspicious. He called his lookout. "Holy shit man, you see that?"

"Yeah."

Anthony sat down in between some bushes right by Safeway. From this vantage point he could see about seventy-five percent of the Albertson's parking lot, but not the bank. The morning dew was still out, and his pants were halfway soaked. He switched to his driver, "You there?"

"Yeah, where you been?" his driver replied.

"Good. Just stay there." Anthony switched back to his lookout's channel, just in case he had more to report. The minutes were ticking by, but to Anthony they felt like hours. He just couldn't sit still with the drugs running through his blood. He got up to walk around, but out of the corner of his eye he saw two guys in blue jeans and blue shirts, one holding a bright yellow safety vest, following him. *Oh shit,* he thought, *these guys are probably waiting for their supervisor to show up, and they probably think it's me. Or at least they think I work for the company that hired them for this phantom job.*

Anthony's lookout piped in over the CB, "Hey dude... dude."

Anthony replied, "Yeah I know. Shit!" Anthony was trying to shake the would-be landscapers off his tail.

He heard over the CB, "Here it comes man. Just around the corner. Another day, man."

Anthony looked up and saw what his lookout was talking about. Then he heard the rumble of the Brink's armored truck. Anthony could hardly deal with the amount of adrenaline pumping inside. He called his lookout, "Are they still there?"

The lookout answered, "What? What's still there?"

"The fucking cops man!" Anthony replied.

The lookout replied, "I don't know man, I left."

"What?" Anthony yelled back. "Tell me if they are still fucking there!"

"All right, hold on."

As if he wasn't stressed enough, his lookout was dropping the ball!

Then he heard, "You should just do it another d—."

Anthony angrily switched off the CB. The lookout didn't know that it was now or never. There was no "another day." He turned it back on and said to his driver: "Hey, I need you ready now! It's here."

Back to the lookout: "You there? Are you there?" No response.

Back to the driver: "I need you to give me a visual of the bank now!"

"What?" the driver asked.

Anthony replied, "Fuck! Make sure there's no cops at the bank parking lot. I'm a sitting duck. Hurry up." Anthony switched back to the lookout, "Where are you? Where the fuck are you?"

"I'm almost there," lookout answered.

Anthony shot back, "God dammit! Switch to channel three!"

The lookout replied, "Huh?"

"Switch to channel three, you fucking idiot!"

Anthony flipped to channel three and heard, "Why'd you want me on three?"

The driver heard the lookout for the first time and immediately recognized his voice. They were probably only feet from each other. "Hey, F—."

"No names!" Anthony said to both. "Someone tell me if the parking lot is clear?"

The lookout said, "You're good."

Holy shit! It's go-time!

Anthony walked down the sidewalk to the bank. From about a hundred yards away, he saw the Brink's messenger loading up his dolly. *I'm never going to make it,* Anthony thought to himself. Still, he continued to walk toward the truck at a medium pace. He walked by a few landscapers milling around, wondering what to do. At that moment, it dawned on him that he'd created fifteen or more witnesses to describe the crime. The thought made him break out in a heavy sweat. Just then, the movement and moisture took its toll on the adhesive of the Velcro holding closed the oversized jeans, and one leg popped off. Anthony was close to the Brink's truck, but he couldn't tell if the messenger was ready to start pushing the hand cart into the bank or not. He got a little closer and saw that the Brink's messenger had two hands on his dolly, but the back of the truck was still open. That meant the third guard—with his assault weapon—would see him if he approached the messenger. He was going to be a bit early if he didn't slow down. *Dammit.* Anthony hadn't realized that the window for macing the messenger was so small. He slowed his pace a bit about ten yards out. Then his pants decided to completely let go. As he was struggling with them, he heard a car door slam. He looked up and saw that the back of the Brink's truck was shut.

It was time.

Everything went quiet. All other noise, movements and objects seemed muted and blurred. It felt as if the whole world just stopped.

Within feet of the Brink's messenger, as Anthony was closing in, he said a prayer that would take five years to completely answer, "God, I know you don't like what I'm doing so I won't ask for your help, but please do what's best for my family and take care of them." And He did.

Almost in one motion Anthony tore off what was left of the landscaper pants with one hand and caught up to the guard. He was still outside his macing radius when the guard looked up at Anthony's approach. He dropped the insect pump sprayer, lifted the can of mace and sprayed the guard in the face. Just as he'd anticipated, the guard let go of the dolly and grabbed for his face. He started running in circles, no doubt wondering what had just happened.

Anthony grabbed the two bags of money—one large and one small. They were so heavy, he could hardly carry them. *There's a de-*

tail I should have examined more, he thought to himself. As Anthony began to take off, he fumbled the bags because he was focusing on getting out of there, like a football receiver trying to take off running before he actually catches the ball. He dropped the small bag while crossing Old Owen Road. He felt as if he was moving in slow motion. Anthony ran down the gravel road to the park, gasping for air. He decided to shed his hat, wig, glasses and painter's mask in one quick swipe and chucked it on the dirt road.

He dashed down to the creek. As Anthony reached the inner tube, he threw the fifty pound bag filled with money into the middle and jumped on top. With each pull of the cable, he moved down the stream quickly.

Anthony flicked the radio on, grabbed the plastic wrapped cash and walked up the embankment beside the train trestle near Al Borlin Park to the street behind the local businesses and to his waiting car. Anthony strolled up to the waiting Taurus sedan and asked the driver to pop the trunk. He tossed the money into the back and climbed in after it. Pulling the trunk shut from the inside, he hollered "Let's go!"

In the cramped space, Anthony went to work ripping apart the bag. Carefully, he sifted each stack looking for the GPS locator he knew the armored car company installed in each bag of money. It had to be there, but he wasn't finding it.

As Anthony searched, the driver became more and more panicky. Anthony did everything he could to get the driver to calm down, but he just got worse.

Finally, the driver shouted, "You gotta get out now! I'm popping the trunk!"

Anthony heard the *thunk* of the trunk latch releasing. "I'm not crawling out of a trunk in the middle of Main Street!" he retorted. He tried to reason with the driver, and for a minute, it seemed to work.

Then the car stopped with a jerk, making the trunk pop open. "I can't do this! You gotta get out now!" the driver yelled. Anthony jumped out. *Shit!* The driver started to leave with the trunk still wide open, money strewn all over the back. Anthony had to jog behind the car to shut the trunk, before it sped off.

He didn't stop to look, but assumed people in the area might have seen him get out of the trunk and could give the cops a description. He needed to change clothes again. He jumped a fence to an apartment complex with a co-op laundry room inside and found a shirt. Then he paused to think.

The cops were patrolling the side streets and obviously had every available car looking for Anthony. He had to get off the streets and back to his truck! An idea occurred to him. Anthony walked in the real estate office and awkwardly explained that he needed to use their phone. The receptionist gave him permission and he called the driver, who muttered that he'd be right there. He continued to chat up the receptionist. His stomach turned when he realized his shoes were soaking wet from the creek. He hoped she hadn't noticed when he walked in.

Ten minutes went by, but no ride showed up. Anthony called the driver again, and was told he'd be right there.

The roar of the helicopters circling overhead drew a group of agents outside. To look less conspicuous, he went out with them. It was odd talking about the robbery and acting as if he had nothing to do with it.

Once back inside, Anthony called his driver back for a third time. The guy said, "Hey man, I can't," and hung up. He wouldn't answer when Anthony called again, so he called the lookout, who came over immediately.

Anthony got in the car and quickly explained his situation.

"Do I get half his share then?" the lookout said jokingly.

Anthony snapped, "I'll double yours!"

The lookout seemed grateful, but frightened. He drove Anthony to the apartment where he changed his clothes and drove out of town. He had the lookout follow him.

Anthony called the driver from a prepaid cell. This time, the guy answered. Anthony told him to meet them at the agreed place. When they got there, Anthony got out of the car, walked up to the driver, and said, "I oughta beat the shit out of you."

The driver apologized, but Anthony didn't care anymore. He transferred the cash to the duffle bags he had brought. Then he and the driver went to a Motel 6 in Everett. They counted out the money, but lost count after $330,000. Over $100,000 was in twenties, so it looked like way more. After Anthony gave the driver a cut, he drove to the YMCA where he had a gym membership and put the money in two separate lockers.

He realized he wasn't going to make football practice, which was his planned alibi. He sent a text message to Coach RB telling him he was running late. Then he drove home, just like any other day. Anthony walked into his house and kissed Emily "Hello." Then he ran upstairs to take a shower.

> "Our new baby was only ten days old, so my mom took our older daughter to her music class for me and picked up a pizza on the way back. We were eating dinner at the kitchen table when Anthony came home. He sat down and had a slice with us. Then he offered to take our toddler 'swimming with Daddy' in the master bath because, he said, "my legs are sore." About an hour later, after he finished getting her ready for bed, he mumbled something about needing to finish up at the office and left again. Sadly, his behavior was perfectly normal (for us anyway). I'd seen coverage of the robbery earlier that day because I always set my DVR to record Oprah and it usually caught the first few seconds of the five o'clock news. So, when I was just about to delete the episode, they showed an aerial view of the crime scene and armored car. It caught my attention, sure. I mean, I recognized the area immediately because that's where I grew

up. I opened my first checking account at that bank when I was sixteen years old. But it didn't cross my mind that Anthony might've had something to do with it. At least not right away."

—Emily

Aerial shot of the Brink's truck after the robbery.

Based on the accounts of the many witnesses—who thought they were at the bank for a landscaping job—the police followed the robber's path down to the creek. Downstream, the inner tube was found. It looked as if the suspect had gotten out of the creek and run into the woods toward the Skykomish River. The police had teams of people searching the forest north of the creek. That's when Detective Timothy "Buzz" Buzzell got there. A detective in the Monroe Police Department for eleven years and a patrolman for seven years before that, Detective Buzzell was in his mid-forties, clean-cut, athletic and professional. During his service as a detective, Buzzell went back to school and received his master's degree in criminal justice from Boston University.

Detective Buzzell wasn't convinced the police were right about the suspect's escape. After surveying the scene of the getaway, he asked, "Now why are there stakes with spray-painted tips pounded into the bottom of the creek and sticking out of the water?" No one could answer him. He examined the cables strung over the watercourse, saw that a channel had been dredged out, and the debris shoved up on the embankment. It pointed to a well-planned getaway, the likes of which he'd never seen.

Detective Buzzell testing his theory about where the bank truck robber dismounted.

After pacing down the watercourse, Detective Buzzell figured the robber got out of the creek at the bend near Al Borlin Park. He retrieved the inner tube and let it float downstream. Sure enough, it ended up in the same spot where he guessed the suspect dismounted. Detective Buzzell also surmised that the robber had a car waiting for him near the entrance to the park behind a strip mall of businesses, only a couple hundred yards away from the bank. After a quick search of the parking lot, he found a two-way radio. It confirmed the suspect had help.

It was hours after the robbery, and Detective Buzzell knew the suspect was long gone. He was behind, but he knew he could catch up to his robber. He brought in a mantracker team—which he'd used to help solve a murder some time back—go over the creek bed and area around the park. They confirmed that the suspect had indeed climbed up the embankment and then gotten into a car.

But Detective Buzzell didn't know who the suspect was or where the car went.

Every channel, every program, every paper had headlines blaring "details on the Brink's Robbery." The banks, the bankers and the bailout were not popular at this time, and Anthony's caper was talked about as if he was some sort of folk hero.

The Eleven O'clock News had new information every night. They interviewed the guys who showed up at the bank in response to the Craigslist ad. Their faces were blurred out as they described how they ended up accidentally a part of the biggest robbery in the history of the town.

Both Emily's and Anthony's computer home pages were set to MSN. The "Craigslist Robber" was on the most searched-for person list—which was usually dominated by celebrities like Brad Pitt and Angelina Jolie, Britney Spears—five straight days.

Anthony stopped by his brother-in-law's construction site. No one was working. Instead, they were hanging around his truck listening to the local talk radio show. The host was having people call in to talk about their best "D.B. Tuber" stories. Some of the people talked about heists they'd always wanted to pull off—right on the air. Standing in line at the home improvement store, Anthony heard the cashier comment to a customer buying some ventilation masks, "That wasn't you floating down the river the other day was it?" They all laughed. *Screw it,* Anthony thought, and smiled too.

Anthony gathered up and saved all the newspaper front pages with big headlines like: "Decoys," "Robber Fools Cops," "Thomas Crown Affair" and "Inner-Tube Robber." He enjoyed the attention.

Anthony took Emily out to breakfast one morning soon after the caper. He bought a newspaper to read while they were having orange juice and coffee. The Everett Herald had a big front page story on the Brink's Robbery, comparing the thief to the movie "The Thomas Crown Affair," or as a modern day Robin Hood stealing from the rich. With pride and an inflated ego, he flipped the paper around so Emily could see it, but she didn't seem to get it. Then she started to read. Emily looked up at Anthony, who was leaning back in his chair with an arrogant look on his face, then continued reading.

> "I was beyond disgusted that he was praising whoever committed the crime, saying it was 'so cool.' I remember asking him, 'Those people always get caught and they go to prison; how cool is that?'"
>
> —Emily

To Anthony it had all become a sort of game. He'd always had a knack to stay a step or two ahead. After this, he felt untouchable. It didn't seem to occur to him that robbing an armored truck with the help of his friends in his own backyard with police who knew him might not have been a great idea. To him, the money was more than earned since he had risked everything for it. He felt he'd saved his house and relationship. He was a real man again.

It was Anthony's turn not to get it.

But instead of the money making things better, Emily and Anthony were fighting again. She was not happy with Anthony's behavior—disappearing for days and neglecting the girls.

> "Someone told me a few years ago that the definition of insanity is doing the same thing over and over, expecting a different result. Looking back, it's pretty obvious that I had been deeply affected by Anthony's addiction. But it happened over the course of a decade, so I never thought there was anything wrong with me. He was the one who was screwed up. I was the normal one, right? Not really. We were both screwed up. I had been doing the same things over and over for years, and it never did even a bit of good. If Anthony relapsed, I flushed his pills down the toilet. If he got arrested, I bailed him out. If he lied, I covered for him. And if he didn't come home, I called him over and over and over again, expecting him to answer every single time. He rarely did. I'd lie awake pressing redial until three, four in the morning. I could've been sleeping for God's sake! But I always worried that he'd been hurt or had hurt

> someone else. I wanted him to answer the phone so I knew he was okay, so I could scream at him and tell him not to come home. If that's not crazy, I don't know what it is."
>
> —Emily

"I am never going to make you happy!" Anthony responded. He couldn't understand why Emily seemed ungrateful. His addiction-laden mind saw her actions as irrational. He decided he needed to get out of town, and organized a trip to Las Vegas.

> "I believe Anthony picked that fight with me so he'd have an excuse to leave town and not feel guilty about it."
>
> —Emily

Before he left, he had to find a permanent home for all that cash. He wanted to secure it for his family in case something happened to him, but the problem was, he couldn't trust anyone with that much money. Anthony decided to stash it at a friend's house without the friend actually knowing it was there. He purchased a two-foot by two-foot safe, and while his friend was at work, snuck into his house. He found an access panel into a large crawl space. Working in the dark with just a flashlight, he "walked" the safe into the space and covered it in a black tarp. (The safe was heavy enough that Anthony believes that although the house now has a different owner the safe is probably still there.) Then he brought in the bags of cash and stuffed it into the safe—it just barely fit. Anthony thought it was funny that his friend had a safe full of cash in his crawl space and didn't have a clue it was there.

Anthony couldn't get out of town fast enough. He had a friend purchase two plane tickets to leave in a day-and-a-half. Since most of his friends knew what he'd done, they all wanted their share, a cut or a gift before he left. He felt he couldn't trust the driver with his $30,000 share, so Anthony only gave him $5,000. "You can't spend this in front of people. I know the way you are when you drink." His friend was such an addict and a liability. Just twelve hours later, he asked for another $5,000. Anthony gave it to him just to shut him up. According to police reports, the driver wandered around town flashing his new money when everyone knew he was unemployed.

> "Monroe is a small town and the rumor mill is always churning. So when a group of guys gets together, robs a bank and then heads off to Vegas for an all-expense paid, VIP weekend. . . well, people talk. They could've been featured on an episode of World's Dumbest Criminals if you ask me. I wasn't exactly sure where Anthony was going, but I had a bad feeling about it, so I begged him not to leave. I knew he wouldn't listen to me, so I typed up a letter instead. I told him I suspected that he'd had something to do with the robbery and that it sickened me. I told him that money didn't matter; that there were more important things in life. I gave him the letter as he walked out the door, but he didn't come back. I don't even know if he read it. And I never deleted it from my computer. So it came in pretty handy to the detectives later on."
>
> —Emily

Anthony and a friend flew to Vegas in early October. They had a V.I.P. host pick them up at the airport. They told him their plans for the weekend and the host took care of everything. They looked at two huge mansions to rent off the Strip for parties, and Anthony put a deposit down on one of them. It reminded him of Tony Montana's mansion from "Scarface." Then they checked into the Palms Casino where they planned to stay the night. It was no ordinary hotel room though. Anthony had stayed at some nice hotels before, but nothing like this. The room had no exterior walls on two sides, just windows. It was amazing! He felt on top of the world looking out over the Strip. It cost approximately $2,500 a night, but the V.I.P. host somehow talked to the staff and shaved off a few thousand a night, so that the room was basically comped by the casino. Anthony tipped the host $500. The hotel room was so nice, it just lifted his mood every time he walked in.

Anthony went down to the casino, gambled for a few hours and had some drinks to try to relax. All of his cell phones were turned off, but he had gotten his friend and he a couple of Nextel-capable walkie-talkie throw-away phones with 702 Vegas area codes for them to communicate while on the trip. The next day, everyone flew in to join the party. The host woke Anthony and gave him keys for a rental car for the weekend—a brand new all-black Cadillac Escalade with limo-like interior. A few friends involved in the Brink's deal flew in to join the party and Anthony picked them up at the airport, including one of the girls he was having an affair with. When they rolled up to the Scarface mansion, the host had the catering team provide an elaborate steak and lobster feast. That was how the trip was the entire time.

After dinner, they went out to The Bank nightclub where they quickly became the group to join. It wasn't like buying the whole bar a round of drinks. They had their own booths with security, right in front of J-Lo and Marc Anthony. There were celebrities everywhere who were talking with them and having a good time. There were so many girls trying to get in the horseshoe seating that they were sitting on the floor or the edge of the couch. Every bottle of champagne was $700-800 each, and there were many, many bottles consumed. When Anthony walked to the bathroom, the security guards were falling all over themselves trying to escort him to take a piss and wanting tips.

As the night wore on, Anthony's so-called "friends" were driving him insane. Even though he had given them the entire trip, his friends kept asking for more and more. The longer they were there, the more money he had to dish out. Anthony's friends convinced the host to set up a party at the Scarface house. Everyone thought it was a great idea—except Anthony. The security guards started gathering people to go to the house, and it quickly turned into a crowd. As Anthony and his party crew were leaving the club and walking through the casino, every single person was staring at the drunk and loud trail of people behind him. Anthony was taking all of this in and realizing what money was and the people it bought. A famous hip hop producer asked one of his friends for the address of the house and who Anthony was. Anthony didn't recognize him, so at first he just ignored him. When he found out who the man was, Anthony told his friends, "I don't give a shit who that is. I don't want him at the house!" Famous-record-producer man didn't like that very much since it happened right in front of him and his entourage.

Anthony was drunk, high and disgusted with himself. His anxiety was rising, and he didn't care. He realized he was nothing. Nobody cared about him. None of these people even knew his name—although he was the king of that night. He realized that his self-value came totally from his ability to provide people with large amounts of money and the material things he had.

They reached the valet area, and the black Escalade was brought right up. . . only it was followed by three super-stretch limos. One of his friends kept asking for cash, then another.

Anthony snapped. He pulled out a $100 bill, tore it up, and threw it on the ground. "There's your damned money!" he shouted. Then he picked up an orange cone and threw it at the waiting Escalade. He was screaming and cursing. The host got him in the Escalade, took him back to the Palms suite, and left him alone.

Tears rolled down his face as he stood in front of the large floor to ceiling windows looking out at all the lights. There were flashing billboards, Jumbotrons, cars, the Stratosphere, the Luxor's lights all at his feet. He should be the happiest guy in Vegas! But he was just the opposite. He drank straight from a liquor bottle, getting drunker and drunker. There were knocks at the door, but he just ignored them. He thought, *There are maybe a million people out there, and not one would be willing to take the chances I took.*

For the first time since the robbery, it was quiet. All he could think about was Emily and those two precious daughters at home who didn't deserve any of this. As he finished the last pulls off of the bottle, Anthony thought about all the shit he had done. His image of money and power, was that really success? Hell, he couldn't even get sober. All the horrible things Anthony had done were catching up to him emotionally, and he couldn't stand living in this reality. His poor girls—he loved them so much, but he was incapable of putting them first in his life and didn't even know them. The drugs and alcohol came first, and he hated it. He wanted to die. As drunk as he was, he still couldn't look at himself in the mirror. He hated himself. Anthony remembers, "I couldn't ever escape. I kept drinking. I drank more and more until I remembered nothing."

The host and the friend who came with Anthony on the trip somehow got into the room the following afternoon before Anthony could put himself together. They saw liquor bottles all over, a broken mirror, and horrifyingly, a bathtub full of water and a hairdryer plugged into a nearby outlet with the cord stretched to within a foot of the tub. It didn't take a scientist to figure out the picture.

"I just wanted to die. I wanted it to be over, but I failed at that as well," said Anthony.

Over the next few days, Anthony continued to stay drunk and high on drugs, partly to dull the pain from the broken wrist that he fractured on that first night. He and his friends continued to party with celebrities and people they didn't know. No matter how out of reality he became, it was never enough to stop the ache in his soul.

> "It seemed like there was no escape unless I was passed out and unconscious, because every second I was awake and conscious I was reminded who I was. I hated me. I tried

not to think about what I had left in order to be where I was. I just kept thinking of my wife and two little daughters. I could handle robbing an armored truck. I thought I could handle dying. But I couldn't handle failing my family. I completely failed them."

—Anthony

Photo of the Brink's truck robbery from the Bank of America ATM camera.

Small town Monroe is a place where people seemingly all know each other. This worked to Detective Buzzell's advantage. When Anthony disappeared to Vegas along with most of his friends, it was as if he was saying, "Hey, look at me! Look what I did!" So it wasn't long until Anthony Curcio's name came up as a suspect.

It wasn't the first time the detective had heard of Anthony. A decade earlier, Detective Buzzell used to attend Monroe High School basketball games with a friend who was the neighboring high school basketball coach. His friends' team had to face Anthony's. Detective Buzzell knew Anthony was a star athlete. After seeing the photo taken from the bank ATM of the man spraying the bear mace into the Brink's messenger's face, it seemed likely that the robber was an athlete by the way he was standing on offense—only he was holding a can of pepper spray instead of a basketball. Another Monroe police officer, who knew Anthony, confirmed that the man in the picture sure could be Anthony.

Sergeant Rick Dunn brought something to Detective Buzzell's attention that, in light of recent events, suddenly made sense. Two weeks before the Brink's robbery, a city worker reported a homeless man had told him that he'd found things that were probably for a robbery—a hat, wig, two-way radio and a can of mace—behind a dumpster across the street from the Bank of America. Sergeant Dunn had kept the report on the off-chance they might match a future burglary case.

Detective Buzzell sent his partner, Detective Hatch, to interview the homeless man, who the police later identified as "A.D." The homeless man said he called 911 on September ninth when he found the material, but somehow ended up talking to the wrong police department (in a search for records of the call, it was discovered that he'd somehow been routed to the Arlington Police). A.D. told Detective Hatch that shortly after he made the 911 call, a man in a silver SUV had shown up to take the items from the dumpster. A.D. informed the man he'd called the police, then wrote down the SUV's license plate and provided the number to the detective. He couldn't pick Anthony Curcio out of a number of photos shown to him, since he had been busy writing down the plate number in his crossword puzzle magazine.

Once back at the station, Detective Hatch and Buzzell ran the license plate number. The truck belonged to Emily R. Curcio.

Co-author Dane Batty captured this picture of a homeless man in Monroe, who is probably "A.D."

The party ended back in Vegas and everybody went home, but things just got more hectic. Anthony had written the combination of the safe on the inside of one of his baseball hats, but during his rage he lost the hat somewhere in Las Vegas. Anthony sat for days trying to remember the combination. He wrote out as many combinations as possible that he might have used. He had to wait until his friend left the house, sneak down to the crawlspace, and then try the numbers out. After some intensive guessing, it finally came to him, but he was tired of waiting for them to leave again, so he broke down and told his friend. Anthony asked, "Hey, help me move the money."

"I don't know man. What money? Where? Where's the money?" the friend said.

"In a safe."

"Where?"

"Under your house."

"What!?"

When he opened the safe, Anthony almost cried. The money was wet and covered with fuzzy mold and black spots. He decided to wash all the bills. It was too much to wash by hand, so he stuck it in his washing machine. (Emily later found several large bills that were caught in the lint trap of the dryer.) He had to do it fast because the money was being destroyed quickly— about thirty percent of the bills had been destroyed past using. Once the cash was dried, it was so wrinkled it couldn't be stacked. It took Anthony nearly a half an hour to wrap $10,000, and he needed to wrap forty times that. His anxiety was rising again, and he didn't want to be with the money anymore. He filled two large plastic bags full of cash. There were so many rumpled bills you could sleep on it. He felt he had to get rid of the money, so he started "investing" it around town, and paid off the people who helped him with the robbery.

Anthony had traded up from the Suburban that Emily's parents gave him for a new Range Rover that he was keeping at a warehouse parking lot. He would switch vehicles during the day. The new car hadn't changed his mood: he was still depressed and suicidal. He wanted his life to be over, but in many ways it already was. God was answering his prayer.

Surveillance photo of Anthony getting into a Range Rover in a downtown Monroe parking lot.

Detective Buzzell's small team communicated with the FBI on the case, but Special Agent Malia Llewellyn let Monroe PD continue to lead the case and offered to assist as needed. The Detective asked the FBI to provide a surveillance team to trail Anthony and look for a way to confirm the DNA in the mask found in the park. This they did.

After watching him for a couple hours, it wasn't hard to tell that he was up to something. He would leave the house in one outfit and in one car, and down the road he would have another car and another outfit, pick up friends, make stops at pharmacies, stores and banks, then another change of clothes and a car on the way home. He had one-use cell phones in plastic bags hidden in the gutters of vacant houses.

What they couldn't know was this was normal for Anthony. He'd been involved in criminal behavior so long, it was his natural pattern.

But the cops hit the jackpot when Anthony left a Gatorade bottle of chew spit in the garbage can at a gas station. It was undoubtedly his since the bottle was the only item in the clean garbage can bag.

Once Detective Buzzell had Anthony's spittoon and the robber's mask, he personally drove the evidence to the FBI crime lab to ask for the DNA to be tested, rather than send them through the mail as was standard protocol. There was a chance the lab wouldn't process the evidence, since murders took precedence over robbery, however high-profile. He convinced the lab technicians that this crime was serious enough to be processed in a timely manner. The personal touch was successful, and the lab quickly confirmed that Anthony was the Brink's armored truck robber, based on DNA evidence that matched the traces left in the mask. Now all Detective Buzzell had to do was bring him in.

On the evening of November third, 2008, Anthony was arrested.

Emily recalls:

"It was around 5 p.m. in the evening and I was talking to my mom on the phone when someone started pounding on the front door. I was just getting over a cold, so I was still in my pajamas. Both girls were napping. I told my mom I had to go, and looked through the peep hole. My stomach dropped to the floor. Standing on my porch were three armed police officers wearing bullet-proof vests. That's when I knew, without a doubt, that my suspicions were correct and today was The Day. An odd sense of relief washed over me at first but, instinctively, I still felt protective and a little in denial when they barged inside asking me where Anthony was. They told me he was going to be arrested for the armored car robbery; that he was going to jail and they were going to search my home. They wouldn't let me call anyone, but they allowed me to get my toddler out of her crib and bring her downstairs. My newborn daughter was in the family room, asleep in her swing. The girls and I sat on the couch watching cartoons while they went to work turning my house upside down looking for the money, which wasn't there. Meanwhile, a detective in plain clothes and an FBI agent asked me rapid-fire questions about Anthony's whereabouts. I told them what Anthony had told me that morning: that he was going to Tacoma with John to look at another retail location for their so-called furniture company. 'Well that's not where he went,' they snapped, 'he's been in Everett, shopping all day.' I didn't even flinch. 'Well then, I guess you know a lot more about where he's been than I do. He lies to me about everything, so I don't think I'm going to be of much help here.' That shut them up, at least for a little while. They arrested him two hours later in the Lake Stevens Target parking lot."

The police searched the house and found a few safes with cell phones. Anthony had many safes hidden throughout the house. They took Emily's laptop that had a copy of the letter that she wrote to Anthony before he left for Vegas. Emily knew it was incriminating evidence. She called her mom and told her that Anthony had been arrested for the Brink's job.

The arrest stunned the town of Monroe because everyone who knew Anthony as a kid or as an athlete thought of him as a happy, polite, young man. It didn't surprise any of his recent friends who knew Anthony as a drug addict and a criminal for the last nine years. All of his scams, lies and well-planned crimes had finally come to a halt.

The following day, Emily's dad came over, since the media was relentless. Reporters were knocking at her door at all hours. The police came back again after they found the letter on her laptop. They wanted to know where the money was and told Emily she could lose her kids if she didn't cooperate. Emily's dad stepped in and told the police to leave. Emily told them she was getting an attorney. They said they'd be back, so get ready.

Emily got an attorney the next day.

Detective Buzzell investigated everyone even remotely connected to the case, including the Brink's messenger who got maced. There was a possibility it was an inside job, since most armored car robberies are perpetrated by employees. It was also suspicious that the messenger was actually a replacement, as the regular guy was sick that day. It was finally determined that the messenger who got the face full of pepper spray was in no way associated with Anthony.

This was one of those places where Anthony got lucky. The regular messenger was a former member of an Eastern European military. Mace or not, he probably could have shot Anthony in the back.

Anthony was the only one arrested in the Brink's robbery, even though Detective Buzzell knew there were others involved. Once the federal prosecutor had the main suspect, he lost interest in pursuing the "small fry." If the case had stayed local, Detective Buzzell would have put them all in prison.

> "My lawyer told me that over ninety percent of inmates have reduced sentences for cooperation deals. It was also in my favor that, technically, the robbery was a non-violent crime since I used mace instead of a gun.
>
> "I never said a thing, and I never cooperated. One thing I wasn't and never could be was a rat, and I assumed no one around me was either. I couldn't have been more wrong, but it wouldn't be until after I struck my plea deal that I would actually see who-all was talking. I still don't know all the details. As soon as I went into custody, it was like the 'Great Snitch Hunt.' People and friends I've known since Day One were voluntarily calling detectives reporting what they knew. My wife told me she heard they questioned the driver. This was impossible! How could they know? Then it hit me. My friend who backed out at the last second knew my driver because I told him. He was the only person besides myself or my lookout who knew. Then I heard about my lookout talking. Others, too, came clean without much pressure. Everything I had done on the Brink's job was known. I couldn't really grasp that my friends could do this. Then I realized it was me who was the odd person out. There was no one to blame but me."
>
> —Anthony

Monroe Police Department arrest photo.

When Anthony was handcuffed, it took a while for reality to sink in. He was in the back of the police car sitting on his handcuffed hands on an all-plastic bench seat, sliding from side to side as they went around corners. This was when Anthony started to see the other, non-glamorous side of crime. The luxuries do not matter on this other side. Anthony wasn't special anymore, and he should have thought of the consequences of his actions. Inside the car, there were no seat belts or cushions mostly because a prisoner is not special. Anthony had his Miranda rights read to him, and he was thrown into a jail cell with other idiots and booked into the system. He surrendered his clothes, personal belongings and pride . . . which may someday be returned.

For serious offenses, a larger bail is set, typically ranging from $5,000 to $50,000. A bail bondsman can be called to post these bonds and will usually charge ten percent in cash with the collateral assets attached to the rest of the bond. The judge set bail for Anthony at one million dollars. No one had enough to bail him out, so he sat in jail for about a month.

Anthony had to make a call that broke his parents' hearts. He didn't understand how much he had affected the people around him until he sat behind steel bars. "I embarrassed them in the very town they lived in. They showered me with love, and I dragged them into the mud. This is how the addicted son paid back his loving and caring parents," Anthony said.

He was released on personal recognizance at the beginning of December. Being out didn't mean he was free—he had to wear an ankle monitor. Everyone knew what he'd done and those involved were cooperating with the police. The newspapers and TV continued to blare coverage of his case. His neighbors looked at him, but kept their distance. He no longer had access to all of the drugs he was taking, and was forced to get sober. Even though Anthony was being tested for drugs, he stayed drunk and out of reality. He knew he was going to prison. He just needed to line up the money and a way for his family to be taken care of before he went in.

Anthony thought the money was still with his friend, but with the FBI tailing him everywhere he went, it wasn't available. His friend with the money wasn't talking to him, so Anthony had phones dropped off to him at his work. Still no answer. This guy had nearly $300,000 while Anthony watched his wife apply for food stamps. The anxiety was torture. Finally, he sent the last person he trusted to pass a note on to his friend. In it, he offered an additional $30,000 to hand over the money.

By contacting the friend, Anthony had violated his release.

Later that night, he turned on all the fans in the house and asked Emily to crawl under the covers. He did this because he assumed the police had bugged the house. Anthony told Emily what he had done, and came clean about an affair. She only knew a fraction of the truth and she was devastated.

The next day, they were scheduled to go to their first family counseling session. They were late as usual. Emily was driving, and when she got fifty yards out of the driveway, she started to worry that she hadn't locked the front door in the rush to get out the house. "Did you lock it?" she asked.

Mired in his own misery, Anthony just shrugged.

Angrily, Emily threw the truck in reverse, and drove a little too fast back down the cul-de-sac. She noticed that Anthony was quiet as she did this, but figured he was a little scared of her at the moment. But when she got to the driveway, Anthony was staring straight out the windshield. Then she saw seven cop cars surrounding them, and officers with machine guns out.

She yelped, "What the hell happened?"

"I didn't do anything. I don't know what's going on," Anthony lied.

The cops were yelling at Anthony to get out of the car. It was clear that they were arresting him again. Emily instinctively wanted to protect Anthony, and she started to get out of the car to argue with the cops. The police yelled at Emily to get back into the car. As she did so, she watched as Anthony was put in the back of the police car. It was the last time Emily saw Anthony outside of prison.

The day Anthony was re-arrested in January of 2009, he began to understand just how distorted his own reality had become.

Twelve

Anthony pled guilty to "Interference with Commerce in violation of Title 18," otherwise known as the Hobbs Act (a law that prohibits the robbery of interstate commerce, originally enacted to combat racketeering). The U.S. Attorney (Western District Washington) noted the following about Anthony's case:

> The Honorable James L. Robart "described the crime as fitting of the type of things seen in the movies similar to the 'Thomas Crown Affair.' However, Judge Robart stated there was nothing 'dashing' about this crime. Judge Robart stated he was troubled by the immediate violence. He was equally troubled with Curcio's novel idea of using Craigslist to have others show up dressed like himself, similar to the 'Thomas Crown Affair.' This, however, put those people at risk of being shot by the guards.
>
> Some $220,000 of the stolen money was recovered following Curcio's arrest on November 25, 2008. Curcio was originally released following his arrest, but was returned to custody in January 2009, after he contacted one of the witnesses in the case, in violation of the terms of his release. Curcio pleaded guilty on May 5, 2009.

> In asking for a five year sentence, Assistant United States Attorney Bruce Miyake noted the danger involved in any robbery. "All robberies are inherently violent and serious. This robbery stands out for its boldness, level of planning, and its ingenuity. Curcio was obsessive in his planning. He was very meticulous in thinking of almost all the details. He spent hours watching the bank to determine the schedule of the armored car. He also spent hours setting up his escape route which included stringing up a cable to assist in his escape," Mr. Miyake wrote in his sentencing memo.

Despite eighteen letters from his family and thirty letters from friends and supporters, Anthony was sentenced by Judge Robart on July 27, 2009. Anthony's attorney, Jeffrey Kradel, made a plea for five years. The judge could have sentenced Anthony to twenty years, but gave him only a year above his plea, for a total of six years. Robart said he was angry at Anthony because he'd lured in fifteen innocent wanna-be landscapers and put them in his "circle of danger." Any one of those people could have been shot.

Anthony was ordered to pay $115,000 in restitution. He is required to pay back the money in small payments as part of the government's Inmate Financial Responsibility Program (IFRP).

Detective Buzzell has received a fair bit of notoriety in the law enforcement community for solving the case. In 2012, he gave a presentation on the Brink's truck robbery to the California Robbery Investigator Association Conference in Reno, Nevada.

Anthony was sent to the Federal Detention Center SeaTac in Seattle to await transfer to a federal prison. Two FBI agents drove him on the hour-long trip, and took the opportunity to make conversation with him. They even offered to buy him a McDonald's breakfast on the way. They were surprised when Anthony declined.

He was polite and respectful, but the FBI agents apparently hadn't read the newspapers to know that Anthony Curcio wasn't cooperating with authorities.

Anthony still wanted the hidden money, and he thought the FBI did, too. He believed he could use the money as a bargaining chip in exchange for a lighter sentence. Maybe he could keep it and set up his family until he was released. Anthony had sent out a message with an inmate released from the county jail to his friend who had the money. He entrusted the combination numbers to the guy, hoping his friend would help Emily financially. Anthony was expecting to hear soon that his friend had taken care of everything.

He didn't realize his friend had already returned the money and signed a cooperation agreement against Anthony.

SeaTac was roughly the same physical setup as the county jail, but instead of the average inmate facing a thirty- or ninety-day sentence, most were facing five- to thirty-years, with a few facing life sentences. If you were in the federal system, you were involved in more serious crimes, including bank robbery and criminal gangs.

FDC SeaTac is a detention center where inmates wait to be processed into the federal prison system, so the anticipation of hard time can be deadly. There are a few suicides a year. Anthony's cell neighbor hanged himself. Some inmates facing serious time quickly lose their minds; daily Anthony watched men become unhinged. One guy was talking to himself. Another looked like a zombie. One lunatic wandered around talking about monsters that tried to have sex with him. For those people, there was the seven p.m. pill call, when a nurse wheeled a cart into the common area and dispensed meds.

Anthony realized that he could no longer find the hard drugs that he was used to, but he could settle for the next best thing. He made a deal with the monster sex lunatic: the drugs the crazy was taking for food out of the commissary. After that, there was a pill line that formed outside of cell 218 about five minutes after the official pill line—only the meds were traded for food. Anthony did the only thing he knew how to feel better, he self-medicated. The pain from the past would only affect him six hours a day. Anthony was so drugged, he would enter a coma for eighteen hours a night. Some of his fellow inmates expressed their concern for his health, but he just brushed them off. They were sociopaths, after all.

The Christians he was praying with turned their backs on Anthony because they felt he'd turned his back on God. As far as Anthony was concerned, God had turned His back on *him*.

The first visit to SeaTac was very stressful for Emily. She took her girls to see their daddy for the first time in federal prison. It wasn't something she had ever imagined doing. The building alone was daunting, but her anxiety was heightened because on top of it all she couldn't bring a diaper bag into the visiting facility. What would she do if her daughter had a blow-out? It was a parent's nightmare.

While the kids played on the floor, Emily started demanding the truth from Anthony regarding the rumors going around. She kept hearing things after he was arrested, and persisted in trying to find out if he'd been having affairs.

"No, Emily," he'd say. "There was nothing going on with that girl. The Feds are just trying to flip you to make their case easier against me." Anthony had heard it was typical for an inmate's wife who was fighting her husband's case to be approached by the feds, cops or prosecutors and shown pictures of the husband with other women in an attempt to sway the wife to wave her spousal agreement and testify against her soon-to-be-ex-husband. It was also a convenient excuse.

A week later, Emily had gathered more evidence. He responded, "Well, okay. I will be honest. Something did happen." Anthony tried the play where sometimes you have to admit some guilt to appear innocent to the rest. "I kissed her. Well, actually she kissed me. One time. And I tried to move but someone obviously saw it, got the wrong idea and the Feds heard about it. I'm sorry."

It happened every week. Emily would hear things and ask Anthony about them. He would lie, and then Emily would try to believe him and forgive. Repeat. Anthony only admitted to things that he absolutely had to. This happened so much that every waking moment of his six hours he would be tortured with worry wondering what else was going to be uncovered from his past. What was really killing Anthony was that he was slowly becoming sober, and he could feel the pain after a long spell of horrible decisions. Anthony loved Emily very much, but he was also terrified that she would find out everything he had been up to and leave.

Emily was busy packing up the house getting ready to move, and needed a tape measure. She looked in the shed and found one of Anthony's many cell phones. There was one number with unfamiliar initials next to it, so Emily dialed it. The woman on the other end of the phone said things that utterly demolished Anthony's lies.

After the evidence was presented against him, Anthony admitted to as little as he could. He did his best just to minimize the damage. But Emily put together his answers with his responses to her previous questions. . . and they didn't add up. Anthony had no choice but to come clean on a few things. Emily'd had enough of his lies, and said so. For all her support, Anthony had rewarded her with more lies. He had destroyed her love for him.

> "I had the balls to rob an armored truck by myself, but I couldn't tell my wife the truth."
>
> —Anthony

She stopped answering his phone calls. He felt tortured by her silence. Then one day, she answered. In the fifteen minute phone call, Anthony asked a question that someone in his position never should: "Did you cheat on me?"

"Yes," she replied shakily.

One thing Anthony knew about Emily was that she didn't lie. After all that Anthony had put her through, for the years she had supported a man she no longer knew, this was the moment everything changed. Anthony knew he had hit rock bottom. He had really done it this time. He had destroyed one of the best things in his life.

Emily came to see him. She felt horrible about what she had done, and answered all of Anthony's questions truthfully. They both talked and cried for a long time. Emily told him that she would stay married to him and maybe someday they could get through all of this, but she also told Anthony that she needed to know if there was anything else he wasn't telling her.

"Do I know everything? Are there more lies you need to tell me about?"

Anthony said, "No."

Emily told him, "I might be able to forgive you, but you need to tell me everything. I need to know the truth about our relationship. I can't keep living a lie. If you love me, if you truly respect me, you will tell me."

She was right, but Anthony still didn't tell her the truth. At that point, he really thought there was nothing else he needed to tell her. He'd been telling the lies for so long, he'd actually started to believe them himself.

Emily grabbed both of Anthony's hands and cried. "I love you, and I'm so sorry."

She should be sorry, Anthony thought.

Judge Robart recommended sending Anthony to Sheridan, Oregon for his prison sentence. Sheridan was a medium security federal prison that had a Residential Drug Abuse Program (RDAP) for inmates like Anthony. It would also allow him to stay close to his family. The Bureau of Prison's guidelines say they will keep prisoners within 500 miles of their home. Based on the points assigned for his crime in his sentencing, he was destined to be in a medium security prison—which was in Sheridan. Instead, the Bureau of Prisons assigned him to a prison at Big Spring, Texas, via a six-week stay at the Oklahoma City transfer center.

SeaTac was a dream compared to Big Spring.

In Oklahoma City, Anthony finished detox from the assortment of sleeping pills and handfuls of psychedelic drugs he had been taking. Anthony's official sobriety date is August 4th, 2009.

Once the drug fog lifted, he started becoming emotional and feel the love that he felt for Emily before he started using. There was a voice in his head, and it got louder. At first he couldn't figure out what it was, since it wasn't the same as the Monster's. He heard it louder and louder as the drugs left his mind. Finally, he realized it was his conscience. It had been muffled by the drugs so long, he hardly recognized it. He began to understand how badly he had messed up his family.

He was then transferred to Big Spring Texas. The plane ride on "Con Air" shackled to another prisoner was a bit uncomfortable, but as he stepped off the bus in Texas, he felt the first sun on his face in nearly a year and was grateful for that moment. Big Spring was originally designed to hold 600 Air Force personnel in the 1950's, but it now holds nearly 1,800 criminals. The place was also dirty. As hard as people would try to keep it clean, it just wasn't possible.

The first day at Big Spring was an introduction to prison politics for Anthony. The sixteen people he came in with were assigned bunks, greeted by other inmates and watched carefully by everyone. He discovered that the few white guys that came to the prison were checked out by six groups: the Aryan Brotherhood (AB) and the TAB (Texas AB). Separate from them was the Aryan Circle (AC), the Dirty White Boys (DWB), a group called The Council, and the Hells Angels. But if you were "Good, Standup or Solid"—which that meant you weren't a snitch or had any type of sex offense—you could also be Independent (although being Independent didn't really mean what it implied). The blacks and Latinos had their own groups. There were regular prison rules put in place by the staff, and then there were the rules put in place by the inmates. Anthony discovered quickly which rules you didn't break.

He had learned at SeaTac that every race had a representative better known as a "shot caller." This was the alpha male of the group who ruled through violence and threats, although in time Anthony learned that this system may actually prevent more violence than it seemed to cause. Any race issue or conflict would be handled through the shot caller. When a new guy enters a prison, the first order of business is to get his paperwork checked out by the shot caller.

The living conditions were packed. Anthony lived in a very large, open-dorm style room that was the size of a half basketball court. The ceilings were low, at around eight-and-a-half-feet tall, with six, two-foot square barred windows on the exterior walls. Every inmate had a bunk that was about six feet long and two-and-a-half-feet wide. They are made of steel and rusty to the point of nearly falling apart, and were so close together that if you laid on the bed and stretched your arm out you could touch the bunk next to you. Old, three-inch-thick cloth mattresses were provided. . . until they were replaced by mattresses made of plastic with a leather casing. The old mattresses had so much hidden contraband in them that the prison decided it would be easier to just replace them instead of removing all the shanks and razor blades inside the padding. If you needed any bedding you had to hunt it down. The only bunks available to newcomers were by the bathrooms. To Anthony the scents, noises and sights of the things that happen next to and inside a prison bathroom are reason enough that one would never want to go to prison.

Every inmate had a locker that was about three feet tall, two feet wide and a foot deep with two thin, steel doors to hold all their clothes, personal stuff and items purchased at the commissary. You could purchase a lock for three dollars. Every inmate was issued three pairs of pants, three shirts, one jacket, three t-shirts, three pairs of socks, three boxer shorts, and one pair of boots. Toilet paper, toothbrushes and soap are sometimes issued to new inmates, but usually each race group will take in their own until they are on their feet and earning money enough to buy sundries.

Anthony's first order of business was to clean out his little locker—but only after a thorough inspection to avoid cutting himself on any hidden razor blades or knives left by the previous owner. He learned that the serious weapons were kept in the common areas in case they were discovered by the cops, since getting caught is a serious charge. That way the weapon couldn't be pinned on anybody.

This was Anthony's introduction to the prison way of life that kept him busy and scared. Emily made as many trips as she could and also brought the girls. Anthony felt that he had retained his family.

Anthony filled his time in prison by writing and illustrating children's books for his two daughters that were fun and based on life lessons. He began going to church and attending inmate AA classes. As he got clearer with himself, the guilt inside of him grew. He kept thinking about what Emily said to him at SeaTac: "I may be able to forgive you, but you need to tell me everything so I can know the truth of our relationship. If you love me and truly respect me, you will tell me." Anthony wished he could go back and just answer that last question with the truth.

He confided in a prison friend he had made, and asked his advice as they walked the track outside in the yard. He told his prison friend about all the stuff that Emily didn't know, about his worst offenses, about how much he loved her and how badly the guilt was weighing on his conscience. There was no mistaking what the right thing to do was, but it was how to make it right that bothered him.

His buddy told Anthony to let it go. Why bring up something that would hurt her? It was so relieving to hear, Anthony decided not to say anything.

The cover of Antwiningo and the Pink Cloud, a book Anthony wrote and drew for his daughters.

Later that night, lying in bed when everything was quiet and Anthony was feeling alone, the voice was there telling him something was still not right. It said he was taking the easy way out again. He knew that he had to do something since there were so many lies on top of the lies, his entire unstable world could easily come crashing down if she found out.

Anthony's prison friend had a girlfriend who shared a hotel with Emily during a visit to the prison to save money. The set-up gave Emily some help with the kids and saved money on a rental car.

Anthony's visit with his family was as perfect as a movie script. His youngest daughter fell asleep on his lap for the first time ever, and his oldest daughter and he played hopscotch outside and ate a bunch of junk food from the vending machines. Anthony was also able to sneak a few kisses with Emily when the guards weren't looking. He had finally gotten his family back.

After nearly a year of slowly building things back and earning Emily's trust with daily love letters and constant phone calls, things suddenly came apart. Anthony called home one day, and Emily's questions came pouring in. "Who was she? How many were there? Were you ever faithful to me?"

"Emily, I love you. Who the hell is telling you this stuff?" Anthony asked as he recoiled back into his old smooth-talking self. It was the nightmare he had feared.

"Who was it? Tell me, Anthony!" she demanded.

"No one! There's no one but you!" he swore.

"Oh, my God! You are such a fucking liar! Liar!" she screamed.

The phone went dead as their fifteen minutes were up. Anthony held the phone to his ear in shock. He had to wait an hour before placing the next call. And he did so until the phones were shut off for the night. She didn't answer.

How did she find out all this stuff? Who is telling her? Anthony asked his closest friend to join him on a walk, and as usual he told him everything. Anthony had heard stories of ex-best friends at home who turned on their ex-buddies and moved in on their women after they were incarcerated. In prison they call this person a "Sancho." This person is the most hated person on the planet. "That piece of shit," Anthony said to his friend, and his friend agreed. "I have no choice. I have to come clean now. I just wish I had a long time ago."

Anthony had someone to blame now—he believed his best friend had betrayed him by telling Emily about his past. As long as Anthony had someone else to point his finger at for what was going wrong in his life, he never had to take responsibility for it. But this time, he decided no matter who was to blame, he had to come clean if he wanted to make things right. The next morning, he phoned Emily to answer her questions. Anthony explained all he could in fifteen-minute calls throughout the day. Very quickly he neared the 300-minute maximum for the month. Anthony was still trying to protect himself, and while he answered her questions, he tried to find out where the information was coming from. He came close to accusing her of having an affair with his best friend. He was that desperate.

Finally, Emily revealed that it was Anthony's prison friend's girlfriend! Every conversation Anthony had with his prison friend on the walks around the yard was relayed to the girlfriend. The girl felt obligated to tell Emily that Anthony wasn't being honest.

Anthony had no one to blame but himself. His prison friend didn't have a clue that he was actually the source.

> "It was almost like I had orchestrated all of this secretly to force myself to finally come clean. Looking back, it was hell but beautiful at the same time. The truth always is."
>
> —Anthony

Emily called Anthony a liar again and again. Each time she said it was like a punch in the face. When the phone call ended Anthony sat stunned. "I looked at everything around me. I finally got it," said Anthony.

Anthony realized then that he had nothing. He didn't have Emily, money, power, friends—and hell, he didn't even have any criminal connections left. Then he understood that he didn't even have himself. Anthony didn't even have his integrity. The one thing he did have was that inner voice, his conscience. It had been quiet and meek when Anthony was first getting sober, but now it was screaming at him. Anthony was ashamed. He decided right there and then that he would never be called a liar again. He told Emily he would write down everything and mail it to her. He was done making the easy choice. He had finally come to the conclusion that those are hardly ever the best ones.

Against everyone's advice, Anthony started to write. He kept hearing, "You will lose her," or "You're an idiot," or "She will take the kids and disappear forever." Anthony didn't listen to them. He was trying to reestablish some real integrity and give Emily back her dignity.

Anthony had accepted that Emily and he would be over, and after what he'd put her through nobody could blame her. He thought that if there was any chance that she would ever respect him again that the long journey would have to start now. The damage he'd created would take years to repair.

> "I imagined myself coming to pick up our daughters from their future home without me as a weekend-only dad. I thought of how Emily would look at me then— as someone who never had the courage to come clean and show her the respect she deserved. I had a choice and this was the moment."
>
> —Anthony

He realized he had the option to become a better man, someone Emily could respect. He owed it to both her and himself. The more Anthony wrote down, the more explaining he needed to do. While unraveling the mess he had created, he saw just how many lies were piled up on each other to protect the one underneath it.

> "I thought I was so cool for so many years, but I was finally able to see how much of a coward I had become. I used to talk about the importance of loyalty, but I had none. My

selfishness and lies destroyed Emily. I ended up writing 240 pages answering all the questions. I wrote all day and all night and answered all of her questions. As I mailed the horrible truths off, the feeling really sucked. But the feeling that it gave me was pure and real and something I hadn't felt in years. Regardless of what everyone around me was saying, I knew it was the right thing to do. I had done the right thing, and the voice inside of me told me so."

—Anthony

In the weeks and months that followed, Anthony sent off his truth letters. They were horrible, but he felt he deserved the humiliation it brought him.

Emily went through shock, anger and denial. She released wrath on Anthony like he had never seen. She sent him the articles and letters on cheating spouses with details underlined in red pen. Emily's letters filled with her disbelief and anger were like knives to Anthony. He felt horrible for destroying everybody around him.

But as time went on, things slowly got better. Emily's letters were less filled with anger, and more with sorrow. Anthony was able to look in the mirror for the first time in a long time and like what he saw. Everything started to change for him as he attempted to rebuild his life on the only thing he had, a foundation of honesty and integrity.

Emily moved back in with her parents. She couldn't afford to support her family on just one salary. Along with Anthony's parents, she sent Anthony money on a monthly basis so he could afford his phone and email bill, and his restitution payment. Anthony's ability to pay restitution made him eligible for the drug program he still needed. She paid out the money for Anthony's expenses strictly for the girls. At this time, she didn't want to speak to Anthony. She still cared for him and for their relationship, but she wouldn't have supported him if it weren't for the children. The ten-month long drug program was his recovery tool so he had a chance to get better and be a dad again.

Before he was arrested, Anthony was an absentee father. Ironically, once he was in prison, he became more a part of their lives.

Anthony had sworn off playing basketball and football years before, but he decided to join prison teams in both sports. He developed his passion in drawing children's books for his kids back home and devoted some quality time to it. Anthony frequently went and sat in the middle of the field to just be alone and enjoyed the time by himself. He also realized that he had been ignoring the presence of someone who was always there: God. Two thousand miles from everyone he loved, with absolutely nothing to his name, Anthony had finally found peace.

Good things started to happen. He went to the prison church. He tried to start his own AA group. Three years into his six-year sentence, he discovered he was eligible for a twelve-month reduction in his sentence for completion of the Bureau of Prison's drug program.

> "As much as I felt like a new person, I still felt sadness for all that I had done to Emily. I had completely victimized this wonderful person. For all the sixteen years we had been together she always was loyal, faithful—and no matter what—honest."
>
> —Anthony

Emily says:

> "I haven't worn my engagement ring since Anthony was arrested; I grew to loathe anything material or expensive because it just represented one of Anthony's addictions and reminded me that he was never satisfied; that his greed, along with his addiction to drugs, is what led him to rob the armored car. I stopped wearing my wedding band a few months later, when I first found evidence that he'd been ly-

> ing to me about being unfaithful. There are no good memories connected to those rings. He may have loved me and wanted to marry me, but he was the furthest thing from an honest man. Our wedding day, our vows and our marriage—none of it was real. The ring I wear now is actually just a piece of rope, but it means more than any diamond ever could. Anthony gave it to me when I went to visit him in June of 2011, after I 'came clean' myself. It represents love, forgiveness and most importantly, honesty. So we'll see what happens, if nothing else, at least we have that."

Anthony was told he was going to be transferred again. They planned to move him to a RDAP facility with an opening. During a phone call, Anthony had Emily look at a map and try to figure out where he was going next.

"The nearest facility is in Long Beach, California," Emily said. "That would be nice, and close, too. There's also one in Englewood, Colorado."

"Those would work," Anthony said. "Any place else?"

"Oh," she said. "Here it is. Anthony, Texas!"

"No!" he said with a laugh. "You're making that up!"

"Nope! It's called La Tuna. It's just outside of El Paso, on the border of Texas and New Mexico. You'll probably end up there."

Sure enough, the Bureau of Prisons thought it was a fine place to send Anthony.

Surprisingly, Anthony, Texas was like a dream compared to Big Spring. The facility consisted of old stucco, Spanish style homes that were white and on the side of a hill in the desert. It was hot—116 degrees in the summer time but the visits were a lot easier.

Once he was settled, Emily arrived with the girls for a visit. The guard said Anthony was out of visiting points.

"How can that be? He just got here, and we're his first visitors," Emily said.

The guard replied, "Well, how do you know?"

Emily froze. *He's right,* she thought, *Anthony could easily be lying to me again.* It was certainly possible that someone else had already used up all of his visiting points. "You might be right," she said to the guard, "But can you double check anyway? We just flew over 2,500 miles to see him."

The guard made sure they had a place to wait out of the heat while he went to find someone to help her. Later, after they were allowed in and during the visit, he made a point of finding Emily and apologized for the inconvenience. He made sure to say—in front of Anthony—that there was a mistake and Anthony hadn't had any other visitors.

The visit was a million times better than those to Big Spring. Anthony could interact with his kids at La Tuna. It was less restrictive, and they could play outside and run around. Emily brought the kids three times to visit Anthony at La Tuna, and she came twice on her own.

Life in prison wasn't without its humor. One day, Anthony stood in front of a closed door for a few minutes. He was waiting for a guard to come and open the door for him, as is routine. A line of inmates formed behind him, all waiting for the door to be opened. Then a new guy in the back of the line spoke up and said, "Is the door open?" Anthony rolled his eyes and checked the door—which he hadn't the entire time he was in front of it. He pushed on it, and sure enough, it opened. That was the day he realized he'd become accustomed to the rules and life of institutionalization.

Anthony and Emily set up regular times to call and talk. They were working on their relationship, and the truth calls were much easier to take if they were planned. Emily found the calls emotionally disrupting, and at least she could make sure she wasn't in the middle of something. The scheduled calls also worked better with the kids, who could talk to their daddy.

Anthony was diagnosed as having bi-polar disorder by the psychologist at the prison. His doctor wrote the following:

> "Mr. Curcio is still working on understanding his bipolar diagnosis. There is a direct correlation between his mental health issues and the use of mood altering substances in an attempt to control it. He is in the process of understanding how the manic phase he undergoes is creating an imbalance in his life. For years he has been trying to cope with it (disorder) by using opiates, cocaine and sedatives. By doing so he obtained a short-term ability to fluctuate from one extreme to another, but it eventually led to a complete imbalance. He has been sharing in his process group how the adrenaline rush was a powerful stimulant for him to participate in antisocial and criminal behaviors."

Anthony was starting to comprehend that he tended to use drugs to help level himself out—although he'd done this not knowing his underlying condition. But the drugs also led to complete disaster. Understanding the problem was the first step in his recovery.

Things were going well. But Anthony was about to experience the worst that life could throw at him.

Thirteen

Anthony was lying on his bunk when he saw a guard carrying an inmate's bedding—which was odd. Following him was a very deformed man in his mid-forties with thick glasses, a Down Syndrome-like face and a body that didn't seem healthy. One of his arms looked like it belonged to a two-year-old child, it was hardly down to his waist with a hand that had webbed fingers. He left his bunk to get soap and a toothbrush from an officer, and when he returned his stuff had already been stolen. Inmates from other dorms and other floors were coming in just to point and laugh at him. People were cruel. The guy just looked at Anthony.

At first, Anthony tried to ignore the man. He'd been burned before by fake people inside and had decided to keep to himself. Finally, he couldn't take watching the deformed man's struggle as he tried to move a locker to his bunk. Anthony jumped off his bunk to help him. He also went and bought the guy a cold soda and a honey bun.

Once Anthony got the locker in position and cleaned it out, the man let Anthony see his papers. His name was Richard, and he had Asperger's Syndrome. This was the last dorm for him. He had been checked off every other floor and every other unit. While going through his paperwork, he handed Anthony a few papers with one that read his charge was "intimidation and threatening a government official." Since every inmate blames the arresting FBI agents for ruining their lives, this charge was held in high regard in federal prison. This was elite status. From that day forward, Anthony stood up for him. Some Hells Angels and AB guys came to pick on him, but Anthony talked them into leaving Richard alone. At one point, it looked like Anthony was going to have to fight another guy about Richard. Eventually, the other inmates listened to Anthony and people actually started to help Richard.

With his deformity, Richard couldn't do a lot of things, so Anthony helped by typing letters for him to send back home. After some time, Richard was accepted by nearly all the inmates. Anthony and Richard became fairly close over the next few months.

One day, when Richard was going through his paperwork, they called him over the loud speaker to report to the officer's station for mail. He told Anthony he'd be right back and to watch his stuff. Anthony noticed a paper sitting on Richard's locker that had big, black permanent marker over some text on the other side. He held up the document to the light. "Sex Offender classes must be completed prior to release for RRC placement (halfway house). Probation: Life." The next few pages included details of his crime. He had threatened an FBI agent—but only after being arrested for molesting his niece and nephew. Anthony was blown away.

The worst thing anyone can be in prison is a "Cho-Mo"—the nickname for a child molester (actually all sex offenders fall into the same category). In every penitentiary or maximum security prison in the U.S., a known child molester would be killed immediately by a "true" convict. It's an old convict code.

When Richard came back in he saw Anthony holding the papers. Anthony handed them back to him and left without saying anything. Anthony went outside to the prison yard to be alone and walk some laps. He had stood up for Richard when others said he was a Cho-Mo. Anthony expected there would be some issues for him, once Richard's crimes became known.

Anthony went back in, and Richard waved him over. His whole demeanor changed and he became aggressive. It was obvious

Richard had been playing Anthony for months. Anthony told him to stay away from him. But Richard pointed to Anthony's bunk. "Check your bed," he told Anthony quietly. There was a note saying, "I'm better at finding people than anyone. You shouldn't have fucked with me," written on an envelope that had contained a letter from Emily. Anthony looked up over the bunk and Richard was staring at him over his reading glasses. He had been deceived by a monster who preyed on children.

Anthony snapped. He pulled Richard from his bunk and dragged him into the bathroom. Some other guys blocked the entrance so the guards couldn't see. Anthony pushed Richard's head into a metal sink. He envisioned getting the justice that Richard's sister's kids never could. Richard's glasses were pushed to the side of his face, and his lips were pressed against the bottom of the sink. Richard stared up at Anthony from out of the corner of his eye like a demon. He whispered, "Do it. Do it. Do it!"

People started to flood into the bathroom to see the action. They wanted Anthony to kill the Cho-Mo—and he almost did. But then Anthony thought of his daughters. Attacking Richard would do nothing. It wouldn't heal what he did to those little kids, and it would take Anthony farther away from his own. Killing someone—especially a Cho-Mo—in prison is just as much of a crime as outside. Child molesters are put into the general prison population and everyone is told that causing them any trouble can get you worse time. If Anthony punched another inmate, it was no big deal—a night or two in the Special Housing Unit (SHU). But if he punched a sex offender, the FBI had to get involved because it was classed as a hate crime. He'd get another eighteen to sixty months tacked on his sentence. Anthony dropped Richard right there. The deformed man slithered down to the floor.

Anthony went to bed. Later, he awoke to three officers telling him that he had to go to the lieutenant's office with them. He was handcuffed and taken into the captain's office. The Captain told him he would be catching another charge for the attack. Richard had been up in the office before anyone woke up explaining his story. He was a master manipulator, and he knew that to protect his secret, Anthony would have to go. Anything Richard told them had to be true because how could a crippled man bully a big, healthy man like Anthony?

Anthony was shackled and on his way to the SHU when the officer's radio buzzed. "Please return inmate Curcio to the Lieutenant's office." When he got back to the office, the officer had the envelope from Emily that Richard had written his threatening note on. Someone had run it to the office. The officer said, "You'd be surprised who bailed you out of this one. Don't let me hear your name again, all right?"

When Anthony walked back into the dorm, he heard an uproar, like a football game was going on. There was yelling and a bunch of pissed off people. The door flung open. Six officers were surrounding Richard and trying to keep people back. The inmates looked ready to riot. Finally, the officers struggled through the crowd with Richard between them.

Once things settled down, Anthony found out that several inmates went looking for Richard when the truth about him came out. Someone raided his locker. When the inmates discovered photos of their families and cut-out magazine pictures of young children, that's when the near-riot started. Richard was never seen again.

After a week, things went back to the way they had been. Anthony spent most of his free time creating picture books for his kids and keeping mostly to himself.

One day, he heard, "Curcio to recreation," over the loud speaker.

He gathered up his drawings and headed to the office. The officer sent him on to the Lieutenant's office. Just as he got there, the head psychologist walked out of the LT's office, glared at him and went down the hall. A special investigator for the prison (S.I.S.) motioned him to step inside. The moment he did, an officer shouted, "Extorting my inmates huh?! Why can't you guys just leave our sex offenders alone?"

Another said, "Give me your I.D.!"

Then another said, "Threatening and trying to plan this. You should know you can't organize shit behind my back!"

Anthony didn't have time to respond or to even think before he was pushed to the wall.

"I've got 1,200 two-legged walking and recording cameras here. Cuff up!" the Lieutenant said, referring to the inmates.

"You're going to the Hole," another said, as he snapped handcuffs on Anthony.

Anthony had heard of the Special Housing Unit, called the SHU, and also known as "the Hole," but nothing prepared him for the realities of this prison within a prison.

The instant the steel door clicked shut behind him, the banging started. There was yelling and the sound of metal doors being kicked as he was escorted down the concrete gray hallway with ten steel doors on each side. He was dragged to the end of the row where there was a shower in a cage and thrown in. He was instructed to strip and given a perfunctory cold shower. Then they shoved a pair of boxers and an old orange jump suit at him through a little six inch tall by twelve inch wide lockable, mini-steel hatch centered stomach-high on the door. The little door, known as the "bean chute" was what they used to cuff inmates prior to the door being opened. Anthony quickly figured out that no door was ever opened unless the inmate was cuffed.

"How long will I be in here?" Anthony asked.

"Two weeks max," he was told.

The two officers escorted him back down the hall. Anthony noticed that each door had little windows of about three inches wide and about fifteen inches tall, made of marked up, dirty Plexi-

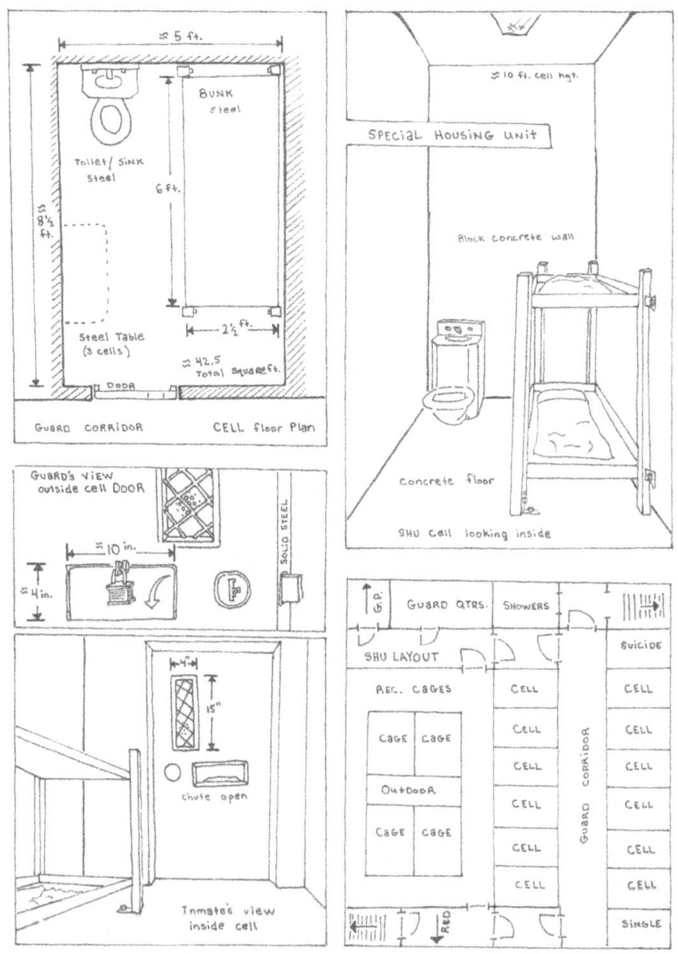

Anthony's drawing of the SHU layout, the cells and the doors.

glas in front of the thick metal mesh. The Plexiglass had six one-eighth inch round holes in it that allowed communication from the guards to the inmates. Most of the time, you could only see a few facial features. But it was the eyes that stunned Anthony. They peered from each cell like vultures looking at a kill that they can never land on.

They stopped in front of cell #108. The black guard kicked the door and hollered, "Wake the fuck up!"

The scuffed Plexiglas quickly filled with the huge face of a bald-headed guy who looked to be about seven feet tall. His scalp and face were covered with White Supremacist tattoos. He yelled, "Let me see him!" Anthony was forced to turn and face the guy. "Is he fucked up?" asked the skinhead. He was asking if Anthony was a sex-offender.

"Listen, James, you want another refusal or you gonna get another assault charge, we don't give a fuck," the guard responded.

Anthony had no idea what the guard meant, but he was thinking, *Please put me in a room by myself if I have to be in here for two weeks.* Later, he found out that solitary is a luxury only awarded to inmates who assault other inmates.

The guard opened the bean chute and the skinhead put out his hands to be cuffed. Once that was accomplished, the other guard opened the cell door and shoved Anthony through. Then they each had to stick their hands back through to have their cuffs removed.

Anthony turned around. He had been hoping his new skinhead cellie had been standing on a stool. The guy later said he was 6'-3" and weighed 260 pounds, but he looked much, much bigger. He had a massive chest and wore only boxers, the better to show off all of his Nazi and Aryan Brotherhood tattoos. In those first moments, an inmate knows to immediately size up the other. Anthony's heart was pumping hard and his adrenaline was flowing. He knew what the first question would be.

"Why are you here?"

"In the SHU or in prison?" Anthony asked.

"Both," the skinhead replied.

"I really have no idea why exactly I'm in here and. . . ."

The skinhead yelled, "What do you *mean!?* You fucked up, you motherfucker!"

Anthony snapped back. "I robbed a fuckin' armored truck! What did you fuckin' do? What I was saying is I don't know exactly why they put me in the SHU. I didn't do anything."

That put him in his place, and he seemed to deflate a bit. "Yeah, join the club."

Anthony looked around. The steel door, with the bean chute and thin Plexiglas viewing strip, was just a few inches from his heels. A foot in front of him were the steel framed bunks with half-inch-thick mattresses, similar to a yoga mat. To the side of the bunks there was a steel toilet and sink. That left about eight square feet for standing. The walls were concrete on all sides that had been painted white about fifteen years ago, but now were more of a khaki color with orangish streaks from drippings off of God-knows-what. Old markings and count-down calendars from previous inmates dotted the walls. *No big deal,* he tried to convince himself, *I'll be out in two weeks*. That seemed like an eternity as he looked around.

He heard the skinhead behind him say, "Yeah, okay, so you robbed an armored truck?"

James, the huge beast of a killer, was actually a big country boy from Minnesota. He thought it was the coolest thing that Anthony was in his cell, because his grandpa had just sent him an article about Anthony's crime—and there he was in an SHU cell with him. The skinhead tried to be helpful, filling Anthony in about the one phone call a month, the guards, the shower every three days, the nasty food, the fucked up shakedowns—and the worst part—the cockroaches.

Anthony made up his bed, such as it was, and looked at his only belonging: a piece of paper showing what time he'd been brought in and by whom. Under "Reason," it said "under investigation."

Then, until the lights went down, Anthony did what he always did in a new cell, listened to someone talk about their life. The skinhead told Anthony he'd been a promising UFC fighter whose career ended because of a meth manufacturing case he was caught up in. He bragged that his grandparents owned lots of oil rigs and were worth an estimated $150 million. He'd been put in the Hole for a few weeks for attacking, in self defense of course, four Mexican gang members who had jumped him with a fire extinguisher. He apparently put two of them in the hospital using the butt of the extinguisher.

All Anthony could think was, *Don't piss this meth'ed-out UFC fighter off!*

Then the lights snapped off. Anthony saw nothing but pitch black. It wasn't just dark, it was inky black. That's when Anthony realized he really was in a deep hole without any windows. He wrapped up the best he could, crawled up to the top bunk and almost immediately fell asleep, he was so exhausted from such an emotional day.

The only similarity of the SHU to the general population is the counts. The Bureau of Prisons mandates a count at midnight, 3 a.m., 5 a.m., 4 p.m. and 10 p.m., with an additional 10 a.m. count on the weekends. It must have been the 12 a.m. count that woke Anthony, because two sets of flashlights flickered in the cell. It was the first light since the overheads went out. By the flicker of the first flashlight, Anthony thought that the wall shifted to one side away from the light. The second flashlight showed things moving all around Anthony. Suddenly, it was as if he'd been given the sense of touch:

They were all over him!

He felt them on his forearms, stomach and legs. He felt them on his face! "Oh my God!" he screeched. It was Anthony's very own horror film, and he was in a pure panic.

Then he heard from the bunk below, "Yeah, bro, you've got to cover up."

"Holy fuck, man! These things carry diseases, oh my fucking God!" Anthony shouted. "How the fuck am I supposed to cover up with this sheet? It's way too short!" The cockroaches were everywhere.

The skinhead said, "They short-sheeted you, so you must have really pissed someone off. Just make sure to cover up your ears." Anthony realized the man's voice was muffled because he'd wrapped himself up in a sheet, head to toe.

Anthony remained in a panic that entire night. He curled up into a ball as tightly as he could, constantly peddling his legs just trying to shake the roaches off. He couldn't cover himself entirely, and couldn't sleep for the terror of the bugs. By the time the next flashlights came by for the 3 a.m. count, he was wide awake. The flickering light illuminated the sheet so that he could see over a hundred cockroach shadows on the other side.

For the next two hours, he fidgeted and squirmed. He tried folding the mattress on top of his legs to block off his bottom half, but nothing seemed to work. He'd tuck in a side, only to feel one on his calf and then movement on his hand. Or maybe he was imagining it. He visualized the legs of a hundred roaches moving and searching for God-knows-what-all around his skin, crawling through his hair, looking for his mouth, trying to crawl into his ear—looking for any way to get in.

The lights popped on after what seemed an eternity of nighttime. Every roach in the world was covering the walls, floor and ceiling. They scattered like vampires running from the sun. They made a noise that was like a tiny hiss and soft tapping of a million bugs from all directions. Then all at once they were gone.

James told Anthony why he'd mentioned the roaches and ear thing. His previous cellie woke up with an itch in his ear, and he instantly knew what it was. After about ten straight minutes of screaming and kicking the door, James's cellie realized the guards would be no help. He decided to try washing the cockroach from his ear, but the roach only burrowed deeper. For an hour straight, the panicked man screamed and cried enough to be removed from the cell. That was the last time James heard of his cellmate.

Breakfast came through the slot, but there was hardly anything inside the plastic three-compartment tray with a lid. The same with lunch. James told Anthony that before the food trays make it to the SHU, they are filled by inmates, then transported by other inmates who take a cut, which are then sold or eaten back in the units. Once the diminished tray reaches the SHU, the guards decided who gets a full tray and who doesn't. James was definitely not one of their favorites, considering the KKK venom he spewed at the two black and three Latino guards that handled SHU duties in any given week.

Once a week, the guards turned on the cameras to confirm the walkthrough and welfare checks so they don't get sued if there was a suicide or something. Their walk-throughs meant some of the inmates would be returned to the general population. But the other inmates—like James and Anthony—were taunted or tricked into believing that release was imminent.

Anthony could barely stand the fact that he had to shit at best a maximum of four- to five-feet from his cellie's head—and vice versa. Sometimes when he and James were out of the cell having their bi-weekly showers, the sadistic guards would strip every bit of paper from the room. That meant that there was no toilet paper, and they'd have to wash in the sink. The constant smell of another man's sweat when the cell's air was shut off during certain shift changes was sickening. El Paso's temperatures often reached 110 degrees, and when the swamp coolers were turned off—as they often were—the walls would sweat so that puddles of water appeared on the ground. The humidity formed a hot film of nasty moisture that clung to his skin.

If it weren't for the lights coming on at 6 a.m. and going off at 11 p.m., he would never have been able to count the change of the day. Meals were the best gauge of time. As the days came and went, Anthony finally neared the two week mark. During the Tuesday walk-through, Anthony figured he would be released back into general population. He heard, "Thomas, Perez, Johnson, strip your bed, you're going back to the compound." He peered out of the window and watched as the three inmates were escorted out holding their sheets.

Anthony's heart almost stopped. *There has to be a mistake!* He asked, "What about me, boss? I was supposed to leave today."

The officer replied, "Talk to your counselor next Tuesday during walk-through."

Anthony broke into a cold sweat and felt sick. He had to get out of there! It was time! He couldn't stand this awful place, the lack of privacy and the disgusting nearness of his cellmate.

He was finally allowed to talk to Emily. They rolled a phone up on a small table and placed it outside the cell door. The bean chute was opened and he had to make his call with his cellmate and the guard listening to every word.

Emily found out Anthony was in the SHU while driving over the 520 bridge crossing over Lake Washington. She had just checked her CorrLinks prison email account to see if he had emailed her. He generally emailed her in the morning, a couple times around noon and a couple times around the evening. He hadn't emailed her all day. They could have been in lockdown or the computers were down, but for some reason she was worried on this day. Something had happened and she could feel it. Emily and Anthony were in a good place at this time and were healing, but they had things they needed to talk about.

While she was headed over the bridge, the phone rang.

> "I've definitely had some weird phone calls over the years regarding Anthony, so my heart still skips a beat when the phone rings and it's a number I don't recognize. Is it the prison? The cops? Another woman? Is there something else I don't know about? The same thing happens when I hear

sirens. It gets better as time goes by; it's way different now. But I don't know if it will ever completely go away."

—Emily

The call was from a woman, a wife of a fellow inmate who heard he was locked up. Inmates set up buddy systems exchanging contact info because the prison doesn't give out information on prisoner status. Anthony had asked his inmate friend to ask his wife to call Emily and tell her that he'd been put in solitary, so Emily wouldn't worry.

She immediately went back to being mad at Anthony. What had he done in prison to get himself in trouble?

The next day, Anthony got the chance to call, but he couldn't explain why he was in the SHU. Emily was on the defensive—there was a good chance he wasn't telling the truth. But she understood that it was only for two weeks and was no big deal, really.

The trouble was when that two weeks ended, there seemed no end in sight.

James the skinhead and Anthony were cuffed and led to another cell that was nearly identical to the one they'd left. While they were in the thin hallway between the rows of cells Anthony, saw an inmate spraying for bugs with a supervising officer. "Thank God," Anthony said. But their cell became infested again right after they were sprayed. Fortunately, Anthony was issued a full-sized sheet that didn't have any holes in it. He could deal with the roaches a little better.

"Wake up bro. Your counselor's a cell down," James said.

Anthony jumped off the bunk. The counselor was four days early. *What the hell?*

The counselor said, "You're getting out this Tuesday. You would have been out today, but we need some signatures from the Assistant Warden."

If there hadn't been three inches of steel separating them, Anthony would have hugged the man. He stayed very positive all the way till Tuesday. On that day he heard, "Lujan, Gardner, Lloyd, strip your bed, you're heading back to the compound." Then another set, "Ellis, Reese, Lopez, pack it up." Then the walk-throughs. They moved through like a tornado. It happened so fast, at the end he heard, "Next week, Mr. Curcio. They need to talk to you. Next Tuesday you will be released back to the compound."

For weeks this continued. And then it was another month. There was another once-a-month phone call to Emily, and then another.

Anthony was talked to by the S.I.S. investigators. They asked him questions about harassment toward child molesters. One asked him, "Do you like child molesters?"

Anthony responded, "Listen, I'm here to take drug treatment and go home. I spend all my time drawing pictures and making books for my kids. I don't pay attention to politics in here, and I'm the least aggressive person you will ever meet. Several people here know me. Don't take my word for it, ask anyone around me."

"We asked you if you like child molesters," the investigator demanded.

"I have kids," Anthony exclaimed.

That was it. He was taken back to the cell.

Names kept getting called, and inmates kept getting released. They got into fights and got caught doing drugs; they all came in and then they all left. A guy smashed another with a brick, and then he was released after three weeks in the SHU. Another spat on an officer, and he only got two weeks. There was an assault on a known child molester. The guys beat him up so badly that the FBI came in to interview the assailants. They were transferred out within a month-and-a-half, but Anthony was still "under investigation."

The roaches created a lack of quality sleep over a prolonged period of time. It began to really wear him down. The cell wasn't big enough to do a pushup unless your feet were on the toilet and your elbow hit the bunk on the way down. If it wasn't for being escorted down the hall twenty feet to the shower cage, Anthony would have hardly walked at all. With the quality and amount of food given, he had little energy left to work-out anyway. Anthony would just lie there all day. Living in the SHU was like living in two stacked coffins just simply existing.

There were ten of the fifty inmates in the SHU that the prison had seemed to forget about. They weren't victims though and surely not innocent. Several white long-stay tenants would chant, "White power!" Occasionally, an inmate would flood their cell using stored up toothpaste to caulk their door jams until the toilet had been purposely clogged and overflowed until the cell had three feet of standing water. Then they would remove the door caulking so hundreds of gallons would flood out and yell, "SHU-namie!" (like a tidal wave). That one always made Anthony smile.

On other days, he was reminded of just who he was locked up with. Using a sheet to somehow pull off the sealed prison-proof light covers, inmates would remove the long glass light bulbs and break them. Meanwhile, cooperating cells would mix soap and water to squirt out their Plexiglas talk holes to make the floor slippery. Then the glass pieces would be thrown out on top of the mixture. An inmate would fake a heart attack, and his cellmate would holler, "Cell 116 is having a heart attack! 116!" The guards would come running. They'd slip and fall into their trap and get dozens of cuts. One time, Anthony watched with dismay as this was done to a fill-in guard who was respectful and minded his own business. As the man stood bleeding and calling for the other guards, Anthony recalled the guy talking to him about his wife and kids. The cheering echoed throughout the SHU. It sickened Anthony, and he crawled into his bunk, closed his eyes and tried to pretend he was somewhere else. As his asshole cellie cheered, he felt more and more alone. That night he really began to lose it.

The guards purposely put rival gang or cartel members in cells with each other. It was like a Pay-Per-View cage fight, except it was free and a lot more ruthless.

Anthony did what he could do to preserve his sanity. He tried to reverse his schedule so he wouldn't be awake during the walk-throughs or the worst of the guards' shifts. Anthony acquired two pens and some paper to draw with, and on the days when the walls weren't sweating he would draw the best children's' books he could for his daughters. Sometimes the moisture in the building rolled up and bled his paper so badly he had to flush them, but he did whatever it took not to lose those pens—which were considered contraband.

It had been nearly three months since he'd been put in the Hole, and he was beginning to worry that the two little loves of his life had forgotten who he was. He never stopped thinking about them, and cried almost every night. He was trapped and scared and couldn't cope any longer.

He wrote Emily a letter every day but two—about 195 letters. Anthony tried his best not to write about his emotions, feelings or truths of what was happening to his family. The ten day turnaround caused Emily terrible frustration. Only a few of her letters made it to Anthony.

The mail was painfully slow from Texas to Seattle, and it was hard to communicate with a ten day delay. They were still working through marital issues, but Anthony was also going through a roller coaster of emotions being in solitary.

> "Some of Anthony's letters were really optimistic and hopeful, almost spiritual. But then there were others that were extremely dark and depressed. I felt helpless and it was scary. But I tried to detach with love as much as possible, because I knew there wasn't anything I could do."
>
> —Emily

During this time Emily was in her support group which helped her get through all of this. She was making sure she wasn't obsessing with it, but most importantly she wasn't trying to fix it like other family members. All she could do was to write him and stay as positive as she could. He had nobody to talk to, and when people would complain to the prison, they treated Anthony worse. One day, she received a letter that was very, very dark and disturbing with statements aimed at Emily regarding things they were dealing with before he went to the SHU, but since her support group was working she was able to respond well and not in anger. She credits her Higher Power for helping her respond to Anthony and help him find some quiet and calm. She sent the letter overnight since she knew he needed to read the letter as soon as possible. Emily also called the prison on this occasion simply because she was afraid he was going to hurt someone or himself, even though she was afraid they would shackle him down and put him on a suicide watch.

It took a while, but Anthony got Emily's letter and acknowledged that his initial letter was crazy. He understood why she had called the prison and thanked her for the nice letter. He was thankful she took action, and was amazed that she could return a caring letter after the devilish one he'd sent. This was evidence that Emily's program was working. It was a big test to her new coping skills she had learned. Her therapy was working.

Anthony was alone, and the negativity from it all and the lack of good heart or compassion from James the skinhead made him feel as if he was in Hell. James had already been broken, and Anthony felt he was well on his way. This is where Anthony learned that in this type of situation—and really in life itself—your own mind is either your biggest ally or your worst enemy.

But it seemed like just a matter of time before he lost his mind in the SHU.

One day, while James was bragging about all the women he'd been with, he told what he'd done to this one girl—the preacher's daughter. He described how he'd been at this party and the girl had been trying to flirt with him. When he started to go too far, she said she didn't want to. That's when he raped her. He went into great detail, then laughed about how the embarrassment from the incident caused the family to move.

The more James talked about assaulting the girl, the more Anthony's heart pounded. Finally, he could take no more. He crawled off his bunk slowly and said, "You have a daughter." James had mentioned the girl, but he was obsessed with exacting revenge on the girl's mother, who he wanted to kill because she never drove the 1,500 miles to visit him.

"It's not like that, bro," James said.

"It *is* like that," Anthony countered. In his mind, there was almost no difference between his daughters and the girl James had assaulted. "Stand up you fucking rapist. You prey on the weak." Anthony could see the fear in James. "C'mon, big UFC fighter, you fucking pussy, get up!"

He replied, "Anthony, it wasn't like that. Anthony, stop."

"Get up!" Anthony yelled. As James got up, Anthony grabbed his neck and pushed him into the mat. With one hand, he held James down, feeling fifty times stronger than the skinhead. He felt as if God had put him in that cell to kill the arrogant skinhead. James' face turned red and his eyes were bulging. Anthony put his other hand on James' throat and the big man's arms flapped at his side. He moved less and less. Anthony let go after a few moments when he realized James wasn't going to respond. He just lay there quietly.

> "Months after this I could still feel the adrenaline when I think about this moment. The whole scene lasted only a few minutes, but I thought I had killed him but didn't really care. I never wanted to fight, but I snapped. I didn't

have any fights in high school, and really the only times I've been involved in fights is when I tried to break them up."

—Anthony

A few minutes went by, and Anthony heard James' sheet move. Anthony started to cry and cry. He hated the evil he'd just heard coming out of James' mouth, and he wanted them both to die.

He looked up and saw James, this weak sexual predator, staring at him with a terrified expression. Anthony said "You're moving out. *Now.*"

James was at the door in an instant, yelling for an officer. He kept looking back at Anthony, as if he expected to be jumped at any second. Somehow he got himself out of there within minutes.

For the first time in a long time, Anthony was alone. Slowly, he could hear the voice of his conscience again. He could see the value of surviving prison, and especially the SHU, with a purpose and a connection to God. He went back to drawing stories for his daughters, and talked constantly to God. At certain moments, he reached an unbelievable peace that he'd never thought possible. For five days, he tried to regain his hope and stay positive.

Then a new cellie was thrown in with him in the middle of the night. They didn't cuff Anthony or anything. He woke up, and the door was being slammed shut. It wasn't until morning that Anthony could see his cellmate, and discovered he was black. They usually only housed blacks with blacks. If there's one thing Anthony learned, it was that prison has to be the most racist place on the planet. He guessed that, since he'd scared a skinhead, the guards were looking for a little "fun" and expected Anthony to fight the guy. Maybe that would allow them to hold him even longer.

His new forty-two-year old cellie, Saget, was from Ohio and seemed okay . . . except for his habit of talking incessantly and being a classic "one-upper." If you ran five miles, he ran six. If you had two cars, he had three. Saget would tell Anthony of his greatness at every moment possible. He was an ex-professional boxer who was supposedly God's gift to women, had a ton of money and it was his second time in prison. Saget was also a Muslim, as was one of the guards; they would call each other AHK, meaning brother by Muslims. His odor was sickening and he never showered. His fingernails were over an inch long.

After a few days, S.I.S. pulled Saget out to question him. Anthony was thankful for the sixty minutes he could simply sit in peace. When he came back, Saget said, "They kept asking me if you ever talk about being involved with organized crime. The whole time they asked about you, really. I didn't say shit. I just told them you was cool. You my niggah boy."

"Organized crime? What the hell is this?" Anthony answered.

"Yeah, they said you and some other niggahs here are involved in some fucked up stuff and possibly facing charges," he said.

Organized crime? Where are they getting that? he thought. All he did was draw children's books and walk the track with a friend from Utah who was in prison for real estate fraud. Then he put together what they were saying. He'd made friends with a member of an organized crime family whose bunk was near his. He ate dinner often with the guy, and they were always joined by two more Mafia guys—one of whom Anthony was sure was still actively operating business from inside prison. Anthony had no interest in any of their stuff. He just really liked their cooking and was welcomed at their table when others weren't. If that's what S.I.S. was after, then why weren't the "good fellas" in the SHU as well? And why hadn't they asked Anthony about them? And what was all this sex offender and extorting child molesters crap about?

The guard pulled Anthony out to get questioned again by the S.I.S. The investigators told him they had no idea why he was being held, since their investigation had been completed weeks ago.

The Assistant Warden wouldn't sign off, but it was pretty clear that Anthony wouldn't be released to the compound because of involvement with certain individuals and staff.

What the hell? No timeline, no nothing and no wrong-doing. They had nothing on him, but they weren't letting him go. Apparently, he'd just have to exist until they changed their minds.

Once every three months, they brought a barber to the SHU to give inmates a haircut. Anthony was cuffed and escorted out to the rec cages. The barber had been on Anthony's prison basketball team. Pleased to have a friend to talk to, he and Anthony chatted freely, even though a guard was present. Then the guy asked if Saget was in the SHU.

"Yeah, he's my cellie," Anthony told him.

"What?!" he replied. "Dude's fucked up, Ant! Dem niggaz checked him in, (meaning the other inmates forced him to go into the Hole off of general population). He's a fuckin' baby raper, dog!"

Anthony paled. "Maybe there's another Saget? This dude talks about dealing drugs all day, bro."

The two guards who were standing there gave out a chuckle.

The barber explained that Saget was selling drugs and getting underage girls cracked out. He used their addiction to control them and sell them as prostitutes.

Anthony exploded. "What is it with these people!? All these under-cover sexual predators, I have daughters! I hate these sick fucks!"

There was a lieutenant nearby who overheard the conversation. Before Anthony could get out of the barber chair, Saget was removed from his cell. They moved him so quickly he didn't have time to get his toe nail clippings off of Anthony's bunk.

Anthony walked into his cell and felt relieved, but also disappointed. All those weeks with Saget seemed to have stolen the momentary peace he'd attained. He felt worthless and far away from anything close to God.

He'd spent the last four months—night and day—with James and Saget. When he'd thought he knew them, he realized everything was a lie. Everything.

Then it hit him: *This is how Emily felt.*

He was starting to see all the craziness around him as merely a distraction. He tried his best to block it out. It seemed more important to him to figure out how he'd turned into a monster and strangled James. He focused on trying to ignore what others were up to and just stay calm.

Anthony was moved into a cell with a fifty-five-year old white guy, named Kaiser. He told Anthony he'd been a sniper in the Marines and a war hero with thirty-six kills (the number depended on the day he told it). He wasn't sure which Colombian drug lord he'd killed in the Nineties, but it probably was Pablo Escobar. He also currently owned and operated—from prison, Anthony heard him say—an 800-plus employee construction company that spanned six states. It was worth an estimated $54 million (and again, the figure changed depending on the day). This dude was serious.

Anthony had heard so many stories by that time that he felt like the old lady waiting for the bus who'd had to listen to Forest Gump—except he didn't want to hear any more. *Where the hell is the nice music and floating feather? End the movie, please.*

His cellmate went out to medical one day. Anthony couldn't stop from going through his papers. He wanted to make sure his cellie wasn't another rapist or child molester. The guy turned out to be a crack addict, and that was pretty much it. So when he returned, Anthony tried to talk with him, explaining his addiction and all the pain he'd caused others, the depression he went through. Anthony prayed the guy would open up as he spoke about his own failures. For days, Anthony tried telling him about the miserable points of his life.

Then it hit him. There are no admitted addicts in prison. There are only tough guys. Addiction is a sign of weakness and shame.

At the next counselor's meeting, he said Anthony was going to be put in for a transfer. *Finally!* This had to be the light at the end of the tunnel. He mailed letters out feeling that this was it. He used his monthly phone call to say he'd be able to call soon. But the next week, the counselor told Anthony through the Plexiglass that he'd never said anything about a transfer.

"What's my status then?" Anthony demanded.

"You're still under investigation."

Behind Anthony, there was a chuckle that turned into light laughter. He glanced back to see Kaiser smirking at him. It was the first time Anthony had seen him remotely happy in three- to four-weeks—and it was because of Anthony's misery.

Anthony felt the rage build up again. He tried to ignore the aggression and take the higher road. "Listen, my little daughters don't get to talk to their daddy because I've been in here for no reason now for nearly five months. You laughing is pretty fucked up especially when you've been in here for less than five weeks."

No sorry, no nothing. Tough guys don't apologize. Then he heard, "You know when I was at the medium and was put in the Hole I was in there for longer than you. This is nothing."

Anthony'd had enough. He shouted, "Listen you fucking crackhead. You are the fakest pussy I have ever met. Shut the fuck up!" And there was the rage that he hated.

For three days, the guy wouldn't come down off his bunk. He would wait until the lights were out, and he thought Anthony was asleep, to come down and use the toilet. That's when he started peeling paint.

After about four months the kids started to ask Emily when they are going to see Daddy again, "Let's go see Daddy in his building," they would say. He went into the SHU in June with their last visit in April, and they had plans to see him over Halloween since they had missed Easter. But now the Halloween trip was in question. The trouble was, Emily couldn't tell the kids when they could go. All she could say was, "I'll take you as soon as I can." After a few more weeks, they were asking Emily every day, and it was breaking Emily's heart. She was losing hope that they were going to be able to visit for Christmas.

Kaiser would pull the paint off the walls for hours at a time. Anthony didn't say anything and tried to stay peaceful after the blowup. He figured Gandhi wouldn't have made it much longer before slapping that sorry, miserable man. Anthony told himself he'd lasted four weeks with this man and bet Jesus could only do five.

A few days later, Anthony's counselor and case manager came by to tell him, "You've been put in for a transfer." He nodded, and even though he was afraid he was being deceived again. He clung to any hope he was given.

Kaiser started arguing with the guard. His previous arguments had ended with them both shackled in the shower and without meals several times. Anthony snapped, "You keep talking and pulling this shit, you've got to go. *I will make you go*. You don't get it!"

Kaiser started peeling paint.

When Anthony woke up the next day, he heard, "Kaiser, Sams, grab your shit, you're going to the compound." The chute opened and they cuffed Anthony up. Kaiser was cuffed with his sheet. A moment later, the loser was gone.

Anthony started to clean up. He put Kaiser's mattress on top of his own—and suddenly saw why Kaiser had been peeling paint. They'd been given pork chops for dinner nearly a month before, and Kaiser must have gotten a bone. Under the mattress was a five inch pork bone—sharp as hell—sticking out of a golf ball-sized handle of khaki-stained white paint. Kaiser was planning on killing Anthony! He quickly peeled it apart. As the last piece flushed down the toilet, he heard keys jingling as the guard came running. The guards took him out of the cell and stuck him in the shower while they searched for the weapon Kaiser must have told them about in order to frame Anthony.

A half hour or so later, he was put in another cell that was at the very end of the SHU's hallway across from an exit door. The counselor, psychologist and guards said he would be leaving in two or three nights with seven other guys. At 12 a.m., right after count one night, they came and yelled, "Transfer. Get up and ready, you're leaving." They grabbed seven guys and turned off the lights. Anthony stood in his cell in disbelief. It wasn't so much that he was upset that he didn't get picked to go as he was that he'd let them mess with his emotions again. He promised himself right there that was the last time.

He read the Bible for a while. Later, he crawled on his belly under the bunks trying to kill roaches. He scrubbed the concrete floor and chased the movements he saw out of the corner of his eye. He counted things. He moved his few possessions around. He wiped the walls, deciphering pictures in the movements.

One minute he was laughing. The next, crying inconsolably. He loved everyone; he hated everyone.

Anthony wished Noah's flood would happen again. He prayed the Mayans were right and the world would end soon. He cried and prayed that if there was a God, He would come down and talk to Anthony. *Show me a sign! Fuck, I'd settle for an alien. Something! Light up the room at night. Command me in that deep voice! Comfort me. Show me a fucking sign!* When no miracle occurred, Anthony thought, *I don't blame Him. I wouldn't come here either.*

For days this continued. Finally, he was given some paper and a bendable—so he couldn't stab himself or others—three-inch long SHU pen from an officer tired of watching Anthony's insanity. He started to draw, but then stopped. He thought back to a time when he wasn't in prison. He asked himself, "What the fuck happened to my life?" Minutes became hours as he stared at the blank white paper.

Anthony realized he'd let his addictions destroy his life. He cried thinking of how he would rush out of his house in the morning so that he could start taking his pills, drinking his Jägermeister and snorting cocaine. More times than he could count, he'd wake up in his car with the engine idling and eighteen missed phone calls. No cop ever woke him, but he wished they would have. Perhaps that would have been the wake-up call he needed. *Look at what my drug use caused. Look at where I am. I couldn't stop the fucking Monster, and then I became one.*

Anthony realized that at some point, he had chosen to be in that place, that Hole. All of his life decisions had led to that moment. He chose cocaine over everything, over himself. He chose painkillers over everything, over himself. *Alcohol, benzos, I chose all of them and for what? I chose them to avoid painful reality and to escape something?* He was in a place that had no escape, all alone in that concrete cell with the pen and paper.

Suddenly, he remembered that saying from the prison movie "Shawshank Redemption": "Get busy livin' or get busy dyin'." Anthony realized he wanted more than anything to *live.*

Maybe he wasn't alone. Maybe God was there with him. So he started to write. In putting his thoughts into words, he decided to change his life. And just maybe, if he could change his life around, he could help others do the same.

It would be another month-and-a-half before he was finally released from the SHU. His counselor said the investigation found that he was guilty of absolutely no wrong-doing.

Anthony was shackled and handcuffed, then led outside where the sun hit his face. It had been almost two years since he had seen the Bureau of Prisons bus. It seemed like a limo as he stepped on to it to be shipped out of La Tuna immediately.

The gratitude and perception each person has for what they experience determines their attitude, and this attitude will determine their life. Anthony went in to the SHU a certain man, but he wasn't the same man when he left. He decided he would determine his life from there on. He believed he'd found his purpose way down in the bottom of that shithole.

They shipped Anthony to the Oklahoma City transfer center. He was able to make a call home a few days before Christmas. By the time Emily answered, she was already crying. For a few seconds, neither said anything, but they knew they were connected.

"Those were the greatest few seconds of my life," Anthony says.

Since the prison system didn't transfer prisoners over the holidays, Emily had resigned herself that she and the girls would have to wait until next year to visit Anthony. Then Emily checked her phone one day and realized she had missed a dozen calls from Anthony. The nightmare was over. He was in Oklahoma on his way to another facility on Christmas Eve. It was a Christmas miracle. They didn't know if he was going to Miami or Coleman.

> "There are low security facilities with the RDAP Program in southern California, Arizona and Colorado. Any one of those would've made life a lot easier (and cheaper) for me. But instead, he was shipped from Seattle to Texas, from Texas to New Mexico and from New Mexico to Florida. You can't get much further from Washington State than that."
>
> —Emily

Just after New Year's, Emily got the call from Anthony in Coleman, Florida. Within a week, she had purchased a plane ticket for late January.

Emily has recently found herself thinking more and more about Anthony and their younger years. Sometimes, when she's leaving work, the street musicians in downtown Seattle spark these memories.

> "There's a drummer who sits on the corner by my building. His drums are really just a plastic bucket, a metal can and a wood block, but he is amazing. I'm told he's been there all along, but the first time I actually heard him was about a year ago and it startled me; something about the sound of those drums and the cold, crisp evening air. Like a jolt, I was seventeen years old again, time for our Friday night pep rally before the big game. I pictured Anthony in his letterman's jacket, me in my cheer uniform, his arms wrapped tight around me. It was the first time in forever that I looked back on that moment—any moment from our past—and actually smiled. There was so much bad, it completely overshadowed the good, and I let it. Maybe that's why I never heard the drums.
>
> "I've learned that the key is not to focus only on what's bad, but to find what's good in the bad—the blessings in disguise—and to use the darkness to see the light; because without the bad, we cannot truly appreciate the good. There is no joy without sorrow. I took things for granted before (like everyone does) and I didn't think twice. Now I know and I remind myself just how lucky I am in this world. I am truly blessed. We are truly blessed. Anthony is alive. He gets another chance. We get another chance. It might sound crazy to some, but this entire experience has been an opportunity, a priceless miraculous gift for which I will always be grateful. No matter what happens between us, we will never be the same. We are forever changed. We are better."
>
> —Emily

In Coleman, Anthony was able to work on keeping centered, despite living in close quarters with nearly 2,000 inmates who are busy repeating the same day for years and years until someday they will be released. As the men walk around the outdoor running track, they talk and laugh about their great conquests—both sexual and criminal. Sitting almost unnoticed in the middle of the field by himself is a man who has finally grown up and is no longer a boy. Anthony talks to himself in positive terms and also listens clearly to his inner voice. As he looks around at everything going on around him, he no longer dwells on his mistakes. After years of torment, his parents are still in his life and visit him in prison. His wife waits for him and makes sure his daughters stay in contact with their daddy. Anthony wonders how he was so blessed to still have them in his life.

> "I dream of flipping pancakes, going to parent-teacher conferences, being around them, coaching their T-ball games and embarrassing them in front of their friends without understanding why. I know unconditional love because of them."
>
> —Anthony

But this was a special day, and after only a short time, he got up and went to his cell to grab his equipment. This was the day of the big prison divisional basketball playoffs. The three game series was tied at one all. Anthony's team and their opponents were considered the two best teams in the league of around ten teams. The team they were playing had a seven-footer and a lightning fast point guard.

A decade after being the hottest high school athlete, Anthony was the starting point guard on his team. He was also the only white guy on any team in the entire basketball tournament. The announcers called him "White Chocolate," after the great point guard Jason Williams who'd played in the NBA for over a decade and elevated passing the basketball to an entire new level. Anthony had come to hate being called that, but it had stuck. On the inmate-run scoreboard and stat sheets, he was third in scoring and led the league in assists. Prison basketball might be the easiest place to lead in assists considering no one passes the ball. Anthony was the only point guard who passed the ball in a league of ball hogs. Before he'd joined the team, they'd never filled in that statistic. But the inmates, like all men, need some sort of purpose in life, so there were statistics for everything.

Money was an underlying element in prison sports. The baseball team wanted Anthony to play with them. He was offered $200 in commissary and new cleats to play shortstop. They wanted Anthony to play for them because of his athletic ability—even though baseball wasn't his skill set. In the end, it was about upping the advantage in gambling on the team.

He walked through the gates separating the recreation yard from the dorms carrying his much-worn basketball shoes that he'd purchased from another inmate eight months ago. The cracked and holey soles had been repaired using dental floss strung through the rubber and sewn back through the leather. At courtside, he slid a knee brace onto his bad knee that he had once blamed for destroying his football career. He put long socks that had the feet cut out of them over his forearms to protect himself from getting cut by the long fingernails of his prisoner opponents. His heart was pumping hard. It didn't matter that this was "just" a prison game. It felt like any attack of nerves he'd had pregame.

The wind started to pick up in the yard. There were bleachers on one side of the court, and they were packed. Bleacher seats were mostly reserved for those inmates who were placing bets, while regular spectators stood, surrounding the court. Some inmates sold cold sodas for stamps. Two Latino guys were selling burritos, as well. At center court were three referees, an announcer and a guy running the game clock. The guards permitted the men to set up the sound equipment. A small tent was set up for the announcers and bookies to stay under.

Little white pieces of paper were being exchanged at both ends of the bleachers, gambling tickets for every scenario, event, score and statistic possible. The typical bet was a book of stamps worth about seven dollars. There was also major street action that had no wagering limits, with thousands of dollars trading hands after the games. Anthony was also sure the guards were placing bets, but he knew better than to ask.

The gambling element had brought some tension between a few players on Anthony's team. Gambling was an excuse to rig games, shave points and place bets on insider knowledge. Prison is filled with crooks, after all. Anthony stayed out of the whole thing. Never once had he been approached by the bookies, but the kicker was that you never really knew who had. One game, there had been so much action on their backup point guard—who was cocky as hell even though he never played. His point total was set at a three-point over/under. He came in for an injured player and took off on a breakaway, scoring two on an easy lay-in. Apparently, he'd also taken himself on the under, because at the end of the blow-out game Anthony found him wide-open under the basket. There was no one around this guy, but he wouldn't shoot the ball. Anthony had never seen anything like it. Anthony followed the play, and as soon as the ball left his hands to another player, the bleachers erupted over a meaningless pass in a meaningless game.

Anthony's over-and-under was set at thirteen points, or so he'd heard when the clock stopped. Lay-up lines went after. Anthony was a slasher, and he had gone off for twenty-five points the game before, so it was pretty likely that it would be a safe bet on the over. The way stat-betting worked, was that a gambler bet five books that Anthony would score fourteen or more points on the "over" with the push being thirteen, and anything under went to the house. The bookies knew Anthony though, and they knew he would never be corrupted. Anthony took it as a huge compliment.

As the wind picked up, the odds on the game changed. Three point shooters who shot the long ball from outside would no longer be a factor throwing up prayers in the wind—which at times could even steal your dribble. Anthony's team would be forced to drive the ball to the hoop, which wasn't their strongest suit especially against a seven-footer acting as a shot blocker.

The game started, and the first time Anthony drove to the basket he was slammed down hard.

"Punish that white boy!" snarled an officer.

Anthony went to the free throw line to shoot two, only it was like a carnival game with the wind. He took a second for the wind to calm down while counting down from ten to make sure he shot the ball in time to avoid a violation. He missed it, and then he missed the second. He could feel that this was the way the game was going to go.

Anthony could see that the other team's speed-demon point guard had trouble with his left, and so Anthony pushed him left, shutting him down. The game started out with a box and one defense against them. Anthony was targeted as a threat and constantly double-teamed until they realized they didn't need to. He'd beat his guy off the dribble and pull up for an eight-footer . . . air ball.

"Air ball! Air ball!" the inmates shouted.

He could feel the anger building from the inmates in the stands. They were losing money because of him. *I'll shut em' up,* he thought to himself.

Next time down the court Anthony showboated—going behind his back with the dribble, then again to the other side, then a quick step to the right with a cross dribble between his legs backward to the left. As his defender recovered, Anthony spun around back to where he had just left and now had a wide open lane to the hoop. He took off for the basket; it was going to be an easy lay-in. He took a quick step. . . and dribbled the ball off his own foot and out of bounds.

There was loud, angry laughter. The boo-birds were out in force, too.

Wide open jump shots *clanged* against the battered metal rim.

More booing.

It seemed as if every one of Anthony's passes were thrown two feet behind his teammates. Everything was off. His confidence shaken, he started listening to everybody around him making fun of him and yelling obscenities. Instead of being aggressive, all his energy was directed to not screwing up. There was a steal made by a teammate, and had Anthony taken off it would have been an easy, wide-open lay-up. But he was afraid to miss, so he didn't follow the play. Anthony played stupid and tired, but his teammates seemed not to notice. The problem was that he noticed, and half-time couldn't come fast enough.

Coach said it would be a different half during his half-time pep talk. He reminded his players that if they won this game, they would move to the semi-finals.

The second half started just like the first half ended. Anthony dreaded getting fouled, since it would put him on the free-throw line shooting in front of all those people heckling him, so he didn't take any chances. Although he was still wearing a uniform on the court, he had effectively taken himself out of the game. He felt slow and stuck to the ground. It was by far the worst game he had ever played in his entire life. Anthony was the leader of the team, but he was being shunned by his own teammates. One player on his team—with about four minutes to go—took off his jersey in disgust and quit. The refs gave his team a technical foul. The other team took the ball. Not like it mattered though. The season was over, and they were out of the playoffs.

Then he recalled what Dave Brekke, the Monroe High School head basketball coach used to say to his players: "Get to the next play." Sometimes Coach Brekke, with his red face and spiky hair, would say this to the entire team in a pre-game speech, but sometimes he would scream it directly at Anthony. "Next play!" meaning that he needed to forget about the bad shot and get his ass back on defense and have fun. His message meant not to dwell on the bad shot but to focus. Forget about whatever it was and put it in the past so Anthony was focused on the next task. Learn from your mistakes and move forward.

Anthony was sick of failing. He felt that he created a life on being a failure. But maybe it was time to take Coach Brekke's advice.

They were down by nine points, but with 3:20 left on the clock Anthony decided to at least go out on a better note and lose trying his best. His teammate went to the line and shot two free-throws. He missed the first, but with a little under three minutes left, hit the second. The bleachers slowly started to empty. The gamblers had seen enough.

Anthony yelled at the other guard to "press." The guy looked at him like he was an embarrassing idiot, but jogged unwillingly behind Anthony. Their big guy inbounding didn't look up before tossing it in to their guard. Anthony stole the ball and hit the other guard for a wide-open, flat-footed lay-in.

Two minutes, twenty seconds and Anthony's team was still down by six.

The ball was being brought down by the other team's guard when they got another steal and got fouled. They were in the bonus, which meant one foul shot and one free-throw, with the clock stopped at two minutes. He hit the first free throw but missed the second.

Down by five.

The opposing team's next possession was a relatively quick shot and miss as they were simply trying to end the game. Anthony brought the ball down and gave it to their big guy, who was relatively uncoordinated, but did an out-of-character turn around five-foot fade-away and hit it. He got fouled in the process and hit the free throw.

Down by two.

The inmate fans who'd been about to leave were rooted to the spot. Guys who'd left came running back.

With a little under a minute left to play, their point guard was waiting for the inbound pass. Anthony jumped in front of him and pushed him to his bad hand. When the speedy point guard went right, Anthony reached around him and grabbed the ball. A few steps later, going for the lay-in, two arms grab him from behind sending Anthony back to the free throw line.

Two shots. That's all they needed to tie the game.

Anthony stepped to the line with confidence. The wind had died. He had this. The first shot left Anthony's hand. He could feel it was dead on . . . but it rimmed out. The second was even worse. He had confirmed what everyone was thinking—that he should quit embarrassing himself.

The other team took the ball down and burned some time off the clock, nineteen, eighteen. . . past fifteen seconds. Their guard decided to shoot. As if the basketball gods wanted to taunt Anthony further, the ball hit the rim and bounced right to him. In every other game Anthony couldn't get the ball in his hands enough, but in this game that's exactly what he didn't want.

Suddenly he was alone and afraid and prayed that someone would get open as he took off with the ball. His other guard was a bit in front of him, and they were paralleling each other running the floor and soon found themselves in a two-on-one crossing half court. Then the opposing guard caught up to Anthony's teammate. The guy guarding Anthony stepped up to stop his progress, but Anthony went easily around him and prepared to go to the hoop again. He had a wide open lay up to tie the game.

Six seconds left.

Just as he was about to take off, something changed. That inner voice he'd been talking to earlier in the middle of the field, the voice that always believed in Anthony even when the outside world and Anthony didn't, told him:

Get to the next play.

"As many times as I failed, all the missed shots in life, the air balls, the turnovers, as bad as I played that day, something told me to just take one more shot." Anthony says.

Five seconds.

Picking up his dribble, he gathered his body behind the three-point line. Anthony made one last look to get rid of the ball and saw the crowd. Without caring anymore what they thought, and with good form, he elevated—rising above the defender who was still trying to catch up.

Four seconds.

With his body perpendicular to the basket and with the balance of a pure shooter, he released the ball from his fingertips.

There was a roar of disappointment from the bleachers: "No!" "Shit!" "No!"

Anthony had already tuned them out, listening to that inner voice and confident once again, as if his Emily was cheering him on.

Three seconds.

Everybody watched as the ball floated through the air. Anthony closed his eyes and prayed. He finally got to the Next Play.

Last Thoughts

Dear Reader,

I have spent a lot of time locked in prison looking through razor wire fences at a world I could not touch, time being my punishment and time being my greatest asset.

Only after first getting past my own self-pity was I able to change my perspective. Originally, I saw these walls as keeping me from everything, but the longer I sat still and the closer I came to peace, the more I realized that I was not ready to face anything until I was able to face myself. I finally accepted responsibility for my life. I quit blaming others, I quit blaming events and I quit playing the victim. It was me. I was the problem. I was wrong about everything. I was an addicted criminal with this selfish sense of entitlement. It was all about me. I came to despise who I was and hated it all, and realizing I would rather be dead than go back to living like that, I decided to change. Therefore I shut my mouth and opened my eyes, searching what I saw in the mirror. This is my reflection:

I found that whatever I showed to life was shown back to me. I learned that whatever I wanted, I first had to give away. If I wanted forgiveness, I needed first to forgive. Forgiveness was also the only solution for my resentments. I saw that true success had nothing to do with money, power, or material things. Through many conversations—and a few arguments—with God I discovered that truth and love held the secrets to my happiness. I took control of my attitude and my thoughts and became the creator of my own experience. I learned that what I focus on becomes my reality. I've witnessed that it isn't the fear of punishment that makes someone do the right thing, only the desire to do so. I also came to see the value in my failures, learning the best I can from them, moving on and getting to the "next play."

During the depths of my darkest moments is when I experienced my greatest growth and also when it became clear what I wanted to do with my life: I want to help others. I dream of being a children's book author who brings smiles to the faces of little ones. I also want to speak to students, the upcoming generation, about the dangers of drugs, the truth of crime, the importance of making good decisions and doing the right thing. I want to encourage them to follow their dreams and never quit being themselves.

My addiction and the choices that I made robbed my parents of a son, stole a husband from my wife and left my kids with no father. I broke everyone's heart and I pray I can glue all of them back together. These choices also put me in prison, where I write this now. But long before I ever was arrested I was in a prison much worse than the physical kind. It was a prison where I was entrapped by my addictions, my insecurities and my negative thoughts. Only with an extreme desire to change was I able to escape. As the gates are about to open, releasing me back to the world, all I can feel is gratitude for everything.

My story is not sad. I was given a second chance at life. What is sad is that my story is not uncommon or unique. Millions like me are trapped in their own prisons. If this is you, I pray you find the courage and steal your life back. I'll be cheering for you.

Sincerely,
Anthony

About the Authors

Anthony Curcio (right) served his Federal Prison sentence in Texas and Florida and was released in April of 2013.

Dane Batty (left) is a technical writer, biographer and designer. His last book was the award-winning *Wanted: Gentleman Bank Robber. The True Story of Leslie Ibsen Rogge, One of the FBI's Most Elusive Criminals*. He is a proud husband and father of two and holds an MBA from George Fox University. He lives near Portland, Oregon.

www.ingramcontent.com/pod-product-compliance
Lightning Source LLC
LaVergne TN
LVHW020706110826
845149LV00012B/2123

* 9 7 8 0 9 8 5 7 9 4 5 0 7 *